I truly wish this book had been around when I was a young Christian! In this brilliant work, Rev. Jonathan Fisk discusses the very fundamentals of the Christian faith in a fresh yet profound manner. He lets the Word of God dispossess the fallen *Me* of all thought of being able to save myself. But then he allows the Word to bring me the certainty of salvation by grace through faith in Jesus Christ. This is the message that all Christians, young and old, need to read, hear from the pulpit, and study time and again!

HARRI HUOVINEN,
*pastor, the Evangelical Lutheran
Mission Diocese of Finland*

A retired Australian pastor once said to me that ours is not a truly confessional church unless our theology counteracts the world around us. Jonathan Fisk has done a fine job in providing both a biting critique of today's culture and a hearty presentation of the twenty-four-carat Gospel. Using the classic structure of catechesis, this book is an engaging read with plenty of salt, written in a unique and witty style. Thanks, Jonathan, for a terrific resource to share with friends and inquirers!

PASTOR STEPHEN VAN DER HOEK,
*Maryborough-Childers Lutheran Parish,
Queensland, Australia*

Pastor Fisk writes in such a way that the reader has time to reflect on the profound truths of God's Word. Responding in faith, the reader learns to echo that Word back to God. Unlike *A Passage to India,* where Mrs. Moore's "God loves you" reduces to an incomprehensible "ou-boom," God is clearly speaking His changeless Word as Pastor Fisk echoes the word of the cross over and above the meaningless noise of this world.

PASTOR GARRY HEINTZ,
*Église Évangelique Luthérienne de Woerth,
France*

Catechesis means to "sound again" or "repeat"—echo!—the core tenets of our holy faith from catechumen (disciple) to catechist (teacher). *Echo* presents the very best of Jonathan Fisk's catechetical teaching in his own authentic and distinctively contemporary voice, fraught with common idioms, witticisms, and edge. Aimed to thoughtfully instruct a younger generation of readers and guide them in character formation, *Echo* reverberates the biblical worldview and Christ's vision of His disciples—be they never so young—pursuing truth, beauty, and goodness. Every junior high student, high school student, and collegian would do well to own these pages to the end that these essential and ever-relevant truths might echo in this generation.

REV. JOHN J. BOMBARO, PHD, LCDR, CHC, USNR,
Grace Lutheran Church
San Diego, California

ECHO

UNBROKEN TRUTH.

WORTH REPEATING.

AGAIN.

BY JONATHAN FISK

CONCORDIA PUBLISHING HOUSE • SAINT LOUIS

Published by Concordia Publishing House
3558 S. Jefferson Ave., St. Louis, MO 63118-3968
1-800-325-3040 • www.cph.org

Manufactured in the United States of America

Library of Congress Cataloging-in-Publication Data

Names: Fisk, Jonathan (Jonathan McAdam), author.
Title: Echo : unbroken truth worth repeating, again / Jonathan Fisk.
Description: Saint Louis : Concordia Publishing House, 2018.
Identifiers: LCCN 2017051832 (print) | LCCN 2018011228 (ebook) | ISBN
    9780758657886 | ISBN 9780758657855
Subjects: LCSH: Theology, Doctrinal--Popular works.
Classification: LCC BT77 (ebook) | LCC BT77 .F53 2018 (print) | DDC
    230/.41--dc23
LC record available at https://lccn.loc.gov/2017051832

1   2   3   4   5   6   7   8   9   10   27   26   25   24   23   22   21   20   19   18

For you,
as always.

And also for my father,
who has been patient with me.

*God Himself is not ashamed to
teach these things daily. He knows
nothing better to teach. . . . Can we
finish learning in one hour what God
Himself cannot finish teaching?*

—LC Preface 16

TABLE OF CONTENTS

Introducing You, the Special (Melting) Snowflake

This is you. An average, run-of-the-mill, everyday (boring) person. I know, I know. It's insulting to call you boring when I don't even know you. *You're special. There's no one else like you. You're a snowflake.* It's all very beautiful. Please feel free to draw a snowflake around your head in the picture above. But after we've each taken the time to do that, then the boring fact of the matter is that we all still look like the same average "special" people. Just like everyone else.

We can argue the point about how your snowflakiness is more snowflaky than mine if you think that would be fun. But it's best to just get this out of the way right at the start: **this isn't a book about you**. It's about **unbroken truth** worth repeating so many times that you can't tack enough "agains!" onto the end of it. For that reason, it is about things wonderfully less average and less boring than you. It's about the real big picture. The total expression. The exhaustive metanarrative. That kind of uber-jazz.

You are a part of it. But you are not what it's about. You are way over on the side, trapped in the borders, quite a bit removed from

ECHO

the middle. But there is a line between the middle and you, and that's important. Because the middle is Jesus. Who Jesus **is**. What Jesus has **done**. What Jesus is **doing**. What Jesus is still **going to do**. Not only is all that significantly more interesting than you, but it also has far more power to change your life than any edge of your snowflakiness could possibly hope for.

Now, I'm not making any promises that this book will make all the bad things in life go away. It will not grant you superhuman willpower or magically increase the virility of your righteousness meter. But you will learn the distilled, unbreakable Christian Echo, the very thing that has radically changed humanity in every nation and tongue where it's ever been repeated. You will learn why these Three Foundational Realities—the Ten Important Things about Being Creation, the Three Elements and Five Results of the Gospel, and the Seven Edges of Christian Holification—are more than just a series of boring stuff that old boring people make you boringly memorize on boring afternoons so that you can stop having to go to boring Sunday School. They are a total operating system for your brain. They are the most astoundingly complete description of what life is and why it is worth living. They are the golden nugget of ultimate spirituality that will give boring little you the conviction to stand with your head held high, no matter how boring the evil days around you might be or not be.

> **That you may be able to withstand in the evil day, and having done all, to stand firm.**
>
> Ephesians 6:13

The first step to standing firm, the first step for having your mind and psyche unleashed by the unbroken truth of Christianity, is not fighting too hard against what it has to say about you.

Exciting.
 Boring.
  Powerful.
   Weak.
    Energetic.
     Lazy.
      Broken.
       You.

Take a good long look in the mirror if you need to. Being honest with yourself is just about the most courageous thing a human can try to do. Greatness and horribleness, magnificence and blahblahblahpbttt—whoever you are, whatever you've achieved or left undone, you're pretty much just an average person like the rest of us. A snowflake who is, soon enough, going to melt. Stuck right here. Not in the middle of it all, but enough in the middle of something that's clearly going on.

Being honest with yourself is often disappointing, usually overwhelming, and filled with plenty of fear. It's also sometimes wonderful, strangely consistent, and filled with plenty of inspiration. This isn't because you're special. It's because everything else is perfectly normal. Except for the bad parts. Those are **im**perfectly normal.

But before we get to that, and to its **supra**normal solution, we need to start back at the borders of the picture, where there is you. And then, waaaay over there . . . is God.

PART ONE

THE TEN IMPORTANT THINGS ABOUT BEING CREATION

THE FIRST THING

There Is a God

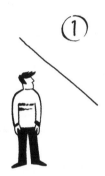

(1)

This is the First Important Thing about *Being Creation*. It seems sort of obvious on the surface, but don't let the stick figure drawing above fool you into thinking this Important Thing is simple. This stuff isn't obvious to your soul. It isn't childishly simple in your **heart**.

This single important thing, all by itself, makes rocket science a breeze by comparison. It's not that the math of the matter is so terribly hard. Intellectually, the picture on the page above is easy to understand. A child can make sense of it. But deep down, at that nethermost average root of who you are, you don't **believe** it.

This is why, especially if you do believe it, it's worth repeating over and over again. Even if you do believe **there is a God**, even if you accept it, confess it, and teach it, the inmost average-just-like-everyone-else part of you isn't going along for the ride. No matter how much you actually do believe **there is a God**, you still don't want to, because believing there is a God means that **you are not Him**, and that's quite a bit more than your psyche really wants to handle on an average Monday morning.

YOU ARE NOT IN CHARGE

Think back to the last time life didn't go the way you thought that it should. Monday mornings are good for that. But any time or day will do. In fact, the more inane the memory, the better. Just think of the last time you got annoyed. You were frustrated. You got angry. It doesn't matter what caused it or if it was justified. The point is, life didn't go exactly as you planned it, and then what happened next?

On that day, during that moment, you were less than perfectly happy, and the reason you weren't perfectly happy was that for a single moment the world around you gave you an experience that made abundantly clear this obvious fact: **"You are not in charge;. You can't control everything. You don't rule the universe. You are not God."** There was nothing you could do about it, and **that** was why you got mad.

There is a God, and you are not Him. Facing that fact, not just intellectually but **spiritually**, really throws the average human off. Nobody wants to believe this. None of us take this sitting down.

It's kind of funny in a way. Here we are, incredibly average not-gods living in a broken world (that we broke) generally managing quite poorly. Then this crazy-actual ALMIGHTY GOD (the one who made both us and this world before we broke it) whispers into the midst of our dark chaos some astonishingly good news: **He is still out there**, and He is so much bigger and better than us that **He can fix everything** we've ruined. Better: He's planning on it. It begins with Him whispering, **"There is a God, and you are not Him."** But then! *If* we believe it at all—and not everyone does—we have the gall to go and assume, *Well, duh! Of course I know that I'm not God. That's obvious. I've known that I'm not God since I was a child. This is child's milk. Give me some meat to chew on. Can't spiritually mature people like me move on to some real truth?*

The First Important Thing: **There is a God**, but you don't believe it.

If only we could just believe it, file it, apply it, and never forget it. If only it were so! Someday we will. But not yet. That day is coming, and looking forward to that day is one of the Five Results of the Gospel. For that reason, like the rest of Christianity's unbroken truth, it is especially worth repeating again and again: "**There is a God.**" This truth is the source of powerful hope, an infusion of forward-looking confidence that can inspire anyone who looks to it with the ability to stand firm in the midst of whatever dark and evil times they might find themselves.

Encourage one another with these words.
1 Thessalonians 4:18

But that hope will always be undermined bit by bit by thinking that you've mastered the First Important Thing about Being Creation. Just because something is theoretically obvious after one sitting does not mean it's equally obvious to your **heart**.

FUNDAMENTALS NEVER DIE

Think of it like learning the most basic forms of swordplay. A novice, once gaining a handle on those forms, becomes exponentially more capable on a battlefield than an untrained sluggard swinging his sword like a boy with a stick. But the master is not someone who has graduated from the most basic forms. He is precisely a master **of them**. He never moves beyond them, never discards them, always uses them as the foundation of everything else.

The goal of this book is to get you to that place where you can stand firm, even against your own heart. We're going to go to battle together and discover the tools for beating down the thorns you find growing there. We're going to arm you with the firm conviction that expects to find those thorns sprouting new every day, but which does so underneath the unbroken truth that is equally as new every morning. That Echo is far greater than both you and your heart combined.

This means that there are a number of things this book will not be. This book is not an apologetic for the unbeliever. This is not a book for answering skeptics. We're not trying to answer every broken accusation being blabbered about the world these days.

"You can't prove that there is a God!"

"All gods are the same god."

"I'm spiritual not religious (and that means I'm better than you)."

Not everyone who echoes these irreverent claims does so out of malice or with cruel intention. Those who bring up such objections deserve to be cordially heard, taken seriously, and answered with care. But this book will not be the place for that. This is a book for empowering Christians of goodwill. It is a whetstone for Christians who can tell that the sword of their religion is growing dull and want to find the everlasting way to sharpen it again. I have one goal here: to invest you with confidence that you can know and understand the nucleus of Christianity in its entirety. No fluff. No frills. Just clarity. Substantiality. The core distilled down to its fundamental essence. Subtract the distraction. Multiply the understanding, and be certain that this will exponentially increase the trust, the tenacity, and the unbreakable will to echo it again yourself.

> **The fool says in his heart, "There is no God."** Psalm 14:1

HALF TRUTHS ARE TOTAL LIES

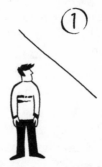

Christianity starts and finishes with the fact that **there is a God, and you are not Him**. Believing this truth is no simple idea. It can't just be picked up or discarded at will. It is so profound that no matter how well you might know it, you must also know that you don't believe it well enough.

All the other spiritualities out there rattling about the world are also echoes, but they echo the opposite of this unbroken truth. They echo the broken lie: the Ever-Lie. Some religions are built on rage and attack. Others float like butterflies on the breeze of stretching exercises and oxygen highs. But all of them root and twist their way back to the Ever-Lie so that the little line between average you and the almighty God isn't nearly so definite as the one in our picture. Atheism to Eastern mysticism, the New Age to Mormonism, crass paganism to those that bear the name "Christianity" but are not—all these on the surface appear to be diverse theories about who God is and how to get to Him. "*I am*

God" is not something that many religions are honest enough to teach out loud, although a few do. But at their core, they are all teachings about how to get **to** God, how to be **like** God, how to **join** God, how to be on God's level.

Every time, they blur that little line, which is all the encouragement your heart needs to start believing that it isn't really there.

> **Then they said, "Come, let us build ourselves a city and a tower with its top in the heavens, and let us make a name for ourselves."** Genesis 11:4

The Muslim imam would never claim to be God. But his average human heart, just like yours and mine, has no problem using his religion's rules and statutes to his own personal advantage, to get what he wants out of life, to live every day as if he were *almost* God anyway. The average human just wants to feel in control. He doesn't have to openly introduce himself to his friends as "God" to achieve that. He just has to have enough power to be able to act like he is God when he wants to, to be able to make what's around him submit to his will.

MY WILL IS WHAT I WANT

Internal subterfuge, self-distraction, and the appetite for half-truth are all far more effective than the open lies, and man is always best deceived by the lies he wants to tell himself. There is nothing harder about Christianity than learning to be honest with the thoughts inside your head and the emotions inside your heart. Not the ones that you like to pretend are there. The ones that are really there. The ones you don't want to admit even to yourself. Being upset, moment by moment, about being "not God" is one of those thoughts. In fact, the louder you dispute it, the more likely it is to be true. The more you claim that you really love God and would never put yourself above Him, the more likely it is that every time the world doesn't say to you, *"Thy will be done,"* every time the world instead says, *"You are not God. Deal with it,"* your heart's regular, average, thorny response is, *"Oh yeah? Just watch me* **make** *it so!"* If you're truly immersed, you'll even convince yourself that you're doing it **for** God.

This average, everyday spiritual war happens all day long inside every single human life on this planet. Nobody is special. We all wake up with the same needs. Whether you wash your face, drink your coffee, or eat leftover cold pizza, **you spend every moment doing whatever it is you believe you need to do in order to take the world you've been given and make it the place you'd rather have it be**. All the way along, right there with you, hanging on your neck, is a very wretched, very disgruntled, very self-absorbed, dirty old man. He's got yellow teeth (just a few), a soiled white T-shirt, and a squinty eye. Each time you do something, anything, everything, he pulls on the thorns growing out of your heart, hanging onto them with all his might until the tremors he starts in there ripple up to your head, where they convince you that what's going on inside your own gut is the only thing that matters. It's usually far more subconscious than intentional, but the question he echoes is the creed of all the little wannabe gods struggling about this dirty earth: *"What about Me? What about Me? What about Me?"*

"Me might not be almighty. But Me is important. More important than them. More important than Him, too, when it comes down to it. Of course, Me is not physically everything, but Me is spiritually everything. Even if Me isn't God, Me should be God. Even if Me isn't God, Me will act like I am God anyway."

> For although they knew God, they did not honor Him as God or give thanks to Him, but they became futile in their thinking, and their foolish hearts were darkened. Romans 1:21

ME SPOTTING

The First Important Thing about Being Creation is learning how to spot this *Me* inside you. *Me* is always right there with you, but even after you've become a Christian, *Me* will never be one. *Me* is your thorns, your own personal bedeviling, that thing the Bible calls **sin**.

Even in the most committed of Christians, truly saved, truly believing, ardently praying, "Thy will be done," *Me* will never stop trying to drag you back down into yourself, where *Me* can rule as your own god again.

Christianity does not unleash you from this thorny experience. Christianity gives you the confidence, conviction, and trust to be honest about it, to admit it for what it is. It takes a Christian to believe that every time you do wrong, *Me* is the reason you **wanted to**. It takes a Christian to believe that the thorns in your heart and the old man around your neck are not somebody else's problem, but the all-too-average spiritual condition of both you and all the other *Mes* who have ever lived.

> **We know that our old self was crucified with Him in order that the body of sin might be brought to nothing, so that we would no longer be enslaved to sin.** Romans 6:6

The First Important Thing is **there is a God**. This is the last thing any of us actually wants to believe. It takes a Christian to believe that **there is a God**. It takes a Christian to believe that this First Important Thing about Being Creation is not nearly so simple as it may first appear. It takes a Christian to insist the sad history of all humanly derived spiritualities is that of the blind leading the blind, the story of an endless stream of leprous souls waging a recalcitrant war against the most obvious unbroken truth that ever was or could be. Your old man, your thorns, your *Me*, stands devoted to its own endless spew of broken lies, always asking the most natural, average, boring, evil question in the world: *"What's in it for Me?"* But the power of Christianity is born in its honesty to admit that this is the heart of our problem.

> **Without faith it is impossible to please Him, for whoever would draw near to God must believe that He exists.** Hebrews 11:6

THE FIRST THING IS ONLY THE BEGINNING OF EVERYTHING

The Christian never stops training with the Echo, never stops practicing it, never puts it down. Like the good swordsman, the Christian knows that every flourish, parry, attack, and final strike finds its root in the fundamental forms. The master of his art is not the one who can dazzle his enemy with the most complicated moves, but the one who in the deep heat of battle is readied to rely on the novice's training that has seeped into his very blood, not hesitating when it matters, readily relying on what is sure, steadfast, and therefore worth always repeating again, until it is more than habit, more than a memory, until these words are **who you are**.

Again. And again. And again. You cannot stop learning what God is not done teaching. Who could be more learned than God Himself? The person who claimed to be more learned than God would be immediately proven wrong by the fact that he has not yet faced this most basic truth! He would need to start all over again, once more becoming a child with his memory work, practicing the Echo that even the most mature swordsman readily admits he cannot master: **There is a God, and you are not Him.**

> **I think it right, as long as I am in this body, to stir you up by way of reminder.** 2 Peter 1:13

It can be drawn with a few simple scratches on paper, but its depth of meaning is endless. The simplicity is profound beyond all we could ever dream or imagine. Wherever this Echo is alive, the Three Foundational Realities will always sound forth again. They are like a raging fire in the bones, impossible to contain. They burst forth, real spirituality, set apart and at war with the world in a battle of endless words.

(1) And then, there is Him, waaaay over there.

You are over here.

The First Important Thing about Being Creation is the fulcrum. All our unbelieving thorns cannot diminish the foundation of this unbreakable truth. The more you drill yourself in it, the more the poisonous infection of self-security diminishes in comparison to it. The more the pride of your heart rises up to push back, the more you are compelled to devote your heart to believing this truth.

You begin by finding out how much you still need to know. You end by experiencing that no matter how fathomless the depths of your *Me* might be, the deep, deep truth of **there is a God** is more bottomless still.

That is where we are going.

THE FIRST IMPORTANT THING
ABOUT BEING CREATION

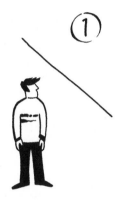

There is a God.

* THE FIRST IMPORTANT THING: THERE IS A GOD.

THE SECOND THING

God Has a Name

A DIFFERENT KIND OF BEING

Once you realize **there is a God** and you are not Him, the Second Thing should be almost as obvious. Sadly, it is not. Those thorns run deep. There is little in us that has not been bent. No matter how boldly we claim we are a "just the facts" kind of people, our stubbornness beats the facts to death when the cards are down.

Even when average, ordinary you begrudgingly admits the fact that **God is not *Me*** and that **God is way over there**, there is still no end of trouble coming to terms with just how far away **waaaay over there** actually is.

ECHO

Typically, we try believing God is only *sort of* way over there, somewhere *just on the other side* of that line (and that line *isn't really* as thick as it looks). So even though we believe that the other side of that line is where the almighty God more or less lives and moves and has His being, we also hold out the lingering hope that we can surely get across that line if we have to. The old man is right there cheering us on, echoing common sense. *"With a little elbow grease and some authenticity, you can breach that gap if you need to. You could poke a hole, sneak around, or conjure up some access, since, after all, you may be average, but among the average, you are still particularly special."*

The problem with this echoing of common **non**sense is that that little line isn't really a little line at all. The line is a scratch on the paper meant to help visualize a distinction. It is there to symbolize a fact: there is a separation between you and God that is cosmically large. The two sides of that line are about as far removed from each other as the east is from the west. This is not a bad thing. It is not the result of the fall or sin or any such nastiness. That line is the difference between being God and **not** being God, a difference that is so vast, so astronomical, that it denies our puny brains even the ability to comprehend it. A "god" whom you could understand wouldn't be God after all.

As the heavens are higher than the earth, so are My ways higher than your ways and My thoughts than your thoughts. Isaiah 55:9

REALLY, REALLY SPECIAL
(NOT LIKE A SNOWFLAKE)

"God is **hidden**," said Isaiah the prophet. (See Isaiah 45:15.) Don't blink or you'll miss the extreme radicalism of that thought. It runs counter to everything that all the spiritual-not-religions in the world brandish about the airwaves these days. They all say that *God is everywhere*, that *God is everything*, that *God is in everyone*, and *you are a part of God*. But "no one has ever seen God," said John the apostle (John 1:18). He "dwells in unapproachable light," echoed Paul (1 Timothy 6:16). That is not the kind of "over there" you can get to just by hopping inside a rocket ship. There aren't dimensional portals or wormholes available for getting to God, and that's because **God is not somewhere to be found**.

The God who made you and everything else is beyond even **heaven** itself. The heavens are where the seraphim sing and where the prophets were carried to, but the heavens also were **created** by God (see Genesis 1:1). As much as God has revealed Himself to His heavens, they are not "where" He "is." He is considerably more significant than all that. He is **holy**, which is the Bible's word for saying **really, really special**. So special as to be not like anything else ever at all. So contrasting, so disparate, so *set apart* that nothing in all the universe can be averaged with it.

> No one has ever seen God.
> 1 John 4:12

Nothing can ever be averaged with **Him**.

We'll come back to holiness later in the book. Holiness, this set-apartness, is an essential part of the Christian experience. It is intimately connected to these first Ten Important Things about Being Creation. But it is most definitely **not** one of them. What is important for now, as we work toward the second of these Ten Things, is not your holiness but **God's holiness**. That special, unique, not average, set-apartness of God is entirely tied up with God's hiddenness, with God not being findable, with God not really needing to be "somewhere" at all.

GOD IS THE JUDGE OF EVERYTHING

By definition, your thorns can't stand this. In your quest to be God, without necessarily letting your conscious mind know that's what he's up to, that old man hanging around your neck always wants to reserve for *Me* the right to be the judge of everything. He wants *Me* to believe that *Me* can hold all knowledge in your hand. *Me* can look it over, comprehend it, and then decide whether any of it is true. This makes the waaaay over there of God—who is not actually somewhere findable at all—something *Me* would rather die than believe.

> Do not say in your heart, "Who will ascend into heaven?" (that is, to bring Christ down). Romans 10:6

What this means is that the spiritual life of the average human spends the better part of every day taking good hard runs at that line between you and God, believing that if you can manage to ram into it in just the right way, you will puncture a path through and find yourself "being" where God is. Or more precisely *Me*-focused, you'll find Him being where you are.

I don't think I need to draw the results.

There are lots of special ways to smash your head against that line, but they all boil down to three categories of ways. First, it's always popular to use virtue and good works. That's what we call *moralism*, which is trusting in what you do to be good enough to get to God. But these days, happy experiences and mountaintop feelings are making a good claim at number one on the charts. This is *mysticism*, which is trusting in what you feel to be good enough to get to God. Not too long ago, the third competitor, *rationalism*, was in vogue. This is trusting in what you think to be good enough to get to God. But rationalism more or less thought itself out of prime time somewhere between 1914 and 1969.

It doesn't really matter which spin you put on your works, your thoughts, and your feelings. The incredibly everyday ways of trying to get through that line still have the same spiritually catastrophic results. Your old thorny man says to you, "Hey, *Me*, you know what would be really awesome? Run as hard as you can at that line over there. Use all the heart, mind, or body you can muster. It'll be **sweet**."

Woe to the foolish prophets who follow their own spirit, and have seen nothing! Ezekiel 13:3

The dastardly average thing is that no matter how often this little scheme leaves *Me* lying flat on my patootie—dazed, broken, frustrated as all get-out—the old man just keeps telling you not to believe that this is because it can't be done. He keeps whispering what *Me* wants to hear, and *Me* is more than willing to believe it: *"God would never have or think or be something that Me can't ultimately understand, experience, or do. God* **cannot be** *hidden."*

IF YOU CAN'T BEAT 'EM, MAKE IT UP

Long before *Me* will admit that *Me* can**not** get to the other side of that line, *Me* will pick himself up off the ground, look at the world around *Me,* and proceed to claim that *Me* has actually made it to the other side after all. It won't be one whit true. But *Me* will begin to believe, teach, and confess that the line doesn't actually exist.

"There! I've done it!" the old man will cry from deep within. *"I always knew I could get to the other side of that line, where God is. This is great!"*

Admitting the technicality that **there is a God, and you are not Him**, the old man still sets up images, dreams, and ideas that he calls "God," even though they are not. It doesn't matter that you are not where God actually is. You've latched onto something else to call "God," and that is usually enough for your thorns. So long as you can understand or experience or have a chance at achieving the self-deception, you will keep pointing to this other thing and saying, *"This is God,"* or *"This can get me to God,"* or *"This is my relationship with God."*

> **Woe to him who says to a wooden thing, Awake; to a silent stone, Arise! Can this teach? Behold, it is overlaid with gold and silver, and there is no breath at all in it.** Habakkuk 2:19

In doing this, the old man succeeds at his most important goal. Whether he sets up one "God" or many "gods," he never really serves them. By insisting on the right to name them himself, he demands that these "gods" exist to serve him. He has kept *Me* the measure of "God." He has kept you God's judge.

SO MUCH SOMEONE THAT HE IS NOWHERE

No matter what the old man says, you are never any closer to crossing that line. It remains more impenetrable than an army of angels holding swords of molten lava. It is a great divorce, an everlasting segregation. **And** contrary to the intuition of our thorns, this is **not** a bad thing at all.

> **For I am God, and there is no other; I am God, and there is none like Me.** Isaiah 46:9

The line between you and God is **not** evil. It is true that being tied to the old man has certainly made the situation more dire than the original created order. But that line between you and God was always intended to be there. When God made the heavens and the earth, He never intended for the creation to be part of Himself. He didn't break off little pieces of Himself and sow them into us. He **did** want us to know Him. He **did** make us to trust in Him, even to identify with Him. But from the beginning, God made us to have an identity that is not "God."

Only **God** is who "God" is. This is the Second Important Thing about Being Creation, and it is why creatures like us can never get through that line to Him. The other side of that line is not "where" God is, but **who** God is. God is no "where" to begin with. He doesn't need to be. But He is still some**one**. **God has a name**, and this *who God is* is what makes Him truly set apart, truly holy, truly God.

The Second Important Thing is that **God has a name**.

Like our earlier problem with **there is a God**, the challenge is not the idea's complexity. The struggle is its infuriating simplicity.

The thorns in us want to argue that God not being "somewhere" diminishes His glory, or some such, *"God **has** to 'be' more than just a name. A name can't have substance and power and eternity in itself. That's ridiculous!"*

But it's all just a ploy. It's not God's glory that we're really worried about. It's our own. It's the thought that God is so different from us that we will never have the chance to be like Him that threatens our pride. But the real God doesn't care about your pride. He cares about your faith, your life, and your true joy, and these are entirely different things.

God did not make you capable of understanding Him for the same reason He did not make you capable of being Him: He made you to be you. Then He gave you a gift. Rather than wasting your time chasing the impossible made-up fairyland of "where" God is, or of understanding "what" God is, God revealed **who God is**, because that's the real deal.

WHAT'S IN A NAME?

If this is a tough nugget to swallow, don't worry. You're nothing special. Everyone has trouble with this. The Bible is filled with people who wanted to understand God, who wanted to see God, who tried to ascend to God, to figure God out, or even to control Him. Through all of it, God deftly turns aside every attempt to reach Him and consistently hands out the Second Important Thing about Being Creation instead: **God has a name.**

"I AM WHO I AM," He said from the burning bush before giving Moses the proper name by which He had already been called for generations: "Say this to the people of Israel: 'The LORD [**YHWH**], the God of your fathers . . . has sent me'" (Exodus 3:14–15).

In most English Bibles, YHWH is translated as "**the LORD**" with small caps. Modern scholars pronounce it as *Yahweh*, though a typographical misunderstanding led scholars in the 1800s to call Him *Jehovah*. How the name

> I will sing praise to the name of the LORD, the Most High. Psalm 7:17

is pronounced is far less important than recognizing that YHWH is the Old Testament name for **who** God is. All the histories, the prophets, and the psalms call on this name, adore it, and consider it to be far more substantial than a mere title.

"**The name** of **the LORD** is to be praised," they sang, and "May **the name** of the God of Jacob protect you," they prayed (Psalm 113:3; 20:1). "Sing praises to **the LORD**, who sits enthroned in Zion," they shouted (Psalm 9:11). Even the great praise word *alleluia* carries the name built into the "*ia*," which is the **YH** of YHWH.

From the time of Seth, the son of Adam, "people began to call on **the name** of **the LORD**" (Genesis 4:26). When David, son of Jesse, stood before Goliath with five stones and a sling, he shouted, "I come to you in **the name** of **the LORD**" (1 Samuel 17:45). When Malachi, the last of the old prophets, wrote his final prophecy, he promised, "For you who fear My **name**, the sun of righteousness shall rise with healing . . . on the day when I act, says **the LORD**" (4:2–3).

When God is angry, "**the name** of **the LORD** comes from afar, burning with His anger, and in thick rising smoke" (Isaiah 30:27). When God saves, it is so that "you shall know that **I am the LORD**, when I deal with you for My **name's** sake" (Ezekiel 20:44). When the people of Judea received Jesus of Nazareth as King and Messiah at the great Feast of the Passover, waving palm branches in triumph and letting their children sing in the streets, they sang, "Hosanna to the Son of David! Blessed is He who comes in **the name** of **the Lord!**" (Matthew 21:9).

This same Jesus, when He established His New Testament Church, sent out eleven men saying, "Go therefore and make disciples of all nations, baptizing them in **the name** of the Father and of the Son and of the Holy Spirit" (Matthew 28:19). When John on the island of Patmos received his vision of the risen King, he saw a rider on a white horse, who was "called Faithful and True" and "The Word of God," but who also on His chest "has a **name** written that no one knows but Himself" (Revelation 19:11–13).

Therefore God has highly exalted Him and bestowed on Him the name that is above every name. Philippians 2:9

That **name** that no one knows, which scholars cannot understand or pronounce, God has nonetheless given for all the world to know and call on now in the name of **Jesus**. Just like with the word *alleluia* above, the name *Jesus* has YHWH built into it, though it is harder to hear due to traveling through Aramaic, Greek, Latin, and German to get to English. The short version is that *Jesus* is a Greek pronunciation of the Hebrew ***Joshua***. That "**ua**" on the end is the same "**YH**" of **YHWH** that you saw tacked onto the back end of allelu-"ia."

In *alleluia*, the YH is attached to the root of the word *praise*, so that *alleluia* means "**praise the name YHWH.**" But with *Joshua*, the YH is attached on the phrase "**He saves,**" so that, every time you say the name *Jesus*, you say, in very poorly pronounced Hebrew, "**YHWH saves.**"

Quite literally, "in Jesus' **name**" is the place where God has said that **He is**.

GOD HAS ALWAYS HAD A NAME

Beyond our comprehension, God has always **been** His name.

Treatises and endless tomes could be (and have been!) written on the power of this identity, on the immanence and transcendence of this presence, on the complexity of this God. But long before you can get to those things, you will need to move from the Second Important Thing about Being Creation to the Third. Truth be told, we've been in, with, and under this Third Important Thing all along. There is no way to know or talk about any of what these first two chapters have echoed without it. But now we are going to go there in theory too.

> [Jesus said,] "Father, glorify Your name." Then a voice came from heaven: "I have glorified it, and I will glorify it again." John 12:28

To be a Christian—to hear from God and to know Him according to His **name**—God is going to have to do more than simply **have** a **name**. If you are going to learn to fear God's **name**, to love His **name**, or to trust it, if you are going to call upon it in trouble, pray to it, praise or give thanks to it, even if you are only going to abuse it, curse or swear by it, lie or deceive with it, then God's having a **name** must make its own way through that line between Him and us, in order to tell it to you.

That **telling** is the Third Important Thing about Being Creation: **God speaks**.

THE SECOND IMPORTANT THING
ABOUT BEING CREATION

God has a name.

* **THE FIRST IMPORTANT THING:** There is a God.

* **THE SECOND IMPORTANT THING:** God has a name.

THE THIRD THING

God Speaks

JUST WORDS

"Let there be light," God said (Genesis 1:3). He spoke, and it came to be. A billion, billion years of mysteries happened in a second. In an afternoon. Before an evening without a sun yet created to set. Since then, a great deal has changed, including cataclysmic events that make it impossible to look back and understand it. But it did happen. "There was light," and so it was.

Nothing—not science, not history, not human reasoning—gets in the way of believing this so much as the old man's

> **By the word of the LORD the heavens were made, and by the breath of His mouth all their host.** Psalm 33:6

deep-seated hatred of the First and Second Important Things' hiddenness. The old man wants more than what the Third Important Thing has said about them. He is not content with knowing that God did something. He wants to do it himself. He is not content with knowing who God is. He wants to be God himself. It only follows then that he is not content with what God has said He has done and will be. The old man wants his own say.

So our real problem with a six-day creation has very little to do with any actual present-day scientific observations of cataclysmically decayed footprints, radioactive slippage, or the life-cycles of burning balls of gas. Our problem is the far more elementary truth behind it all that we consider ourselves too sophisticated to accept the truth. The threat to our pride is not that there might be a God who could scientifically create a universe in any amount of time that He wants. The real threat is if the way He does it is by merely **speaking**. If God built the world with science, then we can study how He did it, understand it, and ultimately replicate it. But if God just says stuff and then it happens, then it all becomes immediately beyond our ability to manage, to hold in our own grasp, to control.

God's speaking creation into existence is unacceptable to the average man because it only further demonstrates the fact that the average man has no chance of ever really being like God. Doubly so, if we were to admit to ourselves that God could speak, what would happen if we then found out we don't like most of what He has to say?

MORE THAN WORDS

It's easy for us to take for granted how essential words are to our lives. Words define us and life around us; they distinguish us from the animals. Words are the means by which we build all our relationships; they are the only way to know who anyone else is. This is the reason God speaks. God speaks because He wants you to know who He is. He may still want His eternity hidden from you, but He does not want His identity hidden from you. He wants you to know Him because He knows you. He created you to be in relationship with Him, and like all truly valuable relationships, this relationship is founded on meaning. For that meaning to exist between two people, it always requires **words**.

The age we live in has rejected the power of words. We take them for granted. But more than that, we doubt their ability to even mean the things we used to think they did. The failures to communicate in the history of societies and philosophies has led many to believe that words cannot actually convey truth at all. You've heard it before: *"After all, that's just your interpretation."*

Yet, when we say that words on a page have no meaning apart from your personal understanding of them, we inadvertently meet the hypocrisy of the argument. Words may not always work the way we want them to, but so long as we're still willing to use them to reject the interpretations of others, we confess

> **Every word of God proves true; He is a shield to those who take refuge in Him.** Proverbs 30:5

their power to have real meaning. We confess our trust in them to adequately bridge the gap between me and you.

This need for words isn't a coincidence. God built words into creation. More than this, He built the creation **out of** words. As He spoke the distinctions between light and darkness, land and sea, His words did not merely describe what He saw. He prescribed what would be. He bespoke things that were not, and that made them the things that are.

It is the refusal to believe this that makes an otherwise reasonable person look up at the stars streaming their ancient powers across the night sky and say, *"This came from nothing. The nothing made it all, longer ago than we could even imagine."* What is really going on, deep within the soul, is a willingness to the old man's insistence, *"The sun is not a word. The stars are not words. Words are what I can speak. Words are local noises, passing only from mouth to ear. Light is not a word. Water is not a word. Plants are not a word. Because **I am not a word!**"*

Except that you are. You are your **name**. But that is for later.

WORDS THAT ARE MORE

As much as postmodern scholars might boast about words having no real meaning, postmodern people still expect our words to "do what they say." From announcing to your friends where you'd like to go out for dinner to telling your four-year-old to pick up his toys, we all desire our words to have creative power, to go forth from our mouths and accomplish their purpose. It is this fact that seems to be the real source of our problem with God's words. While God's words always create whatever He says from the moment He speaks them, our words only reflect the intention to create.

We don't much like this. Just as we are always trying to get across that line between us and God, we are also always wanting our words to act more like His Word. Whether it's looking in the mirror and trying to bespeak a positive future into existence or trying to talk about "what I think God is like," we want our words to be creative. When they are not, we try to gain enough power, fame, or money that we can make it so.

You may not be personally trying to amass enough influence to make everyone and anyone actually hop when you say "hop," but every one of us one way or another is trying to make our words do more than they really can do. We tell ourselves what we'd like ourselves to be, and then we try to prove it to be true by telling other people that "that" is what we are. Listen carefully and you will find that we all have a rather self-inclined habit of describing ourselves not as what we are, but as what we'd prefer. Yet we rarely grant others the same charity. Instead, we spare no effort making sure to describe everyone else, not on the basis of what they say they are, but on the basis of what we see them actually do.

All mankind are liars. Psalm 116:11

Because this quest to make our words into **creative** actions is always coming up short, we are constantly pressured to deny God's words the power to create as well. The thorns of our subconscious can't allow God to be so far beyond us that we could never be like Him. One way of doing this is to conclude that God doesn't speak any real words at all. All those times in history where God audibly revealed Himself to humanity? *Fantasies!* The atheist bases his rejection of God's existence almost exclusively on the fact that he personally has never heard God speak. Armed with this, he assumes that therefore God has never spoken at all, and therefore does not exist, even with the visible words about *being creation* all around him.

Perhaps more dangerous is the Christian mystic. She doesn't mind believing that God has spoken to people in the past. She just insists that God is also speaking to her. But since she, too, has never actually heard God speak audibly, she insists that when God does speak, He doesn't use real words. Instead of words, the mystic believes that God uses inklings, touches, sensations, and dreamy whisperings. She never pauses long enough to think it odd that the God who could say "Let there be light," and there was light, now doesn't quite have the power to tell you what He wants you to know in a clear and straightforward way. The Christian mystic is the flip side of the atheist's coin. She might believe in spirituality while he does not, but neither of them understands the Third Important Thing about Being Creation, nor the power therein.

> How long shall there be lies in the heart of the prophets who prophesy lies, and who prophesy the deceit of their own heart?
>
> Jeremiah 23:26, 30, 32–33, 36

THE WAR OF THE WORDS

Throughout the history of the Christian faith, the war between God's real Word and the false words the enemy sows has raged back and forth on the battleground of human hearts and minds. It was the attack of the deceptive word against the Creative Word that brought about the breaking of humanity. It was this war that caused the sons of Seth to foolishly marry the daughters of Cain, thinking no harm could come of it, and so wreck the preflood Church's faith through their lust and arrogance. It was this war that caused the descendants of Noah to build a tower to make a name for themselves, only to have language itself destroyed in the process. It was this war that caused the children of Israel in the Promised Land to go off seeking signs and wonders from the witchcraft they found

> Now the serpent was more crafty than any other beast of the field that the LORD God had made. He said to the woman, "Did God actually say, 'You shall not eat of any tree in the garden'?" Genesis 3:1

in the high places and by the Asherah poles. It was this war that caused the medieval churches to put their trust in superstitious notes and statues and finger bones, and so bury the Gospel beneath a purgatory's worth of Greek philosophical constructs.

The back-and-forth war of the words has raged on and on. But for those who would fight for the Creative Word, all along there has been one sure and certain sign of false prophecy. Whenever speaking comes, claiming to be from God even though it is not, it will always also look to the authentic speaking of God that has come before it and call some of it into question. *"Did God really say that?" "Perhaps that's just your interpretation." "The men who wrote the Bible were only human, after all. Maybe evil men changed the texts and the churches forgot and now we need a new prophecy to restore it."*

Both Mormonism and Islam make such claims proudly. But again, notice how the God whose Word created the heavens and earth just by being said somehow isn't now powerful enough to make Himself understood. The God who preached through Peter at Pentecost so that men in every language heard without question that clear proclamation of the Christ now isn't able to handle making Himself clear to us? It is astounding that anyone could believe that human sin is so powerful that even God's Word isn't a match for it.

Armed with this cowardly excuse, a wide and seemingly easy path beckons you to discard what has surely been spoken by God, and to run off looking for something new, something to convince you that your words are more powerful than they really are. The old man will look for God in every crevice and corner, every shadow and penumbra of flittering thought and emotion, in the clouds and the sunshine, in signs and wonders. But he will never look for the real God because he will never look for a **God who actually speaks**. He will only really ever look for himself. He will only really ever look for his own words.

LOCATING THE MEANING

On a shelf in almost every home in the United States sits this book called the Bible. Though it is rarely taken down and read, it is an authentic record of the times **God has spoken**. In a very real sense, that is all it is. It is not an instruction manual for how to live your life, and it is not a grimoire for deciphering the omega code. It is a collection of eyewitness records written down by humans just as boring and broken as you, who happened to be there when the God who spoke the universe into existence spoke again into our fallen reality. And every single time, **He used real words**.

But even though the Bible clearly claims to be a final record containing everything He wants you to know, this doesn't go over very well with our old man. He's a jealous bugger. He thinks it's just not fair that Moses and Elijah got to have visions and we don't. (Forget that those visions were more or less the death of them—no retirement on the golf course for those two!) So he pipes up, *"The Bible is only there to point you to the real words. The real words of God aren't made of letters. They're made of spirit. They aren't local or audible. You can't actually hear them. They come to you secretly. They come still and small. They come within your heart. God's words come from you."*

Slippery as always, without ever officially denying the Bible, it is effectively set aside in favor of the oldest tradition in the history of our thorns: the tradition of making what you think into what God must have said.

Real words are **local**. They are limited in their existence. They are spoken, and you hear them. They hold to a certain time and a certain space. Even these words you are reading on the page are only right here, on the page. And you cannot read them all at once. Your mind must be located with them, one meaning at a time, receiving from their letters a description of an idea that you are then hearing in your head.

Spoken words are only different from written words in that they are carried on sound waves rather than light, and their local existence vanishes shortly after being spoken. This is not a bad thing. This is what makes spoken words so useful! Can you imagine if every word you ever spoke lasted forever, just hanging there outside your head, piling one on top of the other until you simply walked around with a constant barrage of meaningless sounds

> **The precepts of the LORD are right. . . .More to be desired are they than gold, even much fine gold.** Psalm 19:8, 10

41

blasting everyone else in the face? The **locality** of words is their strength, and it is from this locality that we can be confident in the power of all words to communicate meaning.

Imagine, for a moment, trying to have a conversation with your spouse or sibling without using any words. Perhaps, if you know each other very well, you might be able to send a signal with a bit of eye contact, a hand motion, or a grunt (but a grunt would be cheating). Imagine trying to have a conversation about whether cats are better than dogs or about how your day was ruined by something unexpected.

Without words, you could not do it. Though you were together, in a very cold sense you would still be entirely alone, trapped in a world full of meaning with no ability to share or understand it with the others around you. But when words enter into creation, suddenly all that trapped confusion changes, bursting forth with interaction, exchange, growth, and power.

All of this was God's idea, which makes it all the more odd that people who claim to believe in God might then consider Him incapable of participating with us on the same level. Why is it that we assume that when God speaks it will not be local and audible the way our speaking is? Why do we think that God could only speak through nudges and hints and not through clear declarations? The Bible, as a book, echoes with the phrase "thus says the Lord." You might think we'd be a bit wiser to the fact that God actually has talked and does talk.

THE PROBLEM WITH THE THIRD
THING IS THE FOURTH

This brings us back to the real problem: when **God speaks**, we do not like what He says. We don't like that His words consistently place us under an authority that is not our own.

When God spoke the world into existence, He spoke a design into place. His local, audible, creative words became localized, physical structures and boundaries— from the spectrum of color to the laws of thermodynamics to the purposes, duties, and limitations of the human spirit. This will be the heart of the Fourth Important Thing about Being Creation, which is the first Thing that ceases to be about who God is and starts to describe what God has given, beginning with the **order** into which God has given it.

> **The words of the LORD are pure words, like silver refined in a furnace on the ground, purified seven times.** Psalm 12:6

There is a God, and being God is what God does. **God has a name**, and because of who He is, **God speaks**. When He speaks, He speaks into being all that is and all that will be. He creates. He makes it so. He **gives**. That is His greatest desire, His highest identity: the God who is, who gives. And the first thing He gives is everything in its place.

THE THIRD IMPORTANT THING
ABOUT BEING CREATION

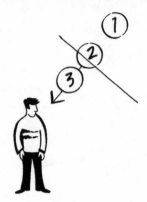

God speaks.

* **THE FIRST IMPORTANT THING:** There is a God.

* **THE SECOND IMPORTANT THING:** God has a name.

* **THE THIRD IMPORTANT THING:** God speaks.

THE FOURTH THING

God Designed You

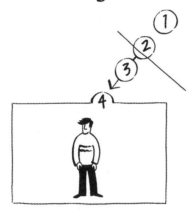

EXISTING ON PURPOSE

When God speaks, His words do what they say. In the beginning, He spoke. Whatever He said, happened. This means that **everything that is** came into being, and this according to His **design**. The Fourth Important Thing about Being Creation is this design, a permanent, physical/spiritual engineering of reality.

The universe is founded and ordered to work with purpose. It is intended to be the way that it is, to such a degree that not even our rebellion against it can truly knock it off its axis. This has as much to do with gravity keeping you from getting flung off the planet

> **When I look at Your heavens, the work of Your fingers, the moon and the stars, which You have set in place, what is man that You are mindful of him?** Psalm 8:3–4

as with the way each individual person is tailored to fit a specific niche in reality. We each are given an individual mind, a unique set of relationships, and a special place to make our life's **stand**.

This is where boring, little you gets to have a few spiffy edges and snowflaky corners to call your own. Average and just like everyone else, you are also designed as a gift to everyone else, given in an exclusive place, composed with your own diversity of experiences, connections, skills, and desires.

But in the same way that the first three Important Things about Being Creation quickly expose our inbred rejection of them, so also does the fact that **God designed you** present immediate problems. To begin with, we cry foul at the very idea of being made at all. To be designed means to be set within boundaries, to be given limitations, to be one thing and not another. The fact that there are things that are not made for *Me*, places beyond which *Me* cannot trespass, is an infuriating reminder that **I am not God**. The result is that all too often, even though God's design is perfectly orchestrated, *Me* often finds myself quite discontent with my particular snowflaky shape.

Yet, just as rebelling against the first three Important Things about Being Creation did not bring with it the power to change them, so our refusal to admit that God designed us cannot dislodge either us or the cosmos from what we are supposed to be. When God laid down our architecture, He did such a good job that even thorns sprouting up in the midst of it all cannot undo its grandly crafted order. It keeps working with all our best interests in mind, regardless of how we might feel about it. No matter how hard we fight against it, we cannot stop being what we are designed to be.

DISCORD IS MY PROBLEM

No matter how rashly we try, we cannot unleash ourselves from God's design. We only thrash headlong against it. The good that

God made never changes, but our war against it does prevent us from receiving it as all the good that it was supposed to be. The "better" design we keep trying to make is always worse.

Imagine that the entire universe is a series of perfectly parallel lines set in endless relationship. Living within these lines does not mean having a cold, sterile, lonely existence. It means that everything in the cosmos is in symbiotic harmony. From the leaves on the trees to the farthest star clusters, within their places the cosmos is a great dance of interconnected meaning. It is this obvious, straightforward, beneficial set of lines that the old man keeps running crossways against.

Me runs against the pattern, thinking *Me* will be able to improve the way things are, mostly in order to better benefit myself (although *Me* will always say that it is for your benefit too). Much like our failed attempts to find a way to God, running against the grain of the universe results in *Me* face-smashing against the changeless truth over and over again. We're all doing this. We bash our collective skulls in endless attempts to break

what was integrated to work perfectly, telling ourselves that we will only make it better. Spurred by our imagined "more awesome than God's design," we use the design in ways it was never intended. Sometimes science lines up with the design and gives us round wheels or gets us to stop eating hydrogenated oils, but the same spirituality goes on all the same. We are all reaching for what "is not" in order to make a better "is," but we more often just ruin things even more than they already are.

Naturally, when God speaks up to point this out to us, we don't want to hear it. We'd rather run away from the sound of His voice, pretending that all this decay is a flaw in the original design, blaming God for all the head-smashing. Hiding in the bushes, *Me* says, "*Me can fix this. If Me can just smash the line a little harder than before, then all the lines will bend sideways the way Me would like it better.*"

There is no authority except from God, and those that exist have been instituted by God. Romans 13:1

So moth and rust take their vigilant toll on what should have been incorruptible, and we find an ever greater discontent in our inability to fix it. The problems we do manage to solve only unearth more impossible ones. But the Fourth Important Thing about Being Creation is that God did not design the imperfection. God did not design the flaws. We have broken it, bending it out of proportion in the hopes of making it serve *Me* better. Yet God refuses to loose us from His good design. To do so would mean unleashing us from Himself. In order for Him to let us truly break through those walls, He would have to cease His constant care and protection, and He doesn't want to do that.

ONE MAN DESIGNED OVER ANOTHER

All of our misguided efforts cannot stop the underlying goodness of God's design from functioning for our benefit anyway. God is simply too good to abandon us without a fight. He is too good to unleash us from His design and let us descend into utter chaos that would happen if the authorities He designed were replaced with the authorities we would rather have.

> **To the only God, our Savior, through Jesus Christ our Lord, be glory, majesty, dominion, and authority, before all time and now and forever. Amen.** Jude 25

But it is our belief that authority is a bad thing. We believe that any kind of power someone else might have over *Me* is effectively the root of all evil. For this reason, we talk a good talk about things like equality, but all the while we're always trying to get a leg up on one another. Petty little tyrants that we each are, whenever we discover that there is an authority *Me* can't have, we try to deny that authority to everyone else as well. In order to protect ourselves from believing that we are not always in charge, we preach that for two people to be fast friends, they must be total equals, with no imbalance in their relationship at all, even while nothing in the universe works this way. In every human relationship, there is always a leader, and there is always a submitter—a follower. Wherever one or more humans assemble to achieve or do anything, there is always a head, and there is always a body. From the lifelong companion to the passing casual conversation, there is always a **master** and there is always a **slave**.

I am not talking about the slavery that involves buying and selling humans as traffic. That wicked act is not the authority God designed for us to have over one another, but a stealing of it. When we broke the world, it wasn't because God hadn't given us any authority at all, but because we were discontent with the authority we had been given and wanted more.

> **Children, obey your parents in the Lord, for this is right.** Ephesians 6:1

But from the beginning, there has always been a good kind of mastery and slavery, one that does not deprive men of their rights, but grants protection by divine right. Such rulership does not abuse the weak in their weaknesses, but serves them in order to make them strong. Such power structure is intimately designed into the best of every set of human relationships, but nowhere is it seen more clearly than the most central of all human relationships: the relationship between a father and his son.

When a son is born and subjected to the arms of his father so that he might lift him high and give him a name, the mastery vested in the man is not given over the boy for the sake of the father. The son is enslaved to his father for the sake of the son, that there might be another power greater than he, another person made master in order to protect his life, to ensure that he is well fed, well clothed, and well loved. In this way, power is never given by God for the good of the one who wields it. It is given for the protection and benefit of the one who is beneath it.

The Bible is graciously clear for us: fatherhood is designed to embody the identity of God the Father (see Ephesians 3:15), and it is the relationship of God the Father to God the Son that forms the crux of Christianity. We greatly err when we treat modern awareness of past abuses of power as a reason for rejecting the powers that God created good. It is not the design that is wicked, but our poor use of it. We will not make better use of it by further trying to deny or destroy it. Better is to recognize that if I am offended by any relationship that clearly demonstrates God's gift of mastery and slavery, power and submission, it is most likely because I will always be deeply discontent whenever *Me* is not the master of all, and any unchangeable reminder of that only strikes yet another blow against the attempts to make *Me* my own personal, almighty god.

True diversity does not despise the ordering of humanity within tailor-made places, roles, purposes, and identities, but relishes them each for the good that they are, precisely because they are different from the others.

THE HATRED OF POWER (WHEN I DON'T HAVE IT)

God made fathers, and God made sons. He made them as an image of Himself, a perfect relation, the ultimate love as the most excellent state of mastery (for the good) and submission (to the good). The Father seeks all good for the Son; the Son willingly receives the good His Father gives.

There is an old proverb that says, "Power corrupts, and absolute power corrupts absolutely." But this is simply a lie. If it were true, then God, who has all authority in heaven and earth, would become corrupted. It is not power that is evil. It is us. It is never power that corrupts a man, but a man who corrupts the power. The power itself is immeasurably good.

When God put some humans over others and called it good, it was because there is something stunning and worthy in **helplessness**. There is something beautiful in caring for the weak, and doubly so when that person can never give you anything in return. He put fathers in charge of their sons so that men might learn selflessness on behalf of others, so that we might find the joy of committing to another's good even if it costs us our own, and so that we might find the blessedness of wielding power to give rather than to receive.

Every authority is meant to work within such relationships. Every power is meant to think of itself as a fatherhood. Every submission is meant to view itself as sonship. The king does not exist for himself, but for those whom he serves by ruling. The husband is not head of the home for himself, but for the stewardship of the wife and children whom God gave him. The employer does not hire workers for his own benefit, but in order that he might benefit them by giving them good works to do.

> You know that the rulers of the Gentiles lord it over them, and their great ones exercise authority over them. It shall not be so among you. But whoever would be great among you must be your servant. Matthew 20:25–26

Power does not exist for the one who has it, but for the one who is beneath it. The only God-given authority is the **authority to do good** to the one under you. The first is last and the last is first. Strength is most perfect when serving the weak. Mastery is never for the master. Slavery is always for the slave, because by "slave" we really mean "son."

WITHIN THE FOURTH THING IS THE FIFTH

God says that He is God and we are not. Our hearts ignore Him.

He tells us that His name is all we need, but we don't want faith. We want sight, so we set up gods in our own image.

He tells us that for our own good He will continue to tell us what good is. But we aren't willing to listen. We imagine we can dream up something better.

So when He tells us that He designed us, naturally we have a problem with that too, little realizing that a world without design, without order, without duty, is also a world without purpose, without meaning, without any real, final goodness at all.

God keeps speaking anyway. **God designed you** is preached from the very created order itself. It's there to be heard, to be felt, to be studied under the microscope or in the symphony of the stars. The old man wants none of it. He points to the thorns, and he encourages the cycle of great evil, especially in the abuses of fathers to their sons, in the poor husbandry of the home by its head, in the poor treatment of the laborer by the one who holds his life in his hands. All along this path of thorns, we find neighbors setting themselves against neighbors.

The entire design is turned on its head by the thorny will of *Me*, who has forgotten how to believe that *Me* is not God, and so is ever trying to prove that *Me* is God, or at least trying to make others treat *Me* like God.

> I write these things while I am away from you, that when I come I may not have to be severe in my use of the authority that the Lord has given me for building up and not for tearing down. 2 Corinthians 13:10

Whether *Me* does this by destroying every authority standing in the way or by scraping and scrapping to wield the authority by and for myself, it blinds *Me* to the deep goodness of the **design God gave us**, the golden chains of our manifold relationships with one another. Within them, all authority exists for the sake of benefitting most the one who does not have it. To see this, you must believe instead that power, authority, mastery, and subjugation are all beautiful, blessed things. It is only our being evil ourselves that has caused them to be twisted. No king is an evil king when he truly believes that he holds the people in his arms, not as assets to be used but as a trust to be stewarded, a sacred fatherhood to be fulfilled for the sake of the good of all.

Thorny as we are, even when we embrace the idea of "loving the neighbor and serving the weak," average humans still have a poor history of knowing what the good of others really means. For this reason, God also speaks to us the Fifth, Sixth, Seventh, and Eighth Important Things about Being Creation. All of them are good gifts given to each of us within the great design. They teach us both how deeply God means for us to receive the good, and so also how best we might seek the good of others.

THE FOURTH IMPORTANT THING
ABOUT BEING CREATION

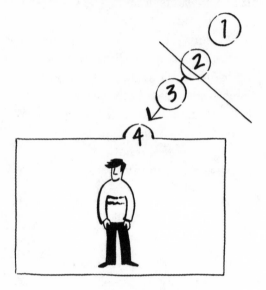

God designed you.

* THE FIRST IMPORTANT THING: THERE IS A GOD.

* THE SECOND IMPORTANT THING: GOD HAS A NAME.

* THE THIRD IMPORTANT THING: GOD SPEAKS.

* THE FOURTH IMPORTANT THING: GOD DESIGNED YOU.

THE FIFTH THING

God Gave You a Body

THIS IS YOU

This is where we started. Even though nothing really starts here, *Me* is the conduit for your experiences of everything. *Me* is not the center of the universe, nor the key to the meaning of life. But it's a lot less likely you would have kept reading the book if the dangling carrot that started it all off was a stick-figure drawing of someone else's dog or donkey.

But it is not as if you are not in the picture of the Ten Important Things about Being Creation at all. It's only that up to this point, you didn't really **need** to be in the picture. Everything about **there is a God** and **God has a name** and **God speaks** and **God designed you** got along fine before you came around. The first four Important Things all exist apart from you, while you exist underneath, from, and within them.

ECHO

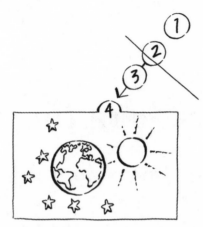

Such is our state that even once we know this, we still have a hard time picturing the existence of God without *Me* somewhere in it. While part of this is *Me's* overestimation of our importance to the system, it is also because the Fifth Important Thing about Being Creation is the fact that **you are in the picture**. You just aren't there from the beginning. You are not the first, or even the fourth. But you are here, right now, sitting in your own special (average) place from which you're viewing it all. Your existence is not a problem, but a gift.

> The LORD God formed the man of dust from the ground and breathed into his nostrils the breath of life, and the man became a living creature. Genesis 2:7

Understanding this has everything to do with seeking the right answers, which means asking the right questions. How you ask a question can have a great effect on the answer that you find. There is a massive difference between asking, *"Where is the true God, and how do I fit into His picture?"* and *"If there is a God, how does He fit into **my** picture?"* Whenever the picture that you try to draw starts with you, or if the God you seek is such a God that His existence rises or falls with you and what you see or feel or believe—that is, when you come at spirituality with the assumption that you are ground zero for everything the universe has to teach—then you are bound to end up slowly meandering down a path that is both limited in scope and bound for self-destruction. You will be boxed into the closed-minded arrogance of believing that *Each person finds her own truth* and *No one can tell you what is right for you.*

This is not a road to wisdom. Rather, it is a highway to ignorance, to division, to separation and despair.

But once you see that you are not ground zero for reality or meaning or even your life, once you learn to ask the right questions, to seek the right answers, to knock at the door of **what God says** instead of the door of *what you think*, then you are walking down the road less traveled. And on this road, you will find an explosion of certainty, unification, bonding, and hope. Once you believe that God really speaks, that what He says is really true even beyond you, then you find yourself in a world where **each person can receive the same *shared* truth**. You live in the freedom of never getting to tell God what is right for you because your eyes can see that **God telling you what is right for everyone** is so much better. It's how we got here! It's what keeps things from being worse than they are. It's how things are going to get better again.

How and where this impacts you always begins with the Fifth Important Thing about Being Creation, a truth that God has said is right for every human being on this planet: **God gave you a body**. This is a shared truth that we each receive, and without which none of us could be who we are. For all of us, it is the most important thing we know of, despite the fact that we are also in some kind of rebellion against it. On the one hand, we treat our body as if it were its own god, quietly worshiping its every whim and passion.

On the other hand, we ignore the pertinent value of our life's real meaning, too

> Man who is born of a woman is few of days and full of trouble. . . . He feels only the pain of his own body, and he mourns only for himself. Job 14:1, 22

often rejecting the clearest designated purposes for which God designed it. While your body—this gift, this thing and place that God made you—has far-reaching spiritual implications, it has significantly less significance than the average person admits.

HUMAN LIFE IS PHYSICAL LIFE

You *are* your body. Your body is how God gave you **you**. Everything that you are begins and ends with your body. You don't just inhabit it. You *are* it.

ECHO

Your body isn't a shell. It isn't some temporary holding place for some other thing you "really" are. You aren't just a bit of spiritual light trapped inside a body, waiting to become something better to come later on. Your soul has never existed without your body. Your body and your soul were created together, in the same moment, when two very special parts of two other people's bodies came together in order to both physically and spiritually become you.

> God arranged the members in the body, each one of them, as He chose. 1 Corinthians 12:18

God did this. He spoke you, designed you, and you came to pass. While it took a while to become all your parts, your eyes and ears, your reason and all your senses, from that instant of conception you were already the blueprint for all of you. You were meticulously engineered, knit intimately together with the mysterious power of what science still can't explain but calls "life."

The universe changed in that moment. There was a new human; that meant a new body and a new mind. From then until now, nothing you have experienced has been outside of both these things. All that you feel and think is done with that physical/spiritual miracle that is your brain/mind. You are a conscious world of thought that both leads and follows your heart, that wakes and rises, feasts and fasts, works and plays, all for the sake of that same body that is not some other thing, but you, yourself.

If you want to know the real answer to the age-old question *Who am I?* look in a mirror. You may not like what you see, but what you see is not the problem. What you see is what God made you. No, not the warts and wrinkles, not the results of decayed DNA or the preponderance of gluttony and sloth's effects. Beneath all that. Behind what the thorns have done, God has given to you, and still sustains, a very clear answer to the question *Who am I?* You are staring yourself in the face. That body is you, an extremely delicate, particular, powerful gift, both to yourself and to all the others you will ever meet. This is not ground zero for everything. But you are ground zero for the remaining gifts God has to give you in the final Important Things about Being Creation. Each of those gifts that follows will always be uniquely connected to you, the person. You, the human. And that means you, the **body**.

HARM AND HURT

When God designed your body, He gave you eyes to see both the world and the other humans in it, ears to hear them, and hands to serve them. He gave you a heart to perceive how you are a gift to them and they a gift to you. He gave you a mind to know that they, like you, are also bodies. As we each keep trying to climb up whatever ladders we've convinced ourselves will get us to where we want to go, seeking to bend all other things to our will to justify our pursuits to ourselves, we often find that all these other human bodies, all doing the exact same thing, keep getting in our way.

The story of humanity is not one of stranger helping stranger by pursuing the best interests of others. It is not a tale of an earnestly peaceful people plagued by undeserved sicknesses and hungers. It is not a tale of striving hand-in-hand to make a better world for us all by sacrificing individual needs for the greater good. No, it is a story of brother setting his face against brother. It is a history of neighbor arming himself in

And when they were in the field, Cain rose up against his brother Abel and killed him. Genesis 4:8

defense against neighbor. It is a tragedy of men slaughtering men.

"The wages of sin is death" (Romans 6:23). This is our doing, the effect of cutting ourselves off from the source of life. What is astounding is that we cannot even wait for it, but rise up against one another in violent attempts to avoid the inevitable. We keep

ECHO

trying to break down that wall between us and God. We keep calling Him by names He is not and refusing to hear the words He speaks. The things we build to replace the world He gave do not last or stand. The better reality we hope for continually turns out worse. Our bodies decay and time sweeps us away, and the terror that grows within us so distorts me from you that when push comes to shove, one body is more than willing to murder another. Brother murders brother, always in the name of his own body, depriving the other of the same gift, stealing the body he cherishes so deeply.

So common is this catastrophe that every culture in the world has laws against it. Every society has some rule, some code, some path to stop us from going too far in breaking the peace God designed us for. As a rule, those tribes or cultures where this code is not upheld do not last very long. They cannot, for in the end they exterminate themselves. Laws against murder do not exist because we are so virtuous, but because we are so wicked. It is self-preservation that realizes if we allow any man to go about murdering others, then one day he will murder *Me* too, or force *Me* to be his slave under threat of death. In such knowledge, even a bunch of *Mes* can come together and agree that we should have a law against killing another person's body. *Me* knows instinctively that human life is valuable when it is *Mine*.

When Gentiles, who do not have the law, by nature do what the law requires, they are a law to themselves, even though they do not have the law. They show that the work of the law is written on their hearts. Romans 2:14–15

Something is wrong with the world, and it is us. In those awful eras where nations rise against nations and leave in their wake more destruction than the mere slaughter of bodies, even the very soil itself suffers our hatred. Time and science have not fixed this; they have only increased the fallout of our wrath against one another. The more we attempt to bend God's design to our own intentions, the more grave consequences we create. The light in which we were created to live becomes clouded by the darkness of warfare and strife. The better we become at all things, the worse we become at this thing.

Death, whether by God's hand of punishment or the unjust hand of our neighbor's greed, only elevates the centrality of the Fifth Important Thing for you. What does it mean to be you? to be human? to enjoy and produce and serve? All these things happen in, from, with, and through your body. Our abuse of the body, or the murdering of it, does not destroy the goodness of its design as the truest home for you as you were designed to be. It is not having a body that is evil. It is the cutting off of ourselves from the root of life that has made it so we now cannot keep the bodies we were given for ourselves. Average you is left in the precarious position of trying to find an answer to the reason that everything around you, including you, is gradually falling apart.

CAUGHT BETWEEN TWO EXTREMES

There are two popular answers to this question. One school, the zealous religion of materialism, teaches that the human body is all that a human really is. There is no soul, no spirit, no heaven or hell. *Me*, so far as you are, is only a matter of some chemical bindings, a random smattering of particles bumping against one another chaotically. All that is, as far as the eye can see and beyond, is cosmic dust without a cause, a haphazard development that in *Me* has somehow stumbled upon the ability to observe and think about itself.

Most *Mes* traipsing about the world parrot the religion of materialism when they are told to do so. *"Darwin this,"* they say, and, *"Oh, of course, I believe in evolution that."* But while the preachers of materialism subdue the masses to their confession, rarely are they able to win the hearts of the people. Every teenager moping about the mall is wallowing knee deep in the intuitive angst of knowing there must be some ascendancy, some transcending, some purpose to what we call "soul." Sure, we may live as beings made up of dust, but something greater must be trapped within us for us to be so filled with expression, so flushed by desires and pressed by our avid willfulness.

Here steps in the subtle religion of paganism, which well knows that there is something more to human existence than the mere passing of electricity through bits of the periodic table. Whatever the human body is, it is more than the mere passing on of stronger genes forward through a cacophony of randomly generated species. So, masquerading behind the veneer of exercise studios and health centers, paganism preaches its antidote to the ominous darkness of materialism. It teaches that all those artful dreams and doubts that rage against the machines of our age are the longings of a spiritual being chained down within who you are. The real *Me*, it teaches, is a luminous being, more than the crude matter you temporarily inhabit. When that empty shell of your body dies, it is not the end. Then, at last, the real *Me* will be unleashed from its fleshly shell, set free to rise to the greater realm beyond those entrapping chains of this material world.

> Now may the God of peace Himself sanctify you completely, and may your whole spirit and soul and body be kept blameless at the coming of our Lord Jesus Christ. 1 Thessalonians 5:23

These two teachings are entirely contradictory to each other. But the average person has no trouble worshiping them both in their turn, bowing to whichever one demands their attention for the moment. Rare is the mind or soul who holds out to only one while rejecting the other. Rather, one moment we boast of evolving from the accidental linking together of random purposeless particles. The next moment we are searching deep inside for the spiritual *self*, valiantly striving against the existential terror of a life with no meaning. It is a bipolar religiosity as we each, alone, are driven to seek stability for the heart in ever more fragmented and atomized ways. The more we trust that we are nothing but matter, the less comfortable we are with the matter that makes us. The more we insist that the true life is not what you see, but what is *inside Me*, the less I can face what I actually am.

So we gorge our bodies on cheap carbohydrates and then despise them for not being what *Me* ought to be. We insist that *Me* is more than what I see until I refuse to believe that what I see is *Me* at all. *"This is not Me,"* *Me* says to the mirror, no matter what the mirror might say back. Then off *Me* goes on a quest to make the mirror agree with what *Me* wants to see *Me* be. While brazenly insisting that the body is all there is and not there at all, we believe that if we can change the body, we will change the soul as well. The result is a religion of destructive experience, ever trying to both be and deny what we actually are at the same time.

YOUR BODY IS NOT ALONE

It is the Fifth Important Thing about Being Creation that reconciles the problem. **God made *you* a *body*.** This ends the division. You are not *either* flesh *or* spirit. **You** are **incarnate.** You do not "have" a spirit, nor are you only a spirit. You are spiritual flesh. You are meat that breathes. You are a chemical will. Two realms conjoined by God's design, you don't just inhabit your body. You are not a soul within a body nor a body with a soul, but you are a **human being**, body and soul.

> Or do you not know that your body is a temple of the Holy Spirit within you, whom you have from God? You are not your own. 1 Corinthians 6:19

To try to be one without the other is to rebel against what you are designed by God to be. Today, you are here, in this physical place, holding a book made of words that engage your spirit. These are my words, from my spirit, which you know only after seeing them with your physical eyes, written on material paper. As you read them, the gray matter of your brain fires countless shots of electric bolts down potassium-charged channels, and these **are** your thoughts, your feelings, your spirit encountering my thoughts, my feelings, my mind that speaks to you through material fingers dancing across a set of plastic keys.

More than a mere matter of the chemicals strung together, these bodies are who God designed **us** to be—**humanity**, the plural "you," not something other than what we see, but strings of chemicals given life, miraculously also able to believe it.

THE FIFTH IMPORTANT THING
ABOUT BEING CREATION

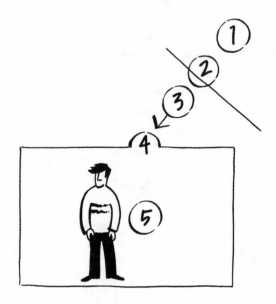

God gave you a body.

✳ THE FIRST IMPORTANT THING: THERE IS A GOD.

✳ THE SECOND IMPORTANT THING: GOD HAS A NAME.

✳ THE THIRD IMPORTANT THING: GOD SPEAKS.

✳ THE FOURTH IMPORTANT THING: GOD DESIGNED YOU.

✳ THE FIFTH IMPORTANT THING: GOD GAVE YOU A BODY.

{ *God settles the
solitary in a home.*
Psalm 68:6 }

The Sixth Thing

God Gave You Family

NOT ALONE

Being a body is a pretty great experience when everything is new and fresh. Humans are born ready. The whole world lies before us. Exploration. Engagement. The chance to build, to craft, to dream. The young child's eyes are active, always darting about for new inputs of awe and wonder. God gave you a body, and through that body you experience all the other gifts God gives.

But it's not enough. After you learn to breathe, to crawl, to know and observe. After you find the sun and learn its name. After the stars, the sky, the dog, the cat, the apple, and the orange are seen and experienced, it turns out this magnificently designed world ends up a very lonely place without the Sixth Important Thing: **other people**.

There are many ways to say it: God gave you **community**; God gave you **relationships**; God gave you **fellowship**. But these are all extensions of the one, central connection at the heartbeat

> **Then the Lord God said, "It is not good that the man should be alone."** Genesis 2:18

of human existence. All relationships flow out from and back to one core relationship. We all come from it, and in it all futures lie:

71

ECHO

God gave you family, and He did so by designing the particular, intimate gift of a husband and his wife.

BOY + GIRL = MORE

But now we have a problem, because this book is written during an age of terminological destruction. We live at a time when the world is trying to **destroy words**. How we got here is less important than that we **are** here. You and everyone else with you—your children, your parents, your friends, and your neighbors—all live in a strange land where humans **no longer believe in meanings**. We no longer believe in **truths**.

Nowhere is this more evident than in the battleground over the simple word *marriage*. It was once elementary, an assumed truth every child could explain. Now many question it, claiming it is too "old" a concept, a relic of religious bigotry and outdated morals. But these new assertions are based on willfulness, not facts. Marriage may be an old concept, but it is only old because it is not a word based on ideas or philosophies but on **events**. Its definition is not a matter of religious fanaticism but a scientific observation of the way things are. The meaning of family has been assumed for so long because it is so obvious. It is a matter of physics.

Like the earth going around the sun or a hot pan frying a raw egg, family is what happens when certain actions have consistent, provable reactions. All the humanity that is or was or ever will be exists only from and through the physical design of **procreation**. It is a law of nature that even an evolutionist has to confess in order for evolution to have any meaning at all. Only a human man and a human woman can make a baby human.

Man is designed to link perfectly with woman and vice versa. It's a unification far deeper than friendship and more substantial than the mere heat of ecstasy. By design, both companionship and pleasure combine in a sacred, carnal act, housing within itself a physically undeniable miracle, a literal **generation**. A piece of one person and a piece of someone else come together. Their very molecular selves join and become **another**. Two bodies come together to produce a third body, who is both of you and neither of you at once. **XX** meets with **XY**, and as a result a new, sentient *person* is created.

With exceptions that have more to do with decay than design, all humans are born with this inbuilt ability to bear more humans. God designed it this way. He molded the physiology of our forms to be capable of and to desire intimacy to pass forward new life. Here alone are all human relationships born. Here alone does the entire species' future flow. **God gave you procreation.**

There are billions of not-yous running about this planet, but only about half of them present you with the scientific possibility of procreation. **XX** needs **XY**, and **XY** needs **XX**. They are for each other and from each other. A man may love his dog, and a woman may rest comfortably against a tree, but they cannot conjoin to form another. For that wonderful effect, for that gift of a future that is not alone, **God gave you family**, and He did it through the designed physiology of **marriage**.

Everything the words *marriage* and *family* have meant is bound up in this set of facts. Though we live in an age when men and women are trying hard to deny it, facts cannot be bigoted. And no matter how great a tantrum one may throw, science cannot be chauvinistic. God's design cannot be unfair or old fashioned. God's design is always good.

> [Jesus] answered, "Have you not read that He who created them from the beginning made them male and female, and said, 'Therefore a man shall leave his father and his mother and hold fast to his wife, and the two shall become one flesh'?" Matthew 19:4–5

THE ULTIMATE ALONE

Physics is built on laws. Water does not run uphill. How we feel about that fact does not matter. In the same way, a man and a man may lie together in the heat of physical passion. A woman and a woman may find comfort in the emotional intimacy of each other's arms. But neither of those acts can change the reality of natural design. Neither can deny that a world filled only with humans who engage in same-sex acts would be a world that has no human future. A world where the last two men marry each other rather than the last woman is a world where that man is one day left all alone, with only death to look forward to.

But homosexuality is not the only way to reject the design of XX + XY = more. Marriage is not only about procreating new children. It is also about raising them. To **bear** a child is not only to **beget a person**—body and soul, mind, heart, and hands—but to beget a person who needs to be fed, loved, grown, and taught. It is to create a person who is **helpless**. Nine months after the sacred act, when that infant's lungs fill up with life-sustaining breath for the first time, a parent's work is not done.

It is from this universal continuation of childbearing that the "till death do us part" of "old-fashioned" marriage came about. The idea that a man and a woman, once married, were **married for life** is no arbitrary stricture imposed upon us by some made-up "holier-than-thou" fundamentalism. It is a recognition of physical reality. Come richer or poorer, come sickness or health, that new, helpless person needs to be cared for. The wedding vow is not only a commitment to care for each other, but more deeply

> Your wife will be like a fruitful vine within your house; your children will be like olive shoots around your table. Behold, thus shall the man be blessed who fears the LORD. . . . May you see your children's children! Psalm 128:3–4, 6

also a commitment to care for each other **so that** they may care for the others whom they will inevitably bring into being. How much easier it is to face the fears of raising a child when you do not have to face them alone!

As much as modern traditionalism may moan and wail about the dangers of homosexuality to society, there has been no more foundational assault on marriage in the present day than long-accepted **deconstruction of marriage by divorce**. There are without question many factors at play in every divorce. There are tyrannical men, and there are harping women. There are fools who marry for lust, calling it "love!" There are bizarre twists of fortune where an illness or injury permanently distorts a personality for the worse. Yet no matter the justifications we throw at it—whether our excuses consist of narcissism drummed up to sear the conscience or the excuse of the truly unavoidable tragedies of a broken world—it is willful blindness to believe that what God has joined together can be put asunder without consequence, both for the individuals involved and for the community in which they have lived. More than even them, divorce consistently and without question victimizes most the very persons the marriage was designed by God to produce and protect: the children.

No matter how much mommy or daddy might plead that it is really "good for everyone," no matter how many candies or toys might be poured upon the soul-deep wound, the child of divorce will forever know with terrible honesty the fearful spiritual consequences of breaking natural law. What God designed so that man might not be alone has now left that child alone after all. The parents will still be there. They will each have a place to call home, and the child will bounce back and forth between them like a tennis ball. But the foundational link of emotional safety is broken. The most secure thing in the world is now insecure.

> [Jesus] said to them, "Because of your hardness of heart Moses allowed you to divorce your wives, but from the beginning it was not so." Matthew 19:8

It is not a matter of reason. It is a scar on the heart. Once two people who promised to love each other forever and to never leave each other do so, what then is to keep them from changing their minds again, and so also leaving *me*?

Divorce has been a slow, terminal disease in the war to deconstruct marriage. The acceptance of homosexual lifestyles is only the icing on the cake. Same-sex attraction is only the logical conclusion of broadly held assumptions that have long divorced marriage from both duty and commitment. Before transgenderism, before abortion, before birth control, our civilization decided that two *Mes* could fuse to each other by solemn vow, permanently fuse to each other through the procreation of children, and then freely change their minds. It is folly to assume such a radical change in direction would have no effect on the civilization as a whole. You cannot tear down a home constructed for love and put in its place a shanty affirming hate without it affecting the neighborhood. You cannot surgically insert into the fidelity of family a "break my word" clause without it having negative results on the communities in which those families live. You cannot say both, "I pledge to you my faithfulness" and, "*I would rather spend the rest of my life all alone than spend one more minute with you*" without it having broad sweeping consequences on the way we view the idea of "human relationship" at its very core.

YOU GET WHAT YOU PAY FOR

When push comes to shove, the Sixth Important Thing about Being Creation isn't very important to American Christians. It is at least not *such* an Important Thing that we would teach our children to pursue it and its fruits as the most laudable goal of this life. Instead, it has become something we teach them is best put off until a later time. Best avoided *until you're ready*. We may not say the words, but the implications are clear: marriage and children are not nearly so worthwhile to you as a good paycheck. Children are not a foundation, but an accessory. A high standard of living is the thing that really matters.

> I would have younger widows marry, bear children, manage their households, and give the adversary no occasion for slander. 1 Timothy 5:14

As a result, what terror faces the parent whose child comes home from college after one semester and says, "**I would like to drop out, get a job, and get married!**" What consternation and effort the family will employ to stop this most disastrous of all possibilities! *Only a fool could throw life away like that!* Worse still, what if they plan to have children right away? What if they refuse to use the pill due to concerns over its abortifacient possibilities? What if she never gets her degree at all? What if they end up living less than middle class? Instead of asking, "*What if our children never have families?*" we ask, "*What if they never have enough stuff?*"

VS.

It is this reversal of priorities that is the real root of the war against marriage. We are all too comfortable in a culture built on placing a higher value on *Me* than on **Us**. Loud voices raise fears of how bad things may become, but few decry the path that brought us here. It is not just homosexuality. It is not just divorce. It is everything that we no longer teach our children about the Sixth Important Thing. It is the fact that for all our rage against the new and shiny challenges to marriage, we are quite calloused and accepting of the challenges that were quite radical less than a century ago.

"Wisdom is justified by all her children" (Luke 7:35). If you want to know what people believe, do not listen to what they say, but observe what they **do**. Our children reflect our doing back to us. Sex before marriage is the result of a generation raised to believe pregnancy is a thing to be avoided. The creation of new people is not a glory to be aspired to but a jeopardy that gets in the way of personal pleasures.

 might dream longingly of

but maybe less often of

 does not equal

at least until there is much more

You may yet find a young woman who aspires to having children *someday*, but extinct is the young man who believes that the greatest of life's ambitions is to have a family. Would you like a new car? *Yes, as soon as possible, even if I can't really afford it.*

> **Therefore God gave them up in the lusts of their hearts to impurity, to the dishonoring of their bodies among themselves, . . . committing shameless acts with men and receiving in themselves the due penalty for their error.** Romans 1:24, 27

What about sex? *Of course I want that. And I'm having it, but please don't tell my parents.* Children then? *Oh no. Not now. Maybe later. But I've got more important things to do.*

The sexual revolution began outside the Christian home, but it has embedded itself in the decisions that young Christians are now making. Our demographics and our pocketbooks speak more loudly than the Sunday School puppets. They have grown up believing that God's only desire is that they have a good time. They think that "*pleasure*" is the measure of truth. They have *I can do all things through Christ who strengthens me* tattooed on their legs and necks, but they think "all things" means "*whatever I want to do most.*" It is no surprise, then, what happens when *what I want to do most* becomes *have sex.*

Modern culture favors pleasure without the begetting, far more than the culture favors commitment and fruitfulness. Rare is the Christian brave enough to question these monolithic assumptions actively. We may still preach to the few sons and daughters we've decided to have that they must resist their God-designed hunger for procreation during its time of peak production, but then we cast them headlong into a pile of pheromonal wolves. Whether they handle the matter by soiling their clothing behind closed doors or by quietly aborting the unintended outcomes, what has truly been stolen from them is the great hope of human relationships: **the freedom to not be alone.** It is less that we have become disobedient to God's will as that we have become undesiring of His gifts.

The children we have are the ones we have raised. Two years of boring afternoons with the pastor beginning at age 12 will not protect them from a world dedicated to pleasure at all costs that we refuse to disagree with. Blaming others is no way to enact positive changes. Madness, it has been said, is doing the same thing over and

> **Fathers, do not provoke your children to anger, but bring them up in the discipline and instruction of the Lord.** Ephesians 6:4

over again while expecting a different result. Repentance is what happens when the preaching of the world comes into conflict with the Important Things about Being Creation, and rather than defend the errors of the past, we embrace the perfection of God's design. Today, this means ceasing to teach our children that the key to happiness is having enough corn syrup, imported plastic, and entertainment to keep yourself constantly satiated. We embrace God's design by remembering that the joy of being human begins with not being alone. It means refusing to let the power of pleasure be our guiding light any longer, and believing again in the call of marital duty.

> **They became futile in their thinking, and their foolish hearts were darkened. Claiming to be wise, they became fools.** Romans 1:21–22

CONCLUSION

The Ten Important Things are not really concerned with how all the varied *Mes* in the world would like the world to be. God's design is not concerned with what we want or what we would rather have. It is the Ten Important Things about **What Is**. The Ten Important **Ways Things Are**.

And they're all gifts! They are important because they are inherently **good**. They are the Designer and His design, filled to the brim with value, worth, and fulfillment. The old man will always argue against them, but he can only do so by pointing to his own thorns. *"What about two men who love each other? What about a couple who cannot have children? What about how much money it takes to raise a family?"*

The thorns are not part of the design. The thorns are what we have grown by our fighting against it. We will not fix anything by further attempts to shatter the gift. Sowing more tares in the wheat field does not remove the tares that are there. You must sow more good wheat.

The things we have abused are not destroyed by their misuse. They are still written into the fabric of our being. **God gave you marriage** to combat the worst possible outcome of life: being alone. He gave you family to bind your *Me* to **Us**, to fuse **Us** together in a world where we are one another's meaning. Each procreation awakens the unwavering power of commitment to **another**. Each generation stabilizes the one that follows by parenting fragile infant consciences with hope for a future of togetherness. Regardless of the hard circumstances, the better or worse of two selfish *Mes* learning how to put up with each other, the marriage of a man to a woman remains the glue from which all humanity's relationships flow.

Whether you are

 or  ,

God gave you

so that you could have

and we might have

"It is not good that the man should be alone" (Genesis 2:18). So God made more. He designed **diversity**. He created an ordered world of bodies with souls, each with inbuilt vocations tailor-made for your physical person to hold securely, to make a good stand in. At the heart of this order, He designed all humans different but the same, two pieces of a puzzle that once joined together can never be divided again, two bits of each other that in the spiritual fire of love become a third.

> Behold, children are a heritage from the LORD, the fruit of the womb a reward. Psalm 127:3

Marriage. It's the Sixth Important Thing about Being Creation because it's how "being creation" happened to you. Even if you are a child of divorce or born of parents who never tied the knot in public, nothing changes the fact that God designed the procreation of you, a gift to yourself and to all of the **Us** who will ever be. Everything in the world is better because of marriage. Dogs and cats and giraffes and chocolates are wonderful things, but they are that much more wonderful when there is someone to share them with.

THE SIXTH IMPORTANT THING ABOUT BEING CREATION

God gave you family.

* THE FIRST IMPORTANT THING: There is a God.

* THE SECOND IMPORTANT THING: God has a name.

* THE THIRD IMPORTANT THING: God speaks.

* THE FOURTH IMPORTANT THING: God designed you.

* THE FIFTH IMPORTANT THING: God gave you a body.

* THE SIXTH IMPORTANT THING: God gave you family.

THE SEVENTH THING

God Gave You Stuff

ALL GOOD THINGS

The first three Important Things about Being Creation were all about **who God is to His creation**. With the Fourth Important Thing, we left that realm and entered the design of **who God's creation is to Him**. Everything that has followed exists within this "big box" of God's design. The Fifth Important Thing deals with your body, how you were created to live and move and have being within the cosmos. The Sixth Important Thing deals with your relationships, how God didn't think it was good for you to be alone so He made you part of a vast race of other people. The Seventh Important Thing now steps out of the sphere of humanity and into the world that remains. The Seventh Important Thing is the fact that along with your body and your family, **God has also given you everything else**.

> And God said, "Let the earth sprout vegetation, plants yielding seed, and fruit trees bearing fruit in which is their seed, each according to its kind, on the earth." Genesis 1:11

85

Some of it is living. Some of it is inanimate. All of it is good. Food and clothing, land and animals, wind and rain, stars and dust, spicy and sweet: they're all particles of the grand design, each inch intimately crafted for mankind to receive, possess, cherish, and understand. Everything that is not you or some other person, all the goods, all the substances, all the materials we can ever find, are all a giant gift from God to us to steward, to share, and to enjoy.

I don't know what your favorite food is, but you know that it is **awesome**. That's not just your opinion, even if not everyone else agrees with you. Your favorite food *is* awesome. God made it that way and gave you the special insight to recognize it. That joy of experiencing the good of creation is not some arbitrary thing, but an eternal reflection of the ultimate goodness of God Himself.

God's greatest desire is to give pleasure to others. Far from being some whiny tyrant in the sky, making the world and us for His own benefit, God made humanity strictly to give His joy to us. The chief end of man is not to give glory to God, but to receive it **from** Him. He didn't need people to worship Him, as if He has a poor self-image without someone to sing about how cool He is. He wanted people to give things to, because giving is the greatest thing there has ever been. We enter God's glory when we realize that He is the giver of all good things to us, when the direction is not up but down, when the worship is not flattery but thanksgiving. He does not need us to take what we find in this world and offer it to Him as if He did not already have it or could not make a million more on a lark. He wants us to take what we find in the world and share it with one another, because that is what He made it for.

ALL GOOD THINGS, BENT

God gave you stuff. The amazing, endless diversity of all the myriad of things in the universe are the designs He laid to bring eternal joy into the material world. Your favorite food, your favorite color, your favorite music, your favorite animal. Your home. Money. Weather. Breath. God planned it all, intimately crafted it precisely so that you could have it, experience it, and use it.

Of course, there are things that exist that you probably don't enjoy. The bad news for you is that this is essentially your fault. Sometimes it is your fault because you're stubborn. Sometimes you just refuse to enjoy something that really is totally awesome. You don't like the crust on your bread or that amazing bitter taste of a cup of coffee or (heaven forbid!) the sweet burn of a splash of sriracha in your burrito. In such cases, something that is fairly awesome has been ruined by your original sin. The rest of the world knows that it is good, but for whatever reason you've become the child of discord on the matter. It's not really a big deal. None of us escape from this. We all do it one way or another. I personally can't stand peanut butter. I'm not going to go to hell for it, but it does contribute to the total experience of life on this planet being less than perfect.

Then other times, what should have been totally awesome is really ruined completely. Something that should have been good for everyone is bad for everyone. This also is caused by our original sin, though it is less directly your fault. Mosquitoes and dandelion roots. Puppy training and high humidity on a summer day. That feeling when you first wake up. The way sugar metabolizes around your waistline. These aren't the end of the world either, but just like our stubborn opinions, they signify that the world isn't functioning like it should. That is, the cosmos isn't acting like there is a good God who designed it all to be perfectly suited for us.

Something is off-kilter. Metal rusts. Concrete cracks. Cat litter never stays in the box. All the good things that God made are, to borrow a word from C. S. Lewis, "bent." They are other than they were supposed to be. Their substance hasn't changed. The molecules and atoms didn't become morally evil. But there's been a shift on the axis of reality. Everything is ever so slightly crooked. The earth totters askew, all the way down to the half-life of atomic decay. Things are the way they "seem" they should be. But stuff was not supposed to be this way. Stuff was not supposed to be bent.

Perhaps the most important thought in all of Christianity is that **it won't remain this way for long**. We'll get to that soon. But before we do, the Seventh Important Thing is seeing that the bending of the big-box design of creation hasn't stopped all the good things from still being good things. Even if we abuse them or don't know what they're good for, God gave us **this** stuff. He continues to sustain it. Sugar and spice and frogs and snails—God still thinks they're all a great idea. Some might be great food.

Some might just keep the ecosystem in line. Some might serve the purpose of pointing out to you personally how things aren't the way they were supposed to be. But none of it is evil in itself. Evil in itself is **our** problem.

All the struggles in the world, from the pricking of your finger on a rose to the smell of sweat in your armpit, are not a matter of the things themselves. The pain and the nasty scent are the bent reflection of what our old man has done to the world. Alcohol and hamburgers, tobacco and fossil fuels, electric guitars and pharmaceuticals, video games and money, they're all **good**. The problem is not in them but in us. In how we use them. In how we **mis**use them. The root of evil is never in the material stuff that God has given us. The root of evil is not in the **mammon**. It is in the way we love the mammon. It is in the way we try to use the mammon to give us the fear, love, and trust we should only be able to find in God Himself.

> [We] exchanged the glory of the immortal God for images resembling mortal man and birds and animals and creeping things. Romans 1:23

TWO TYPES OF AWESOME

Much of the falsehood that exists in every not-Christian religion comes down to this confusing of the creation with God Himself. We have a nasty habit of attributing to the many good things of the world the kind of goodness that it takes to **be** God. As a result, we tend to believe that there is only one kind of goodness in the universe, and that it is shared by everything, including God. But that's just not true.

The kind of goodness that everyone knows about because of all the experiences and stuff we find lying about does come from God. But it only does so **indirectly**. God is the ultimate source of the awesomeness that is pizza. Pizza is a reflection of how totally awesome God is. But pizza is not God. He designed it, but we are a part of it. The plants grow. Humans harvest. You bake. Your friend eats. This is good because God created it that way. They are God's good creation, but they are not God and His own goodness.

The other kind of goodness is radically different. It is the goodness of God's own self: His own existence and substance, the direct goodness from which all indirect goodness flows. This is **who God is**. He is the source of all things existing at all. He is the life by which they are continually sustained. God's own personal awesome is the kind of goodness it takes to **be** God.

The problem comes when we confuse the two. The problem comes when we take the fact that **there is a God**, that **God has a name**, and that **God speaks**, and we try to achieve unity with those things through the orders of creation that were never made for those purposes.

Put another way, there are two places where we exist, two relationships that define all others. We exist before God, and we exist before one another. We have a relationship with God, and we have relationships with our neighbors. This mark of separation is evident in the Ten Important Things, where the first three deliver to us the goodness of God in His personal self as the primary meaning of existence. The remaining Important Things deliver the goodness of what He has created for us to be and share.

All of these things are good, but only one of them can be God or bring God to us. The full picture is not yet developed, but the distinction is clear. There are Important Things about Being Creation that have to do with God (there is a God; God has a name; God speaks). And then there are Important Things about Being Creation that have to do with not God (God designed you; God gave you a body; God gave you family). **God giving you stuff** continues to fill out this second category.

GRANT THEFT CREATION

In our quest to be gods, we are always coming up short. We are constantly running into that wall of God's existence, trying to stake some kind of claim on His own personal goodness as something we can share. Falling on our tails over and over, the old man begins casting about for anything to convince us we still have a shot. He readily starts believing that the various goodnesses he finds in all the stuff can help him get over the hump. *"Me may not be able to ascend to the heavens, but Me can still live as if a god among the rest. Me can still amass enough things to convince myself that Me is greater than they."*

The result is that we take the many gifts of creation given to us by God and use them as replacement gods to bolster our misguided quest for divinity. Whether this happens by funning away the years, by eating away the helplessness, by drinking away the pain, by storing up more future than you could possibly need, or by setting up a statue of a golden cow and calling it "God," the result is always the same. The stuff God gave you is never enough to make you **be** like Him. Nature cannot become what only the supernatural can be. Wood and stone, silver and gold, dust and ashes, none of it can help you ascend out of your imperfections, let alone to godhood. No matter what you call it, the creation can never take the place of the Creator.

That hardly stops us. As soon as your stuff fails to satisfy you, you seek out more stuff, even if it happens to be stuff that belongs to others. In a world as debased as ours, you can still get in trouble if you outright steal things. But *steal* is such a narrow, limited little word. What if you just "copy" it? What if you pay only what you believe is a "steal" of a price? What if you find a way to get it that is totally legal, working the system to your advantage? *What a deal!* But the definition of a deal is that one person takes a loss. Somewhere, somebody is stuck holding an empty bag.

All the efforts of *Me* to consume creation as the answer to its own bentness ends up consuming you. Your wants become needs and your needs dominate. Everything gets subjected to your body's hungers and whims. You cannot be hands to aid while *Me* is being the hands to help myself. You cannot be a heart to care while *Me* is looking out for number one. You cannot be a mind to seek the good while *Me* can only perceive good when it is stored in bigger and bigger barns.

In order to have "enough," you begin to capitalize on your neighbor. Your neighbor is no longer family, but an object, a tool, or at the very least someone to borrow tools from and forget to return them. Authorities, wherever you find them, cease to be benefactors and are seen as your enemies, something to be rebelled against or outwitted. Your vocations, whatever they are, cease to be works done to benefit others and are mangled into means for protecting yourself. All the things designed to bring satisfaction are sacrificed on the altar of your endless appetites, giving way to discontent and discord for all.

Like children who've received a balloon at the store and within minutes are screaming and grabbing and crying out "*It's mine,*" we've ruined what we've been given **to share** by insisting that the things we have are ours **to keep**. In order to get all that you really want, bit by bit you enable a world where someone else does not. For some to have, others must be have-nots. Whether macro or micro, whether done in the name of capitalism, socialism, or the divine right of kings, it's all **theft**.

VIGILANTE GIVER

God gave you stuff, and He has done so **by the hands of others**. His great joy is sharing, so He made the world with sharing built into the system. Creation exists by sharing itself, growing and producing and exchanging in a million and more uniquely designed ways. God is at work behind it all, like a gift-giving vigilante with a million masks. He's not just behind the ecosystem of plants and animals, bacteria and fungi, as they take what the others give and return what something else needs. His love of sharing is also behind being family, working everything a community thrives on in the same give-and-take. As people live their lives, fulfill their pursuits,

ECHO

and produce with their bodies, humanity helps one another to receive the stuff we all need by God's design.

It's such a good design that even our thorns can't stop it. We don't just share only if we want to. We can't help it. Even when we capitalize on others, the others still receive something. It might be broken all to heck by our self-driven intentions and discontent, but even at our worst, the system won't let us harm everyone all the time. In order to take advantage of one another, **we still need one another**. When we barter a hard bargain, scraping every penny from our neighbor in the deal, we still make a trade for something our neighbor needs enough to agree to it. Even as we try to horde it all for ourselves, the system curbs us back to ensuring the group's survival.

> **Everything created by God is good, and nothing is to be rejected if it is received with thanksgiving.**
>
> 1 Timothy 4:4

But it is so much better when we do it on purpose! Creation may be capable of functioning even while we're all working against it, trying to take from and take advantage of our neighbors. But God built the system so that all would serve all with intention. Buried within the heart of that intention is the source of true joy. While *Me* always believes that the meaning of life is wrapped up in getting and using all the stuff for myself, true lasting joy is found in giving good stuff to others to be enjoyed by them. When joy is shared, it is multiplied exponentially. A piece of cake is always better when eaten by two.

Your body is perfectly designed for this. Your eyes don't look at your own face, but are placed perfectly for you to see the needs of others. Your ears are built to hear the "please" of their request. Your hands are formed to hold and deliver the gift. Your heart, even with its thorns, is still more than capable of finding pleasure in the pleasure experienced by somebody else. **God gave you stuff**, so that you could **give it to others**.

THE SEVENTH IMPORTANT THING
ABOUT BEING CREATION

God gave you stuff.

ECHO

* **THE FIRST IMPORTANT THING:** THERE IS A GOD.

* **THE SECOND IMPORTANT THING:** GOD HAS A NAME.

* **THE THIRD IMPORTANT THING:** GOD SPEAKS.

* **THE FOURTH IMPORTANT THING:** GOD DESIGNED YOU.

* **THE FIFTH IMPORTANT THING:** GOD GAVE YOU A BODY.

* **THE SIXTH IMPORTANT THING:** GOD GAVE YOU FAMILY.

* **THE SEVENTH IMPORTANT THING:** GOD GAVE YOU STUFF.

THE EIGHTH THING

God Gave You a Name

WE NEED TO SEE SOME IDENTIFICATION

Identity should not be a difficult thing to find. A glance into a bathroom mirror is all you really need. It might not be as hip as pretending to be whatever you think you want to be. But no matter what you might tell yourself, there in the mirror is that

staring back at you. Your body is a giant raging hint to your identity in multiple ways, beginning with its source in the two other bodies whom God used to make you.

Who your parents are defines you more than you may want to admit. But "not wanting" to admit it won't stop

from defining you too. Before anything else, your body is one flesh formed of the two others who bore you. Not in your genes or because of them but **as** them, you are a chip off the old blocks. Beyond this, as much as you are "just like" both your father and your mother, you are also a lot more like one of them than the other in one biologically significant direction. With rare medical exception due to traumatic genetic disorders, from the moment a human is conceived, you are either man or you are woman. Being a man or a woman, notwithstanding its willful rejection by many people of our age, has everything to do with who you are.

Along with your being a biologically defined sex, you also inherited from your parents a particular combination of gifts, all designed to aid you in finding a place to make your life's stand. This "standing," sometimes called **vocation**, is the way God also identifies you through

Wherever you stand, even while you must still crawl, your hands and mind come into contact with all the marvelous stuff around you. Those materials engage you and begin to reveal to you who you are through your interest in them. Are your hands quick with a wrench or better with a ball? Is your mind a natural for perception or better at convincing your body never to quit? Do you prefer to make things beautiful or to make things tick? Sometimes it's both/ and. Sometimes it's either/or. But as you step into walking and running at full speed, you find yourself gravitating toward toys and tools and productions that further identify your place within God's ultimate design.

But there is more. The gifts you are given for the good of your family and community, your neighbors and the world, are incomplete without the unity of all your vocations rolled into one. Your DNA and your lineage and your sex and the works that flow from your mind and heart and dreams are only pieces of the final identity God has given you. They are a strong foundation, but they need a capstone. Before and after all that you make and all that you say and all that you grow to be, something else goes both before and after you, a source of power and godlikeness that all of us recognize as powerful enough to destroy us, though we often have little trouble wielding it in the destruction of others. That power is **words**.

YOU, DEFINED

Before you were born, when you were but an idea in the mind of your parents, there is a better than average chance they gave you a name. Even if they didn't, they planned things about you all the same. They spoke words about you. They began to define how they wanted you to be. Because how they wanted you to be played a massive role in how they raised you, those words spoken before you were even conceived began to define who you are.

Many alive today would rail against such "constructions" as a form of tyranny or violence over others. Still that rage has not saved them from being trapped in yet other words, other constructions that have likewise bound them by ideas that came before. This is because none of us can be free from words, because words are a good thing. Rejecting hopes and dreams as a matter of principle can only be an eternal war of tearing down the existence of ideas themselves. It is true that there exist many harmful words and ideas. But it is not words' power to define, explain, persuade, and humor that is evil. Like all the good gifts of stuff, words, too, can be used for evil ends. But the power of words is good by God's design, a gift to mankind to set him above all the beasts.

If broken parents have never quite been able to perfectly make use of this gift due to their old man, it is a far cry for the chips off their thorny block to presume to do any better, much less by

ECHO

abandoning all the good of the design itself. So when your parents spoke those words about you, when they gave voice to their hopes and dreams and began to lay down structures and pathways to bring you there, this was **good**. It was the Fourth Important Thing in symphony, the design of powers and authorities crafted for the benefit of those below striving to achieve their created purpose. Nowhere was this hopeful future detailed by them and set forth more clearly than in the one word selected to be your very definition, the set of sounds by which all other people would know you, the identity they constructed for you on God's behalf and as a great gift to you: your **name**.

Guttural sounds. A breath pressed between teeth and tongue. It seems so simple. Yet in a room consumed by a crowd of people, hundreds of other bodies pressing and moving and making all variety of noises, those sounds will pull you from within yourself, causing your eyes and mind to cast about in search of the one who called you. Because your name is **who you are**.

> I hope to see you soon, and we will talk face to face. Peace be to you. The friends greet you. Greet the friends, each by name. 3 John 14–15

Whether you go by the name given at birth, received a nickname from your parents or friends, or insist on being called by something you've made up for yourself, there always will be personal and emotional power wrapped up in "who you are" known by others to be. If your parents named you Rainbow Bright or Fluffy McFlufflemumps, I guess I won't blame you for having changed it. But you had it changed **because** there is **power** in a name.

WHAT'S IN A NAME?

Everything.

George Washington. Julius Caesar. William Shakespeare. Confucius.

In a moment, a name can inspire fear or dread (Adolf Hitler; Attila the Hun) or serenity and hope (Mother Teresa; Jackie Kennedy). A name can be a synonym for wisdom (Solomon; Ghandi) or a curse forever ruined by folly (General Custer; Agamemnon). It can be an enduring symbol of power and victory (Alexander the

Great; Muhammad Ali) or a permanent fixture of betrayal and loss (Brutus; Benedict Arnold; Judas).

Names go before and after us. Even if you aren't going to be an archetype of history, your name still acts in the same way for all those who have met your body, who know your family, or who are familiar with all the stuff you've acquired, built, or given away. It is by your name that you are experienced and by your name that you are judged. For all that any person can ever be in a lifetime, each of us can be reduced to a simple set of sounds that carry huge meaning. Who you are is bound up and tied in a chord, set to sounds that can be a great gift (or a great burden) to all who hear them.

The Eighth Important Thing about Being Creation is that God made you a word when **God gave you a name**. By this word, you are distinguished from everything else that has ever lived or been. The ancient world recognized this reality more fully than our current age does. In many civilizations, you find a deep belief that everything's name is intimately connected to its design, either as a reflection of it or a prescription for it. For this reason, what people named their child or called their friend was more than just a pretty sound. More than just a symbol, the name was a **meaning**; it was a true description of who someone was, so much so that a name could change when and if anyone became someone else.

So the sound *Esau*, given in Genesis as a name to a baby who came out "red and hairy," is actually just a play on the word *red* in Hebrew. They named him Red Guy because **that was what he was**. Red Guy's twin brother, who came out clutching at the firstborn's ankle, earned himself the name Heel Grabber, a Hebrew word pronounced by us as *Jacob*. But later in life, when God chose Jacob in order to set him apart and fight on his behalf, marking the event with an actual wrestling match on a riverbank, God also renamed him *Israel*, which can be understood to mean either "God fights" or "he fights God" (or both!).

"Heel Grabber Whom God Fights For" had twelve sons. One of them, whose name was Joseph, ended up a slave in the court of the King of Egypt, where he eventually interpreted several visionary dreams for the king and his court. As a result, Pharaoh renamed Joseph as Zaphenath-paneah (a real mouthful!). But whenever he was seen about the palace and spoken to, he didn't hear all those

ECHO

funny sounds. He heard a sentence of words strung together that meant "He Speaks with God." Joseph then married a high-ranking priest's daughter and had several children, effectively replacing for him the family he'd lost many years before. He marks their identity and the events of their life by giving them the names "I Left My Family Behind" and "New Day."

> "Hello, He Speaks with God! Nice to meet you! How goes it?"
>
> "Things are great except that my boy New Day keeps complaining that I Left My Family Behind gets all the best privileges."

Constantly throughout the Bible, a person's name is a confession of who he is. Adam is just the Hebrew word for dirt, and Dirt names his wife Eve because God promises the antidote for death would be born of her womb. *Eve* means "life."

Jesus looked at him and said, "You are Simon the son of John. You shall be called Cephas" (which means Peter). John 1:42

The modern person usually gives a name because it runs in the family (its own form of deeper meaning) or because they like the sounds the letters make together. There are names that are given that are never intended to have any deeper meaning at all. Yet, naming your child Starlight or Daffodil is, in its own way, a throwback to naming your child Red Guy or New Day. It's calling children what they are or what we hope they will be, defining them as words that hold the characteristics we desire them to have or sounds that make us feel the way we want them to feel too. All of it is a continual hint at something we all know: human identity truly exists within your **name**.

BAD WORDS

If you steal a petunia from your neighbor's yard, he will likely be upset. But if you steal his credit card number and use it to buy a petunia, it will likely throw him into a panic. This is because a lost credit card represents not only a potential loss of money, but more important, the potential loss of the good name you've earned that allows you to borrow money. Credit is one way that our civilization shows that it's not just who you are that matters. **What other people think of you also matters.** It is one way in which we publicly acknowledge that there is power in your name. Something that threatens that power, like a stolen credit card, is often far more disturbing than something that threatens the many good things you might own.

In fact, many of the things that we like to own we only desire because of the good they bring to the reputation of our names. Petunias are certainly put in the front yard for your enjoyment, but it hardly needs to be pointed out that half of what we do to our yards is about fearing what the neighborhood might think of us if we don't. The same goes for the way your children behave, the desire to marry a beautiful person, and the goal of keeping your body in shape. All these things aren't just about preserving or having good experiences. They're also about ensuring that we have a good name for ourselves.

This is why words are such a phenomenally powerful thing. With words, you can do terrible damage to your neighbor (or he can do damage to you), even though you've never actually taken any physical action against them. All that it takes is for somebody to straight up **lie** about it.

> A good name is to be chosen rather than great riches, and favor is better than silver or gold. Proverbs 22:1

Lies are so powerful that they don't even have to be true to have long-enduring effects. If I tell you that so-and-so at church is a gossip and that her husband only showers twice a week, it doesn't matter whether my words are golden truth or a tall tale like Pecos Bill. Unless you happen to be so-and-so's best friend or mother, the next time you see so-and-so, even if you've chosen not to believe me, a small hint of what I said will remain with you, ever so slightly diminishing the value of her name in your eyes. That diminished value will then affect how you treat her. She *might* be a gossip, so you don't open up to her. Her husband might smell, so you don't sit by him at the potluck. Far beyond these somewhat tame examples, on the basis of a lie, a man may lose his career, his wife, his house, or his life. All of this, only because of words.

The capability of false words to destroy only exists because of the power put into words as a marvelous gift to mankind. Words are part of our being made in the image of our Creator. They are there to make us like God, able to name the things we see, to distinguish between one and another. Sweet and spicy, rain and shine. Would a rose by any other name smell just as sweet? Yes, no doubt, because it would still be a rose—and that is the power of the word. The word captures the thing in order to share it with all. The sounds don't matter a millionth so much as the truth the sounds represent to you and me, calling to mind a reality that does exist, that can be experienced, that is given for our good.

WHO AM I?

This has become a far more complicated question than it really needs to be, largely because we've tangled up the search for self with the search for meaning. We are starving for real names, but the age we live in wants to convince us to search for identity everywhere except in who we actually are. With our bodies denied and our parentage rejected, there isn't enough identity left in "stuff" to do much more than try to get and keep as much of it as possible.

The result is that we spend most of our searching for self trying to consume ourselves into existence. We act as if what we absorb with our bodies or what we hang on them or the size of the rooms we rest them in can actually confirm the meaning of who we are. But the suit never makes the man. The diet cannot give peace to the heart. Finding out you have the same favorite TV show might spark off the start of a good friendship, but something as superficial as entertainment is not in itself a bond that will endure the testing that a life filled with thorns is bound to bring.

All of this floundering in the shadows is an attempt to create what God has already given in this:

We use God's good gifts in the worst possible way, but those gifts still reflect the good that God built into them in the first place. We try to find our identity in the gifts of our body, our relationships, and our stuff, but we do it in twisted ways that reject God's original design. No matter how much we try to escape who God made us to be, we won't find our identity without Him.

This is because there is no real and lasting meaning in *Me*. Identity cannot define itself, much less define itself through the things that perish. Lasting identity is always defined in its relationship to everyone else. That means **through** your body, **as** your family, and what you do **with** the stuff you have been given. What your body is, the people you are related to, and the things you enjoy have much to say about what God identified you to be when He made you. Our thorns will always be there to contend with, but even the old man can't utterly destroy the great idea— **the good word**—that is meant to be you, which the rest of us are only ever able to know by the sound of your **name**.

> Thus says the LORD, He who created you, . . . "Fear not, for I have redeemed you; I have called you by name, you are Mine." Isaiah 43:1

THE EIGHTH IMPORTANT THING ABOUT BEING CREATION

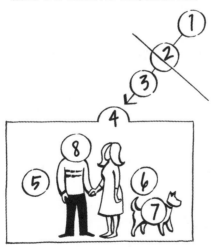

God gave you a name.

* **THE FIRST IMPORTANT THING:** THERE IS A GOD.

* **THE SECOND IMPORTANT THING:** GOD HAS A NAME.

* **THE THIRD IMPORTANT THING:** GOD SPEAKS.

* **THE FOURTH IMPORTANT THING:** GOD DESIGNED YOU.

* **THE FIFTH IMPORTANT THING:** GOD GAVE YOU A BODY.

* **THE SIXTH IMPORTANT THING:** GOD GAVE YOU FAMILY.

* **THE SEVENTH IMPORTANT THING:** GOD GAVE YOU STUFF.

* **THE EIGHTH IMPORTANT THING:** GOD GAVE YOU A NAME.

THE NINTH THING

God Gave You Happiness

YOU'RE NOT HAPPY

That much is obvious. If it is not obvious to you, then it is obvious to everyone else around you. You can argue about it if you like, insist what a total bundle of joy you are on all occasions. But do me a favor first and start paying attention the next time you watch a few commercials. How many will it take before you find yourself interested in—wanting—something that you don't already have? Do some online shopping. How many moments until you find that thing you've been hoping you could buy for so long? Then ask yourself this important question: what do you hope to gain by getting it? What are you seeking that you don't have right now?

Happiness.

It's not that you're never happy. You get moments here and there. You might even be a genuinely chipper person overall. But it is not complete. It is not total. You are not perfectly happy. You want. You desire. These, at

All things are full of weariness; a man cannot utter it; the eye is not satisfied with seeing, nor the ear filled with hearing. Ecclesiastes 1:8

root, are the opposite of happiness. You have unmet needs, and filling those needs, whether they are real or imagined, is the most important thing in the world to the average *Me*. No one wants to keep that feeling of need. You want to squash it. Like a bug. Like a fly buzzing around the room while you're trying to focus on something more important. Like a fly when you can't find the fly swatter so you just have to deal with chasing it about with a roll of paper and all the while not . . . being . . . happy about it.

NOBODY IS HAPPY

Nobody.

Everyone is discontent. Anyone who says otherwise is likely selling something. That's why we have online shopping and commercials and fly swatters: the discontents sell them to other discontents in order to try to make contentment. It works. Sometimes. For a while. But it doesn't last because it is a fact of the universe that every day every human being wishes that at least one other thing in the universe (usually lots of them) would be different.

All the many religions of the world hinge on this one fact being true. They might not care about snakes and gardens, forbidden fruit or flaming swords. They might have no place for walking on water or being swallowed by a big fish. But every religion, by definition, admits that there is a center to a target called **happy**, and no one's really hitting it. Not for long. Not hard enough to stay put. Not true enough to last.

> And I applied my heart to seek and to search out by wisdom all that is done under heaven. It is an unhappy business that God has given to the children of man to be busy with. Ecclesiastes 1:13

Every day, every person gets up and takes aim at happy. Month after month. Year after year. We try to hit happy so hard and so often, that gradually we begin to covet hitting happy more than anything else in the entire world. It becomes all consuming, an itch that can never be scratched enough, a hole that can never stay filled. The ear is not filled with hearing. The couch potato is not filled with entertaining. The athlete is not filled with winning. The executive is not filled with succeeding. The stomach is not filled with eating. All streams keep running into the sea.

There is a target, a goal, a meaning, a waaaay over there that keeps staying off the edge, out of bounds, beyond a saving hope of our getting there. It's like our aim is **bent**. It's like the arrow fletching is compounded with **thorns**. So over and over again, we seriously **miss the mark**. There is a line we want to stay inside of, a border, a demarcation of the good that would satisfy us once and for all, but all we ever manage to do, from the soul out, is find ourselves back on the other side of that line. We find ourselves continually trapped in trespass, even in our own attempts at happiness.

AND . . . IT'S (VERY SLOWLY) KILLING YOU

If you can't admit it, if by some herculean accumulation of hubris you've made it this far through the book without seeing this coming, then you're probably royally miffed right now. No doubt the other eight Important Things gave you some trouble. But nothing can make a conscience bleed like being exposed to its own covetousness. That's what the Ninth Important Thing does: the dirty work. It points out your mess once and for all, shoving your animosity with your God so far down your throat that you either finally fess up and admit the problem—that **you** are the problem—or you rage-quit, go home, and take all your toys with you.

Happiness is the final idol. It is all other idols combined. Its greatest power is that it never admits its own existence. It won't admit that the reason you want a better name than your neighbor is that you think it will make you happy. It won't admit that the reason you want more money is you think it will make you happy. It won't admit that the reason you lust after that person is you think it will make you happy. It won't admit that the reason men harm one another

> **The righteous has enough to satisfy his appetite, but the belly of the wicked suffers want.** Proverbs 13:25

is that we think it will make us happy. It won't admit the reason we riot against authority is that we think being in charge will make us happy. It won't fess up that the reason we don't want to hear God's words is that He will force us to admit that we are not happy, that happiness is not attainable by us, and then the entire glass castle of our clichés and platitudes and pretendings will come crashing down as its sandy foundation is swept away.

ECHO

Our unwillingness to admit it—the adamant vehemence with which we refuse to acknowledge how desperate things really are, how little they can change, and how much *my soul* is tied up at the root of it all—is the purest demonstration of our blind devotion to false happiness. We hide from the truth of our unhappiness with nigh-superhuman, reality-defying insanity. Since we can't change the reality, since the hopelessness will drive us mad if we think too deeply about it, we revert to the personal fantasy that what happens today will make all the difference, willfully ignoring the fact that whatever happens today will be gone tomorrow. So we complain about unhappiness. We try to escape from it. We medicate it, polish it, buy a new one, bury it, or burn it. But all the while we insist to ourselves that the unhappiness isn't really here. It's a mirage. It will soon go away. We parrot the world and ourselves, endlessly professing today's sandcastle will be different than all the other sandcastles that came before it.

> It is better to go to the house of mourning than to go to the house of feasting, for this is the end of all mankind, and the living will lay it to heart. Ecclesiastes 7:2

This is nothing new. Long before you got here, everyone else who has ever lived in the whole wide world has already tried and done everything imaginable to turn this collapsing universe around. But they have all **failed**. They have failed **so hard** and with such consistency that the only remaining avenue of hope has been to quietly agree that it's best if we just don't talk about it anymore. *Best not to scare the children!* It's too hard to face the bare, brutal truth of the matter. *Better to have faith!* Better to tell ourselves that the problems will go away if we ignore them hard enough. Whatever is wrong with the world can't be *that* wrong. *"Peace! Peace!"* they yell. *"Surely, we will find a way to make it better!"*

> What has been is what will be, and what has been done is what will be done, and there is nothing new under the sun. . . . What is crooked cannot be made straight, and what is lacking cannot be counted. Ecclesiastes 1:9, 15

It has never worked.

Something is diabolically wrong with the world, and it takes a supernatural arrogance to refuse to believe it. No matter how much cheap talk fills up the air, no matter how sanctimoniously the pious pretend they can catch the wind in their hands, every person on the planet lives each day acting as if everything is fine. We can't admit that we have not fixed the real problems in the world. Instead, we fight to do whatever it is we want most to do because we are starving for happiness and we can feel in our bones how little yesterday succeeded at smothering the discontent with all those temporary fixes. We spend today again getting what we can while we can because we know with tactile, soul-deep certainty that the survival of the fittest is catching up with *Me*. And *Me* is not. *Me* is not fit enough. *Me* is suffering. *Me* is frustrated. *Me* is stuck with yesterday's regret and today's limitations and tomorrow's taxes. And after all that, death is coming.

> I considered all that my hands had done and the toil I had expended in doing it, and behold, all was vanity and a striving after wind, and there was nothing to be gained under the sun. Ecclesiastes 2:11

SOME PEOPLE BLAME GOD FOR THIS

It's a pretty common routine. But it's just as misguided as it is common. After all, **God designed happiness**. He came up with the idea. Blaming Him for your lack of happiness is like blaming your cat because you're chasing your own tail. When God designed the world, He designed it with you in it, and the "you" He designed was built to be utterly happy. This is why you expect happiness. This is why you long for it. You're **supposed** to be happy. It's the **right expectation** for a creation made by a good Creator.

> And God saw everything that He had made, and behold, it was very good. Genesis 1:31

As certain as the body that He made you is sitting there reading this book, the rest of the world was built so that you would receive from it and in it, as a gift, forever and ever, the most constant and endless stream of perfect happiness, every moment of every day, all the time, both with and from everyone and everything else. You are tuned to receive constant and intuitive contentment.

The problem is that this contentment is to be received strictly from the knowledge that God is God, and that He is the ongoing source and sustainer of everything.

It's not like you're supposed to just sit around thinking, "God is God," over and over again. It's more about truly knowing that God is **your God**. That means knowing, beyond any shadow of a doubt, that the Almighty is always using all things both to take care of you and to keep you connected to Him. It means that **you are His own**, that you live under Him, and that this state of being is a source of eternal, breathtaking blessedness.

This is the Ninth and (almost) Final Important Thing about Being Creation. **God gave you happiness.** Just like your body. Just like your family. Just like your name. Just like all the good stuff in the world. The God who built you engineered you to receive everlasting happiness from it all. But this, more than anything before, begs the real question. If the God who is, who designed everything else, who by the power of His name spoke it into being, not only made you what you are but also did so with the gift of always being totally satisfied with everything else, then what made everything go so hell-bent wrong?

THAT'S THE POINT

That is what these Important Things are really here to expose and help you to see. They don't need to be taught just because they are a perfect outline of what human life is supposed to be (although they are certainly that too). They are spoken to us because by them and their perfection you can recognize that there is a problem. With them as your measuring stick, you can see the great rift that exists between what **should be** and what *actually is*.

All the many religions of the world run around huffing and puffing until their faces are blue, preaching up excuses about how nothing is really as bad as it seems and how all of it is a grand plan or test or tool for getting better. They preach that what "shouldn't be" is the way it is supposed to be, as if being broken and needing to be fixed is a good thing.

This is where Christianity breaks the mold. Christianity doesn't waste time trying to justify the all too obvious bentness of all our shots at the perfection targets. Christianity doesn't mince words pretending that things aren't really as out of proportion as they seem. Christianity throws its money down on the curb and calls out the Ninth Important Thing because it demonstrates, over and over again, that what "should be" is **not what actually is**.

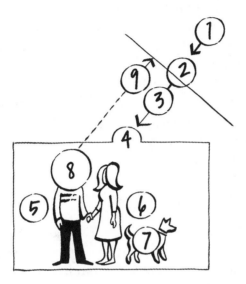

Our way of being is nasty and messed up. Happiness is what everyone is looking for. Happiness is what the pursuit of life and liberty are all about. We wake up every day, and we chase it. We go to bed every night trying to cling to it. Whatever promises to deliver it, it must be worth it. *As long as it makes you happy.*

All the sources and styles and endless streaming of stuff and things and peoples and places

Again, I saw vanity under the sun: one person who has no other, either son or brother, yet there is no end to all his toil, and his eyes are never satisfied with riches, so that he never asks, "For whom am I toiling and depriving myself of pleasure?" This also is vanity and an unhappy business. Ecclesiastes 4:7–8

that we pressure ourselves with are all bound to the hope that they will give happiness to us. We trust in our dreams and our hopes because we imagine they will stabilize us in a constant stream of happiness. Everything we desire is only desirable as a path to it.

Just about the only thing more certain than the fact that we're all trying to get happiness is the fact that none of us really have it. But this never stops us from spending nearly all our time trying to convince ourselves and the rest of the world that we have happiness . . . or that we can get it . . . or that I can sell it to you.

God **did** give you perfect happiness. When He made you, happiness was how He knit you together. The fact that now you don't have it is the final shot across the bow of your thorny boat. He is still speaking about what He meant you to be because He wants to wake you up to see what is really going on now instead. You should never have had to spend a moment of your life wanting things to be other than they are. Ever.

But you do.

Constantly.

That's how sick you are. That's how badly you're missing the mark of real goodness. Real goodness, even if it had to live in a world as jacked up as ours, would be so good that it would smile and thank God for everything, go home perfectly happy, and never utter a murmur of complaint in the world.

But you don't.

Because you're not.

That's the point. And that's the Tenth Important Thing.

CHRISTIANITY IS NOT FOR PEOPLE WHO ARE HAPPY

Christianity is not for the joyful either. "Joy" spends way too much time these days freeloading as a sanctimonious version of happiness. Happiness labeled "joy" is not to be trusted. Trying to make believe our spiritual bankruptcy can be overcome with a few reality-denying platitudes is not to be trusted. Joining the world in mutually enabled insanity steeped in obviousness-avoidance is not to be trusted.

Christianity is not an antidote for people who are not happy. God **did** create us to be happy. But we're not, and the first step out of this catastrophe is to stop pretending we are something we're not.

Christianity is for people whose lives are not good, whose emotions are not doing all right. Christianity is for people who are tired of pretending to believe in a bunch of inner-light mumbo jumbo.

Christianity is for the person who knows the biggest thing standing in the way of happiness is *Me*.

If you're doing fine, then you don't need a doctor.

If you've got all you need, then you don't need something more.

If you're happy with life just the way it is, then you don't need someone to save you from it.

If the eyes have gone bad, then there is no way to see. If the salt has lost its flavor, it must be tasteless forever. If the light has become overshadowed by darkness, then how terribly great is that darkness!

> **Draw near to God, and He will draw near to you. . . . Be wretched and mourn and weep. Let your laughter be turned to mourning and your joy to gloom. Humble yourselves before the Lord, and He will exalt you.** James 4:8–10

Christianity is for people who know the Important Things aren't working out. Not like they're supposed to work in this world. Not really. Not inside of *Me*.

Christianity is for people who are not happy, and they are happy to admit it.

Christianity is for the sad.

Christianity is for the broken.

Christianity is for the discontent.

Christianity is for the poor in soul.

Christianity is for the humiliated.

Christianity is for those starving for goodness.

Christianity is for those who know they've missed the mark.

Christianity is for sinners.

It is immensely freeing to be able to admit that the world is not the way it's supposed to be, to honestly see that whatever is wrong with the world is no mere smudge or little dent but something horrible and diabolical. It is doubly freeing to admit that *I* am not the way I am supposed to be. And it's exponentially freeing to admit that there is no possibility of us fixing our brokenness. Once you admit that you can't fix anything, there opens the possibility that there exists Someone (who is not you) who can.

THE NINTH IMPORTANT THING
ABOUT BEING CREATION

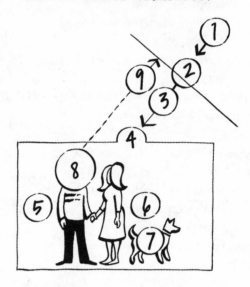

God gave you happiness.

* THE FIRST IMPORTANT THING: There is a God.

* THE SECOND IMPORTANT THING: God has a name.

* THE THIRD IMPORTANT THING: God speaks.

* THE FOURTH IMPORTANT THING: God designed you.

* THE FIFTH IMPORTANT THING: God gave you a body.

* THE SIXTH IMPORTANT THING: God gave you family.

* THE SEVENTH IMPORTANT THING: God gave you stuff.

* THE EIGHTH IMPORTANT THING: God gave you a name.

* THE NINTH IMPORTANT THING: God gave you happiness.

THE TENTH THING

You're Not Listening. Yet.

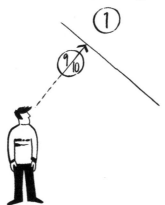

THE SHADOW UNDERNEATH EVERYTHING

The **brokenness of the world of man** is the Tenth Important Thing about Being Creation. All the other Important Things, when combined and held up together, form a perfect picture of what the world is meant to be. But by being that perfect picture, they also reflect what this world is missing. Like the highest definition camera, they capture us as we actually are. Every detail. Every flaw. Every "should have been" that is **not**.

> Cursed is the ground because of you; in pain you shall eat of it all the days of your life; thorns and thistles it shall bring forth for you. Genesis 3:17–18

The world designed by **one God** is instead a world filled with many gods. The world designed to know Him **by name** is instead filled with people who do not. The world designed to live from **every Word** that comes from God's mouth now experiences a famine of that Word, an age in which that Word can hardly be found.

A world intricately structured **in order** now lives under the reign of chaos and decay. The harmony built of hierarchy is filled with tyranny and oppression at every turn. Humanity, intended to be its own greatest gift to **one another**, finds brother fighting brother and "neighbors" defined as people we build fences between.

In a world beautifully diversified by male and female, the distinctions of **sexuality** are rejected, and sex itself is used as a weapon, a tool, or a toy for anything that serves the passions of pleasure. In a world filled with more **stuff** than anyone could possibly need, each of us wants even more. In a world where **names** are given to our children in order that they might be blessings invoked by others, instead we hasten to tarnish all names but our own, thinking thereby to build a better future for *Me*.

It was a world made so good that it would always be good enough. But now, it is not. Our failure to be **happy** is only the tip of the deeper darkness. We stand at the maw of death, with a world at war, wracked with famine and disease, filled with life so impoverished that it keeps on dying no matter how hard we try to stop it.

Why?

THE FALL MUST BE BELIEVED

When the Bible's account of creation gets floor time for discussion these days, most people are hyper concerned about trivial tangents, like whether the length of a day was the length of a day, or whether man lived at the same time as dinosaurs. What gets lost in these debates about the age of starlight or the radioactivity of carbon is that the truly **unbelievable** thing in the first chapters of Genesis has nothing to do with the creation at all. It has everything to do with the **fall**.

A perfect man, crafted by the immaculate hand of God, woke up in a perfect world, where all the Important Things about Being Creation were as they were supposed to be. The man knew no false gods. He walked with God, called Him by name, heard His words as nothing but truth. The orders were set; the future of family was guaranteed. There was plenty for all, and all were to be born into this great goodness.

But a radical rebellion was afoot, hatched in the mind of a self-made *liar*. It was a lie to birth all lies and to tear all things asunder in mutiny. A myriad of angels, once nothing but true, wresting their wills away from the Creator, believed that lie and made themselves nothing but false. This would have been bad enough, but that perfect man also believed the lie. By **choice**. By **decision**. With **intention** and **prejudice**, he chose to free his will from the will of his Creator.

Worse still, he was no mere man. He was the king. The son of God (see Luke 3:38). He was the single sentient animal set in place to subjugate all other things. By then subjecting himself to the *liar*, he subjected all other things to the *liar* as well.

This **broke the world**. The havoc is unimaginable. **Everything** changed. It was a **cataclysmic shock** so all-consuming that it is impossible to underestimate it. Everything that we feel to be wrong, everything that we see to be other than it should be, is just the aftershock. At ground zero, everything that was "very good" became "not good." Nothing was left out. Nothing was untouched. The very fabric of the universe was altered.

Before the **breaking of the world**, earth was filled with lions and sharks that ate plants. It was covered by roses and thistles that had no thorns. It was built of metals that never oxidized and mosquitoes that served a good purpose. But more than all this, it was filled with angels who were all perfectly, wonderfully, eternally **good**. Then, some of them weren't. Rust and rot **became** a thing. Decay and destruction took effect. **Death** began to happen.

> **The creation was subjected to futility, not willingly, but because of Him who subjected it, in hope that the creation itself will be set free from its bondage to corruption.** Romans 8:20–21

And we argue about the length of a day.

Not just what we see and what we know, but even **how** we know has been dynamically altered. Science cannot see past this cataclysm to take measurements of what happened before it, no matter how much it might want to. An angel with a flaming sword stands in the way, an anti-miracle so cosmic that our reason cannot explain it, our emotions cannot fathom it, and our works cannot repair it.

So deep is this depravity within us, so much has it skewed even our ability to reason, that from our vantage point the only way to explain the fall is to blame God for it. After all, how could a good and all-powerful God create a good world that had in it the power to become evil? Wouldn't He then be the one behind the evil? Or did He not know it would happen? Wouldn't He then be less than God? Surely, God could have prevented the fall, or created a world that could not fall. But He didn't. Or so we would think with our broken minds.

> He drove out the man, and at the east of the garden of Eden He placed the cherubim and a flaming sword that turned every way. Genesis 3:24

But this is thorny reason. The healthy, brutal truth is that God did **not** create us capable of falling. God made the world so **very good** that becoming evil was, by definition, **impossible**. God did **not** create mankind with a will able to free itself from Him. And yet, we did.

This is only **unbelievable** to us now because we cannot understand it with our fallen reason. Out of one side of the mouth, we decry God (or God's nonexistence) for the evils in the world, while with the other side of the mouth we refuse to acknowledge that our ability to see clearly might forever be subjected to that same corrupting evil. All the while, we are blind to the fact that our reason's need to see evil itself as at least partially God's fault only further demonstrates how horrifically inward our thinking has become. So great is this original sin that it cannot be understood. It must, in the end, be believed. It is the Ten Important Things that teach us to do just that.

THE GOOD THING TO DO WITH EVIL

This **evil**—this thorny, broken, bent, sinful reality—is a **disease**. An **infection**. Aggressive and progressing, it is so encroaching that it threatens the life of everything that is. Even the trees. Even the rocks. Even the atoms. Even the stars.

There is only one thing to do with infections that threaten your life. You kill them. You murder the little buggers. You pump yourself full of antibiotics and take two Tylenol for the fever. But what if **humanity is the infection**? What if humanity is the contaminating agent? What if **you** are the **lethal threat** to every other living being, innate material, and subatomic particle in the universe? The meaning of the fall is that *we are*. We are where death—**all death**—comes from.

Death is the way that God deals with things that are evil. God kills evil. Killing evil is what a **good God** has to do. It is the only thing a good God can do with things that have gone bad, the same way you throw away moldy food or flush the toilet. The miracle, the next unbelievable thing, is that we are still here!

Why? If killing evil is what a good God does, then why aren't we all dead already? Why didn't the good God scrap us and start all over way back at the beginning? Why all the bother about that angel with a sword of heavenly fire guarding the gates of paradise? Why not just burn us all instantly and be done with it? That's certainly what *Me* would do! If something *Me* had made ceased to make *Me* happy, much less rebelled against *Me*, *Me* would discard it like dross and go off coveting something else to take its place. But not God.

Why?

The simple answer is the most commonly known passage of the Bible. But it defies explanation. Reason must truly die at this altar.

Why did God not just end evil at the root, at the moment of its deception? Because **God so loved the world** that even though the world is self-broken into a disorienting evil, God still would rather fix the world than destroy it. Why does God allow all the evil things in the world to go on? Why doesn't God stop all the bad things from happening? Because **God would rather save you** than destroy you. God loves you so much that He is willing to let the whole universe, including you, wallow in its self-made problem of evil, groaning under its weight for a time, rather than abandon you and lose the world forever.

> **Know the love of Christ that surpasses knowledge.** Ephesians 3:19

When God created everything, including us, with the intention of being God **for** us, He meant it. So with great resilience, He refused to put an end to evil at the spot when it first happened. When the first man decided to worship a piece of fruit as if it could raise him to godhood, God intervened in the event and did what a good God had to do. He set death in a placeholder

121

to put a limitation on our evil. But that is not all He did. He also, in the same breath, put into action a plan that spelled an even greater end of evil, but He did so in a way that didn't mean the end of **you**.

A DIFFERENT KIND OF ANSWER ALTOGETHER

The Tenth Important Thing is that being **creation is not the way it should be,** *and* **God has every intent of putting this evil to an end**. In this bizarre way, the Tenth Important Thing is really the First. All Ten Things are one and the same. There is a God, and you are not Him. **But you think that you are.** You can't stop yourself.

He has not been silent on the matter. The only reason we do not hear Him is because we choose to listen in the wrong place. That is our failure. That is our condition. That is the original sin: to stop hearing **God speak**. But our refusal to hear has not stopped Him from speaking. Our evil has not stopped His good. Even from the beginning, even from the first moments of collapse, even as the fires separated us from Eden, God didn't just stand there and let it happen. He spoke. He said something. He told us His plan to save us from ourselves.

The problem is that it wasn't the answer we would expect. It wasn't the kind of plan we could come up with ourselves. It wasn't obvious. It didn't require us to do anything, and, worst of all, it was **slow**.

The perfect world that could not fall broke with a cataclysmic crash. Archangels are in revolt, and time and space are bent with dying. Leprosy and thorns are spreading. Scars are covering the ears of all. And the almighty God's great plan to save evil men from themselves is to tell them a **story**. He left the words of His story hanging there in the ears of the first man. Then He didn't do anything. Nothing at all. No miracles were performed. There were no grand signs. Just words. Mere words. Unbelievable words.

But more than words. This story was made of the kind of words from which God created the universe. This story was made of the kind of words that do what they say. So they did what they said. They were spoken again, moving forward with men from one generation to the next, like an ever-blossoming flower on an otherwise dead tree. Through all the bloody history of man that followed, that story kept being told, the story of an unbelievable promise that would make itself be believed.

When more bending will not straighten a bent board, then you need a new board. When the brambles must be cast into the fire, then you need a new root. When all individuals are cursed to the same evil end, then only an entirely new incorporation can hope to restore what was lost to its place. So God told the story of something different, something outside the seven days of creation that had already come to be and come to be broken.

> God said to the serpent, . . . "I will put enmity between you and the woman, and between your offspring and her offspring; He shall bruise your head, and you shall bruise His heel." Genesis 3:14–15

God told the story of a man who would be born from woman with the full intention of going back to the dust again. But He would not be just another life lived and died in the same broken epoch. Instead, this man would be a life lived in order to die in one epoch and rise again in another. His death would not be just another death that changed nothing but Himself, but in Himself His death would fuse a new dimension with the present one. His body would not be just another broken, thorny man condemned to the same end as all broken, thorny men. His body would be such an unstoppable force as to carry not only itself but all things with it between these two worlds, between the realm of darkness and the realm of light, between the vale of sorrow and the mansions of joy, between the seven days of catastrophe and the eighth day of the brokenness undone.

He would be everything and nothing at once, in the same moment. He would empty Himself and so fill all things. He would make His demonstration of all power perfect in the acceptance of all weakness. He would be so sinless as to be able to become sin and, in so doing, to destroy it by its fusion to Himself. He would be the source of blood that cannot die, the source of water that is alive, the source of cleanness that rubs off on the dirt.

God whispered the story of a second humanity, of a **Son of Man**kind, of a person who as of that moment both existed and did not exist, but who would, yet more unbelievable still, speak Himself into being, not by lessening Himself but by taking into Himself the very man whom He so desired to save.

Christianity, before being anything else—before being a religion, a philosophy, a spirituality, a moral code, or a comfort—is a **history** of *how* God did this. Christianity is a history of how God so loved the world, of how God's story entered the world to save it, of how those words continue as an ongoing declaration of what God continues to do.

Christianity is not really about the Important Things. They are only the preamble to the story. And the story goes like this. . . .

THE TENTH IMPORTANT THING
ABOUT BEING CREATION

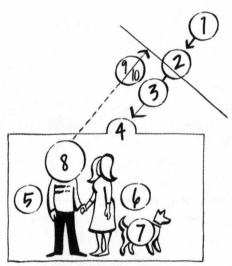

You're not listening. Yet.

THE TEN IMPORTANT THINGS
ABOUT BEING CREATION

* **THE FIRST IMPORTANT THING:** THERE IS A GOD.

* **THE SECOND IMPORTANT THING:** GOD HAS A NAME.

* **THE THIRD IMPORTANT THING:** GOD SPEAKS.

* **THE FOURTH IMPORTANT THING:** GOD DESIGNED YOU.

* **THE FIFTH IMPORTANT THING:** GOD GAVE YOU A BODY.

* **THE SIXTH IMPORTANT THING:** GOD GAVE YOU FAMILY.

* **THE SEVENTH IMPORTANT THING:** GOD GAVE YOU STUFF.

* **THE EIGHTH IMPORTANT THING:** GOD GAVE YOU A NAME.

* **THE NINTH IMPORTANT THING:** GOD GAVE YOU HAPPINESS.

* **THE TENTH IMPORTANT THING:** YOU'RE NOT LISTENING. YET.

PART TWO

THE THREE
ELEMENTS
OF THE
GOSPEL

THE FIRST ELEMENT

Who Jesus Is

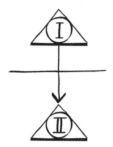

EVERYTHING CHANGED

It was a normal enough day, sometime around the year we call
2 BC (or 2 BCE if you want to insist that the birth of Jesus began the
"common era" rather than the era after Jesus was born). History was
at a high point. The reign of a man named Caesar Augustus, a guy
so famous we still have a month named after him, had effectively
staved off the collapse of the five-centuries-old Roman Republic.
It was a time of movers and shakers, a time of technological leaps
forward and scientific discoveries, a time of medical progress and
religious expansion. As much as things ever could lay claim to it in
the ancient world, things were really looking up. Augustus settled
to busying himself with masterminding the next half millennium,
taking a pit stop here or there to steal a day from February from
himself or his forebear Julius. Meanwhile, in a backwoods corner
of the empire, something unexpected happened.

A virgin had a baby.

This was all quite a bit behind schedule. It was so far behind
that even people who had spent thousands of years waiting for it
had largely forgotten how it was supposed to happen. They were
immaculate record-keepers, but even pristine copies of ancient

ECHO

books don't always stop bad ideas and misinformation from skewing the way you read them. For centuries, there had been false starts and misguided claims. To some, it looked as if key pieces of the puzzle were still missing. For others, how many generations can pass with something not happening before you start to doubt whether it will ever happen at all? One way or another, you start rethinking what it was you were hoping for in the first place. Often enough, that means replacing what you were hoping for with a more thorny, slightly bendier shadow of itself.

For to us a child is born, to us a son is given; and the government shall be upon His shoulder. Isaiah 9:6

So the hyper-particular, standoffish, ethnically self-referential tribe of people that had been fighting in their own special way to keep this backwoods bit of Caesar's land—*theirs*—were still holding onto shadows of the belief that a son would be born in the line of their now-archaic king, in order to rise up and restore His people's fortunes and glories. But by now, these shadows had been bundled with more than a few extra expectations, not all of them even in agreement with one another, and nearly all of them well usurping any focus on keeping an eye out for a virgin birth.

The current king had a bad habit of expecting anyone and everyone of wanting to take his kingdom, perhaps because he'd come by the power somewhat dishonestly. He was a mighty powerful figure as minor kings of the Roman Empire go, even earning for himself the moniker "the Great." But he certainly wasn't looking for a new king to be born outside of his hard-earned lineage. Any news of such possibilities would be treated with more than a little contempt.

There was also the guild of lawyers and the social justice warriors who had aligned with them, an aloof social class of elitists, many of whom made their livings managing the many copies of their ancient prophecies. Of all people, you would expect them to have a good handle on the special birth of the foretold king. They not only had the texts all but memorized, but they also still believed it was going to happen. The problem was that they also had come to believe that a number of other events had to happen first before it would be possible for the king to be born. More so, these other events rested on them and their fellow countrymen. They had to bring certain levels of effort and valor about; otherwise it didn't matter what other planets or stars aligned. Until they cleaned the place up, the king wasn't going to come.

Their bitter enemies in the culture war were the ruling class of priests who had inherited the right to run all the official rituals of their theocratic religion. Over time, they had really figured out how to keep a good racket going. With a bloodline-based set of rules, they were guaranteed to be the sole proprietors of a host of customs and social rules, all of which they tweaked into one of the smoothest money-laundering schemes in the ancient world. Not only did they firmly believe that this little system of sancti- monious capitalism was good for the common people beneath them, giving them hope and something to believe in an otherwise desperate world, but they themselves largely didn't believe any of the religion actually meant anything at all. For them, there were no angels or demons, no resurrection or afterlife. There was only being a generally good person and keeping the social order in line. Virgin births were out.

Still others grew tired of waiting and took up arms, thinking to unleash the land from its oppression by force of will, to stir the Messiah from His hidden place by their zeal. Yet more of them withdrew from civilization altogether, living in caves and pouring over the most explicit texts foretelling the impending end of the world, as the prophecies of the virgin birth receded into the fog of history.

WHO COULD HAVE PLANNED IT?

So when representatives of several of these powers found themselves gathered together in a room on a cold, blustery night, forced by some weird-as-witchcraft foreign mystics to figure out where the virgin birth would happen—even though they all knew it was clear in the ancient texts that it would happen within the city limits of a little town called Bethlehem—none of them seriously thought to take those Magi's word that the time was now. Some didn't seriously believe at all that such a thing would ever happen. Others believed the time was not yet right because we ourselves had yet to fulfill the prophecies. The last thing anyone expected was that the prophecies would simply take care of themselves.

But that's the way prophecy always works, even in make-believe. Prophecies of the sword in the stone or Jedi to bring balance to the Force never need us. How much less the authentic promise of the holy Creator God? From the moment of creation itself, God's words have always taken it on themselves to do what they say, just as they did with the virgin birth.

While all these various players of backwoods Rome make for enough story lines and plot twists to keep us busy for the making of many books, they are really the boring part of the story. If you're in it for the bizarre, if you're a glutton for the fantastic, if you're addicted to the profound, then you'll have to leave all the expectations (and even the understandings) behind and focus on that intricate, impossible moment when human capacity itself shifted on an axis beyond imagination. Don't look to the power players or politicians or religiophiles whom the story would be all about if we wrote it. Look in the last place any normal, Western, postmodern, civilized person would think to look for the salvation of the world and a king born to rule kings. Look to a no-name, stay-at-home mother whose unplanned pregnancy had without question ruined all her family's best-laid future plans.

> But you, O Bethlehem Ephrathah, . . . from you shall come forth for Me one who is to be ruler in Israel, whose coming forth is from of old, from ancient days. Micah 5:2

DANGEROUS PROMISES

We can't underestimate the extreme threat the angel Gabriel delivered to the maiden Mary when he caught her off guard to tell her, "Remember that promise about a man to be born of a woman, a man who will slay the enemy of the world? Yeah. You're the woman." Sounds great on the surface. It's as cool as a fairy tale about a dragon slayer or the Muad'Dib. But it was a royally offensive and dangerous idea. To be sure, amid the ridiculous license and leisure of morally libertine America, the only offensive thing about a sixteen-year-old girl finding herself pregnant would be any decision to keep the child to term rather than abort him. Both she and her parents might be disappointed at the hassle. They might worry about how if they don't get the matter taken care of quickly and quietly it might ruin her chances at a good scholarship or infringe on their good name at church. But for the most part, the sexual promiscuity of the matter wouldn't be a big deal at all. The only scandalous decision would be following through with motherhood. The evidence would be inescapable. Pregnancies happen only one way. The fact that this was God's archangel telling her about this would not help her much during the moment Mary would need to let her family know. How useful would it be when her fiancé figured out that there was a baby in her womb who wasn't his? What would the village do about not just their right but their command to pelt her with rocks until she was dead? Can you imagine how it would sound? "Hey, everyone. Yeah, yeah, I'm pregnant. But it's okay. God did it."

> [If] evidence of virginity was not found in the young woman, then they shall bring out the young woman to the door of her father's house, and the men of her city shall stone her to death with stones. Deuteronomy 22:20–21

What mad man would believe such a tale, even told to him by the daughter he truly loved and trusted?

It is against all this that the greatest miracle, the most marvelous moment, arises. It is magnificent enough that God chose to bind Himself with man's flesh in order to save us. It is outstanding enough that God chose to dwell with us as one with His creation in order to unbreak it. It is mind-blowing enough that God overcame so many things that according to our reason cannot be: a God, incarnated; the infinite, finitized. But none of these mysteries compare to the even greater wonder that resulted from God becoming a man: Mary **believed** what Gabriel preached.

"Let it be," Mary said.

Let what be?

Let **Who Jesus Is** be.

Neither God nor Gabriel needed Mary's permission. **God speaks**, and His words always do what they say. But

> I am the servant of the Lord; let it be to me according to your word. Luke 1:38

in this case, they did more than just make what they said happen in time, space, and history. God's words also, by their own inherent force, by their God-Spirited essence, also made mankind capable of believing it **without having to see it**. The words about **Who Jesus Is**, the **First Element of the Gospel**, *created* faith.

MATERIAL GOD

What would she tell her parents? **Who Jesus Is** would be more than enough.

How would the town handle it? **Who Jesus Is** could handle that too.

What if they dragged her into the street, strung her up, and stoned her to death? **Who Jesus Is** was the answer there as well.

If her parents handed her over to the crowds, and the crowds killed her and the baby with her, would that stop Him?

No.

Even death would not be able to impede this prophecy. Even death would not be able to contain this promise. Even death would not be able to stop this baby. This was the One foretold to undo the breaking of the world. This was the One who, by the hand of God, was born of a virgin. This was Jesus, and **Who Jesus Is** would handle everything.

"Let it be to me **according to your word**," Mary said (Luke 1:38).

This was the real undoing of the curse. This was God really doing something that cannot be done. Gabriel preaching to Mary was not the first time the promise of who Jesus would be was made, nor was Mary the first to believe in this powerful redemption. But this was the moment when all the beliefs that had been or would be came to their crux as a woman confronted by an angel was not deceived but believed again by the power of the **Gospel words**.

The mystery is explosive. Life of very life, begotten in the Godhead before all worlds, would be born. "Jesus will be His name," the angel told her, because *Jesus* is that name that holds the highest name, now given to be the man who holds the highest God, heir to His own promises, answer to His own prophecies. The cosmos changed as **Who Jesus Is** came to earth. He never in Himself had not been. He in no way was now anything more or less than all He'd ever been, even though He did not add to Himself one bit, as if His being God had been somehow lacking. This was the life on which all the promises to bring life out of death were founded. Without this enfleshing, without this **into-carnal-ating**, the rest of the Gospel, the rest of the story that God has been preaching since the day we broke the world, simply could not and can never be.

"He will be a king," the angel said. "He will save," the angel said again.

She believed.

This gift from God, her faith, lived to see what she believed. But Christianity has always insisted that more blessed are those who have not seen and yet believe, because it is not the sight of the world restored that lies at the heart of man's salvation. It is the ability of man to trust God's Word again that truly needs to be restored.

This trust is restored by being given words to believe again. The **Three Elements of the Gospel** are the beating heart of those words. The First Element is **Who Jesus Is**: the Son of God, begotten of His Father from beyond eternity, and also the Son of Man, born of the flesh of His mother, Mary. But **Who Jesus Is** alone is not enough to destroy evil without destroying you. Humanity didn't just need **Who Jesus Is** for its own sake. Humanity needed **Who Jesus Is** in order for the **Second Element of the Gospel** to take place. The whole reason the Son of God became **Who Jesus Is** was to accomplish **What Jesus Did**.

THE FIRST ELEMENT OF THE GOSPEL

Who Jesus Is

ECHO

* THE FIRST ELEMENT OF THE GOSPEL: Who Jesus Is

- Jesus is God.

- Jesus is man.

The Second
Element: Part I

What Jesus Did

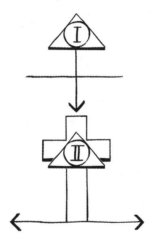

WHO JESUS IS HAPPENED SO WHAT JESUS DID COULD BE DONE

Jesus did many things, so many that writing them all down would take up more space than all the books the ancient world could have held. What we know about Jesus comes from those things that were written down. The acts of Jesus were not written centuries later but by the same generation who knew Him, lived with Him, walked with Him, ran from Him when He died, and yet later died for Him and His cause.

These men chose to tell us the things they believed mattered the most. Having seen it all, they had to boil Him down, summarize Him, and give us all of Him in a picture that would by nature be only part of Him.

In this way, the Gospel was first written, not as everything that Jesus did, but as the things Jesus did that men named Matthew, Mark, Luke, and John saw as essential to understanding the Christ of **Christ**ianity. They each had different takes. The former tax collector and Hebrew highlighted certain things while the Greek scholar and physician zoomed in on something else. But when we take them all together, put them in a single pot, and boil their writings down, we find within them the real meat of the man named Jesus. We find that of all the things He did, both written and unwritten, there are **five** that matter more than the rest. There are five that include, absorb, and flow from all the rest. These **Five Dones of What Jesus Did** do not undo or limit the rest of **What Jesus Did**. They are the reason He did everything else. They are the acts that give the rest of what He did meaning. They are the epicenter, the fulcrum, the finest, surest point.

They are the **Second Element of the Gospel**.

> Just as those who from the beginning were eyewitnesses and ministers of the word have delivered them to us, it seemed good to me also, having followed all things closely for some time past, to write an orderly account for you, most excellent Theophilus. Luke 1:2–3

THE GRAVITY OF THE CROSS

It was the last reasonable place anyone would ever look for Light of Eternal Light or Life of Eternal Life. One incredibly dark afternoon, under clouds of deep shadow and amid cries of hatred and despair, at a desperately unhappy mound of mud known as the Hill of Skulls, one human male had spikes driven through His hands and into the wood of a dead tree.

This was the crux of history.

One man did what every man before Him had eventually done. One man died. He gave up His breath. His heart stopped beating. His blood stopped flowing. The synapses of His brain stopped firing.

One man died, but He did so in a way no other man before Him had ever done. A way no other man but Him could ever do. Jesus of Nazareth, one man, died **as God**.

Not with God.
Not by God's help.
Not as God's example.
God.
Dead.
Pierced and nailed to a cross.
It's impossible.
More impossible than talking snakes.
More impossible than water turning into wine.
More impossible than any ludicrous dream that has ever been dreamed.

Bound to the nature He had chosen for Himself, God was crucified, dead, and buried.

That's **What Jesus Did** to stop the evil. To love the unlovable. To justify the godless rebellion of our personal hells without casting us forever into them.

But in order to do it, Jesus needed to do two other things first.

In Him the whole fullness of deity dwells bodily. Colossians 2:9

THE THINGS GOD CANNOT DO

When Gabriel came from heaven and called out, "Greetings, O favored one, the Lord is with you" (Luke 1:28), he was saying Mary was favored because of the action God was doing in her womb for the sake of the human race. It was a mystery even angels longed to look into. They marveled to watch and burst into song at **What Jesus Did** in order to restore peace between God and the entire cosmos. In order to die on the cross for the bentness of the world, God first had to become a man.

This incarnating, this **enfleshing**, this **Who Jesus Is** is the **First Done of the Gospel**, and there was no avoiding it, because dying on a cross is something that God as God cannot do. Except that He can. **After** He becomes a man too.

Men have been dying since we broke the world. Not a single one of those deaths has been enough to pay the penalty of our mutiny. The endless train of dying has only been the tip of the punishment, a merely temporal justice that limits our evil rather than undoes it. The scales have not been balanced. The meter has not been leveled.

In order for the death of a man to fulfill God's deep desire to undo the evil in His creation without undoing the creation itself, He needed to have a better man, a **second Adam**, so that man could have a better death. This Adam could not be entirely from outside creation. He needed to be of the same mud, born of the same flesh that fell. But He also couldn't be tainted by the creation.

> You, who were dead in your trespasses and the uncircumcision of your flesh, God made alive together with Him, having forgiven us all our trespasses, by canceling the record of debt that stood against us with its legal demands. This He set aside, nailing it to the cross. Colossians 2:13–14

He needed to be free from the inheritance of thorns that would make His death an imperfect payment. A new man, born free of the old man's necessities, could then completely, willingly subject Himself to the penalty, assume its consequences, and stand in your place without in the same moment desecrating the results.

But nothing in creation, not even the good angels in heaven whose wills were untouched by the fall, could enter human flesh and not also be subject to its impurity. No being is so good that evil cannot corrupt him. Except for one. Only one. Only God—the only being who is not only good but is the very source of goodness—could possibly enter a flesh that was evil and be good enough to swallow the evil whole without being tainted by it in the least.

Evil is a filthy thing. It rubs off on everything it touches. Like leprosy. Like leaven. It can't be gotten out just by rubbing it with some soaps and salts. When you rub your finger across a dusty table, the dust might come off the table, but it only does so because it sticks on you. But what if there were a being so clean, so unable to be dirtied, that when He ran His finger across the table the dirt didn't come off on Him? What if instead His pure cleanness came off on the dirt?

This is why it was God who had to die. This is why only God could take responsibility for the evil of creation, even though that evil was not His fault. **What Jesus Did** is become a man. He was born a baby in Bethlehem so that He could grow into a prophet, so that He could be strung up with spikes and thorns upon a murderous tree, so that as God He could take physical responsibility for the evils of creation, so that in His own destruction He could absorb those evils forever, on behalf of everyone else.

THE OTHER CHEEK

God was born as a man so He could die. But until He died, everything else that Jesus would ever do would be part of something else that could not avoid being **Done**. No matter if He were preaching to multitudes or getting fed by His mother, Jesus, the God-man, was also doing something else. This **Second Done of What Jesus Did** is an obvious, constant event in Scripture, yet it remains hidden to most readers. This **Done** is something He did because He was fully human, yet at the same time this is something that humans were never designed to do at all. This **Done** is something we all do, though in large part we have become numb to it. This **Done** is something we now know by nature but God does not, and that is what makes it different.

We don't know the specifics of what Jesus did between the ages of 2 and 12, or 12 and 30, because there are no records of His travels, labors, or teachings. Fanciful speculations about His life as a yogi in India are only slightly less baseless than supposing He spent

His teen years as a hermit on Mars. But there is one thing we can say with certainty that Jesus **did** do when He was a teen. He did it on the day He was twelve in the temple, and He did it the day He turned twenty in anonymity. Born of a virgin and waiting a whole life only to be murdered, Jesus, just like everyone else, had to live on this cursed earth, filled to its edges with rages and decays and sicknesses and sorrows.

> He had no form or majesty that we should look at Him, and no beauty that we should desire Him. He was despised and rejected by men, a man of sorrows and acquainted with grief; as one from whom men hide their faces He was despised, and we esteemed Him not. Surely He has borne our griefs. Isaiah 53:2–4

Jesus, just like everyone else, **suffered**. **Constantly.**

It was only natural. All men do so. The amazing grace of the issue is what it would have been like for **God** to do so.

There are some tall tales that remain from the centuries that followed the Early Church. They are fables of the childhood of Jesus that mimic much of the modern mythological pictures of Jesus that adorn the walls of Christian churches or the pages of Christian children's books. They are stories about a kid who giggles and plays while He raises dead sparrows to life. They are pictures of a shepherd who laughs and smiles as He searches for His lost sheep. They are the visions of a savior who doesn't seem to think there is much in the experiences of this world that anyone needs being saved from.

There is something terribly wrong with this image of God. It is a picture focused on the power and glory that God becoming man brought into the world. But this image of God ignores the deep and abiding pain that coming into the world would certainly have caused Him. The problem is not the curiosity about what the world must have been like around a body who is God. The problem is imagining a perfect God who could become part of a fallen creation and never be bothered by the imperfections constantly around Him. The Jesus of our mythologies and pictures seems hardly bothered by the evils of the world, less bothered than a mild housekeeper is bothered by a few stains and spots.

The suffering of Jesus was no different in the *details* than the suffering of everyone else who ever lived. He found the same troubles, felt the same pains, caught the same colds. But even though the events were the same, the suffering Jesus experienced was radically different in its **effects**. It would have been **worse**. Much worse.

Because He was God.

GOD OF SORROWS

The daily grind, the hourly frustrations, the constant futility that we all labor under would not have been made more bearable by Jesus' perfection. Because He was perfect, these imperfections would have bothered Him **even more**. He was the author, source, and font of endless pleasure, so His pain of living in a world of suffering was so much worse than anything you or I could ever know.

> In the days of His flesh, Jesus offered up prayers and supplications, with loud cries and tears, to Him who was able to save Him from death, and He was heard because of His reverence. Although He was a son, He learned obedience through what He suffered. Hebrews 5:7–8

We children of the cataclysm have never known it to be any other way. It's not that we don't despise the suffering. Obviously we do. We are constantly caught up in our little justification-quests in order to avoid suffering, improve it, or convince ourselves it will eventually go away. But imagine not just *thinking* you don't deserve the bad thing that happened to you, but *knowing* it, with perfect foresight and knowledge. Imagine living day after feckless day in a world of such bankruptcy and agony that it touched your skin, your mind, your feelings. Imagine living in that suffering when you yourself are the source of eternal good and up to this point goodness is the only experience you've ever known.

We strike a foot against a stone and don't hesitate to blaspheme. By cursing the rock ("damn rock!"), we acknowledge that someone, something, must be responsible for the evil of the moment. We can't admit that it is not the rock's fault, but we also can't admit responsibility for being the one who kicked it. But for Jesus, all of that would be different. Every splinter or angry glance would come with the perfect, pristine knowledge that it was totally and entirely undeserved. Being God would not make a stubbed toe easier to bear, but harder. Even if Jesus did strike His foot against a stone, it would be the stone's fault.

It is the cruelest torment imaginable, not only to endure all the wrong and its results that the rest of us live with, but to do so while knowing how right you have made it to be. Jesus' suffering was, for Him, the most backward and wrong experience imaginable. How much better do we have it, never to have known perfect pleasure, and so not having any clue what we're missing? Can we even imagine what it would be like to spend all eternity being the source of pleasure, and then one day you wake up crying for milk and warmth because you were cut off from it? And then remained so?

Most of us can hardly give up coffee or cigarettes or hamburgers. Could you give up never feeling pain or sadness? On purpose? For years and years? Think about how little you can stand it when you see someone take what you know is yours and abuse it. Day after day, for a whole life long, Jesus watched us do just that. With **everything**.

What must it have felt like to have taxes demanded of Him by His own temple?

What must it have felt like to hear lies taught about Him and in His name?

What must it have felt like to have the very authority He bestowed on man as part of His own image used to condemn Him to death?

You and I can hardly bear to not receive credit for the petty good things we sometimes manage to do without whining about it. Jesus lived as God among a bunch of jerk-face, head-up-the-rear, arrogant slimeballs with not a one of us really knowing who He was or how great a thing He was doing for three decades. And He didn't utter a word of complaint. He just quietly went along with it, waiting for the fullness of time to kill Him. When at last He told us, we despised and mocked Him for it.

Worse! Being God, Jesus also had within Himself the power to undo it all. He could snap His fingers, call on ten thousand angels, and make it all go away. There was no eternal requirement that He endure any of this.

Yet He did.

He endured the suffering because He knew that the moment He made His own suffering stop, all the other lives would be abandoned to their just deserts. He knew that getting to that cross would change everything for everyone. He also knew that the humiliation of His powers and rights carried His entire life long and brought to completion in His death was the kind of life that could swallow the curse once and for all. He knew that His suffering was slowly unbending the world.

THE REAL OTHER CHEEK

No more heroic valor is conceivable than that which Jesus of Nazareth showed simply by being born and living among us. These are the first **Dones of What Jesus Did** that summarize all the others. It is easy to overlook them because we would have things differently.

It is easier to focus on His acts of charity. It is more civil to wax on about His teachings of virtue. It is more fun to paint pictures of the miracles. Such things make for the kinds of stories we fallen creatures prefer to tell our children. Stories that hide the disaster of this age. Stories that help us make believe that the evil of this life is not great. Stories that help us believe that **What Jesus Did** is the kind of thing that we could do too.

Our thorny hearts would prefer that the important things Jesus did could at least symbolize the kinds of things we also could achieve. We might not calm storms, but we can overcome turbulent times. We might not heal a beggar, but we can help the people we see in need. But **suffering** is the very thing we are always trying hardest to avoid. **Being born** isn't something we have any control over at all. Both are **passive** things, actions that we do not do but are merely subjected to.

But Jesus actively chose to be subjected to being born and suffering. More. He subjected Himself to a life of suffering as a prerequisite for the final subjection by which He saved the world. He was born into our sorrows and stricken with our torments so that He could receive the finishing smite that would put an end to it all.

> **The foolishness of God is wiser than men, and the weakness of God is stronger than men.** 1 Corinthians 1:25

This is the inverted love: the fortitude Jesus displayed just by opening His eyes in the morning and accepting it; the mettle He demonstrated by courageously staying in this imperfect world day after day, all the while knowing that the only thing waiting for Him at the end of it all was a brutal, tortured, entirely undeserved murder at the hands of hateful men. It makes the magic healing of sparrows or even blind men pale by comparison.

Changing water into wine or walking on water did not save the world. They were signs of **Who Jesus Is**, but they were not the **Five Dones** that Jesus came to do. They are not the **Second Element of the Gospel**. The heart of **What Jesus Did** belongs to the cross, to those things that made the cross possible, and to those things that are a direct result of the cross.

> *Whoever believes in the Son of*
> *God has the testimony in himself.*
>
> 1 John 5:10

THE SECOND ELEMENT: PART II

What Jesus Did

ONE DONE TO DO THEM ALL

God died. That is **What Jesus Did**.

Not as an idea or thought; not as a theory or a story. God died. God died—a dead man hanging nailed to a tree. This was love inverted. This was love making an unlovable world lovable again. This was love, not that we had ever loved in such a way, but that He still loved us in spite of our hate. This was love, that He unbroke all that we, by our hate, had broken. Love took responsibility for the cataclysm that was not His fault. He took the recompense and placed it firmly upon Himself, crown of thorns and all. He took the curse and killed it with the death of His own beating heart. God bled, and in His blood flowed Life of Very Life. It pooled upon the broken earth, dripped with supernaturality beyond the most fantastic of fairy stories.

This was the real story whispered of old. This was the answer quietly left without action for millennia. This was why God let evil continue. This was the price of our ransom. God waited because God wanted to put all things back to the way they are supposed to be. God wanted to save the world, not condemn it. This was the only way for that to happen.

God. Dead. Paradise restored. His blood unshackled the universe from the chains forged by the flesh of the old man. A new man's new flesh now became a shackle for the dominion of darkness, locking up the futility of our age and casting it down into the abyss like lightning falling from the sky.

> **When the centurion, who stood facing Him, saw that in this way He breathed His last, he said, "Truly this man was the Son of God!"** Mark 15:39

But no one knew! Even those staring at God as He died on a cross could not see this greatest of all dos ever done for what it was. When they took God's corpse down, the best of us wept and wailed. Most never made it that far. Most fled or hid or mocked or laughed. Scales covered the eyes of all. No one believed this was the whole point. No one understood this was the fulcrum of all the prophecies, all the stories ever spoke.

Many still do not.

Jesus was **born** and Jesus **suffered** in order to be God the dead man.

Without this, there is nothing. It is the bitter pill that tastes sweet. It is power made perfect through weakness. It is the ultimate sacrifice given in mercy.

But dying was not the end of **What Jesus Did**. The cross is what He came to achieve. It is why He was born and why He suffered. But He also achieved His death in order to make possible the things He would do next. The cross is the end of all things, but not an end unto itself. The first three **Dones of What Jesus Did** make Christianity possible. Jesus was born. Jesus suffered. Jesus died. But the **Fourth** and **Fifth Dones** are Christianity's immediate **effects**.

UNCONTAINABLE

In order to save the world He loved, God needed to die. But God could not die. So God became a man in order to be able to die. Yet even as a man with a spear-pierced heart and a brain so oxygen-deprived that the gray matter irretrievably lost all function, He was still God. Even dead, it was impossible for Him to remain that way for long. As God, even His own wrath against sin could not be greater than Himself. As God, He could become sin in the cursed body of a man, swallow sin whole, and still remain ultimately unfazed by it.

For God, being dead is only a matter of time. This is why **rising from the dead** is the **Fourth Done** of **What Jesus Did**. Because death died in Jesus' death, the resurrection didn't just become possible. It became **inevitable**. Death, having killed God, was now also dead. The resurrection is the only possible result. Not just for Jesus. For everyone.

The result of Jesus' death is the new birth of mankind. When Jesus of Nazareth rose from His own grave, all of humanity rose with Him. His body of clay became a vessel of light to lighten all men. His limited flesh and blood, revealing itself to contain infinity, proved once for all that death is not the end of man. In Him, in His personal humanity, a supernatural ark was built, a new man capable of ferrying all mankind out of this creation and into another one.

> God raised Him up, loosing the pangs of death, because it was not possible for Him to be held by it. Acts 2:24

But even to say **"Christ is risen!"** is to confess that He is risen **from** something. He is risen from the washing of mankind in the eternal wrath of God until the wrath of God was all used up. He is risen from the pit of human brokenness borne in the heart of all mankind. He is risen from a baptism unlike any other, forged of fire and blood and darkness and pain. He is risen from a death died in your place. He is risen from His crucifixion.

No one hangs an empty tomb on the wall. We hang crosses. Even with Jesus taken off the cross, His crucifixion is still there. Hewn of delicate craftsmanship or coarse woods, hidden behind a praying child or a dove or a cowboy hat, the cross still remains an implement of torture, a gory symbol, quietly begging for its story to be whispered again. **Christ is risen from God's crucifixion.** In three dimensions. In time and space. With storms above and quakes below. With wounds and bloody lashes that would forever leave the scars to prove it.

"Here, Thomas, put your hand into My side."

The resurrection of Jesus does not escape the cross. It **preaches** it.

Christ is risen! It is the **Fourth Done** of **What Jesus Did**. It is less achievement than effect. It is less a saving act than a foretaste of salvation's hope. It is less the end of the cross than the cross's meaning extended forward. It is less a miracle than the impossible turned inevitable because of **Who Jesus Is**.

WHERE DID JESUS GO?

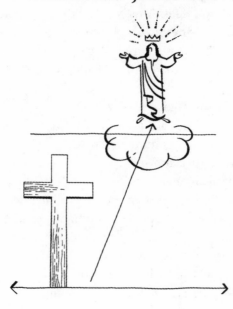

If you're like me, then you've probably wondered why, after Jesus rose, He left. When I was a young man, I would hear the passage read about the Upper Room, where Jesus told His disciples, "It is to your advantage that I go away" (John 16:7), and I would want to shout, "What on earth is He talking about?!" How could it possibly be better for us to be away from Jesus? How could it possibly not be better for Him to be right here in our midst, proving His existence, silencing His critics, keeping His Church on the right track?

The apostles wondered this too. Even up to the day Jesus left, they didn't really believe He was going to go. On the big day itself, the day He vanished for the last time, they asked Him, "You're going to fix everything now, right? Now is the time to end the world and make it perfect again, right?" They still didn't understand that just as Jesus' **crucifixion** was the cornerstone that made His **resurrection** possible, the resurrection was really just the groundwork that made Jesus' **ascension** possible, and the ascension was the real pavement that makes saving **faith** possible.

> **When they had come together, they asked Him, "Lord, will You at this time restore the kingdom to Israel?" He said to them, "It is not for you to know times or seasons that the Father has fixed by His own authority."** Acts 1:6–7

Most discussions about Jesus' ascension are about *how* He did it. Did He fly away like superman or did He just disappear behind a supernatural cloud while more or less still on the ground? Was it a wormhole in space and time or did He wave to the moon as He passed by? Fascinating as it might be, this is a distraction. *How* Jesus ascended is far less important than **where** Jesus went. In the same way, where Jesus went is only important because of **why** He went there.

The **Fifth Done** of **What Jesus Did** is that Jesus, the made-of-atoms physical human, **ascended** into heaven. This doesn't just mean that He went to where the angels are, though it does mean that too. But that "heaven" is just another part of creation. It is what God made when He created the heavens and the earth. Jesus went much **further** than that. He went where even the angels have never gone. Jesus went **outside** of creation. He went to dwell in the "unapproachable light . . . [that] no one has ever seen or can see" (1 Timothy 6:16). He went to the all-seeing, all-knowing, all-being, all-presiding magnitude of where only God can go. He went to what the ancients called the **Immanent Trinity**.

No one goes there.

No one sees that.

But Jesus did. **Jesus ascended** to the **excelsis** of "highest heaven," beyond space and time and even eternity itself, beyond the throne of God to the hidden center of God Himself, reclaiming all of His power for Himself in order to wield it.

As a **man**.

For **you**.

This is tremendously wonderful news. We do not hear about it often enough.

As God, Jesus has put one good man in charge of everything forever. As a man, all history is now moving at Jesus' bidding. As a man, nothing passes His notice. As a man, time, space, and eternity serve the purpose of His will. Nothing is outside of His control. Jesus has grasped the real divine right of kings, and with it He has been exercising full **reign** for over two thousand years.

But it doesn't look like it, and that is because He is not reigning in the way that any of us would expect. He is not reigning to fix the world the way we would like to see it fixed. The fact that we don't immediately understand what He is doing is only one more tribute to our plight. The fact that we assume that if we saw Jesus in charge everything would be better for us only illustrates the essence of our problem.

Our problem is not that we do not see enough proof of God being in charge of the world. Our problem is that no matter what we see, we do not really **believe** God is in charge of the world. That is the thing that needs to be fixed. That is the dilemma that we need to be saved from.

The way to be saved from doubt is not through sight but through **faith**. Nobody hopes for what he already sees. So Jesus ascended to the Father to achieve something even more marvelous than raising all people from the dead. He knows that if the resurrection of the flesh is going to do us any good, then first He needs to take care of the resurrection of our souls.

THE SYMPTOMS ARE NOT THE DISEASE

It is natural for thorny people like us to hear the word *salvation* and think of finding relief from the things we don't like in life. We think of salvation from suffering, division, atrocities, brokenness, and death. But in doing so, we confuse the **effects** of evil with evil itself. We confuse the wages that evil earns with evil's **source**.

No matter how much you throw away the bad fruit that grows on a tree, if you never address the rotting root, you will only get more bad fruit. Unlike the evil side effects of sickness, suffering, and decay, the real root of evil is not a new thing added to creation in the fall and curse.

When the first Adam fell, he invoked on himself and his descendants an emptiness within. He twisted his created state into a new, uncreated version. He chose for us to have a dark hole in the heart, not adding to but always pulling from the goodness of the universe by pulling away from the place that goodness is born. God's words **create** what they say. Always. They make what they proclaim. Adam chose to **unmake** this very thing by simple refusing to believe it.

Adam was not deceived.
1 Timothy 2:14

It is a bizarre thing indeed. Suddenly, here was a part of creation that could resist being created. Here was the anointed king of creation choosing to believe that if he didn't believe God's actual words, then he could make reality even better than the world that God's words created.

But he didn't. He made everything exponentially worse. Yet as bad as those results are, they were only the results. Adam chose to hear God's actual words but not believe them. That choice to not believe remains the real problem. All other problems that have ever been flow from that unmajestic disruption. All decay and dissolution ruins its way back to it.

For this reason, eternal salvation from evil must not only remove the things that currently plague us. Salvation must also restore the very thing thrown away, the lack of which caused the plagues in the first place. For this reason, if mankind is ever going to be saved, truly saved, we can't just be saved from the pains and troubles that bother us. If the rotten fruits of the curse are ever to be lifted, then the unbelief that first infected them needs to be cured. We need to be saved from **unbelief** itself.

The only way to save someone from unbelief is to restore him to **faith**.

JESUS LEFT US WITH FAITH ALONE

Salvation is not just randomly **through** faith alone. Salvation is through faith alone because salvation *is* faith alone.

Everything else is secondary. Life. Resurrection. Health. Peace. These are all the wages of faith. These are all good gifts built into creation by the speaking of God. The problem is not the lack of truth in His words about these things. The problem is that we refuse to believe the truth in them.

> For I am not ashamed of the gospel, for it is the power of God for salvation to everyone who believes, to the Jew first and also to the Greek. For in it the righteousness of God is revealed from faith for faith. Romans 1:16–17

Without faith in God's creating words, all that remains is a world condemned to an existence without God. Without faith, God is dead to us even while He lives and reigns. Without faith, all that remains is the uncreation of self-inflicted destruction and fire.

But once faith is restored to man, then nothing is impossible.

Jesus knew this better than anyone else. After all, He had to live with us all those years, experiencing firsthand not just the problems of a suffering world, but also the godless way we thorny humans deal with it. He had to watch us create the suffering and death that plague us by the unbelief we constantly bring forth from our dark hearts. As Jesus taught and served and did His miracles, He saw what was really in mankind. In many ways, His own ministry was twisted by the people around Him to serve their own selfish ends. Jesus experienced people's need for the real salvation, the faith that could best live and flourish only when He and His miracles could no longer be seen.

He did not leave us as orphans. He did not leave us actually alone. He left us with the one thing that was lost, now restored.

Jesus asked Thomas, "Do you believe because you have seen?" The answer is **no**. Thomas believed because Jesus called him by name. Jesus spoke miraculous, saving faith back into Thomas's unrepentant heart. "Stop unbelieving, and believe!" But then Jesus also said, "Blessed is the one who never sees and yet believes."

Faith *is* salvation. Faith alone. Faith all by itself. Faith without sight. Faith without proofs. Faith that springs from nothing more or less than the words about **Who Jesus Is** and **What Jesus Did**. Such faith saves by filling that empty darkness of unbelief with actual words of God newly spoken to re-create the faith that was lost, to make it possible for unbelievers to believe again.

Faith is what Mary received when the angel preached to her. Faith is what responded, "Let it be."

Faith is what Abraham was given in the promises of an heir to come. Faith is what was reckoned to him as perfection.

Faith is why David was a man after God's own heart, trusting that having been circumcised into the covenant was greater even than his own death. Faith is how David then stood before Goliath, not certain in his sling, but certain in the promise that no nation could overcome Israel because God was fighting for them.

Faith is what Paul was given when God struck him blind and shoved him to the ground. Faith is why Paul was then willing to be shipwrecked, beaten, chased by wild beasts, stoned. He, like the rest, was not waiting for salvation. He had it. Salvation had already come in the fact that he found himself **believing**. Because that faith alone was salvation, anything and everything that could happen to the body afterward, whether it was martyrdom or some evil death, didn't matter. God's words were true. That was all that mattered.

> **Through Him we have also obtained access by faith into this grace in which we stand.** Romans 5:2

Wherever God's words are true, faith alone is more than enough. On the rock of faith, the prophets foretold and hoped in what Jesus would do. They did not see His day but longed for it. On the rock of faith, the Church of Jesus is assembled. People hear His words, and by them trust is created within, a light shining so strongly as to devour that black hole within until its emptiness is powerless before the certainty of God's promises.

By faith alone, we are saved, because salvation happens when lost faith is restored to us. Jesus' being **born** set the stage for Jesus' **suffering**, which prepared the way for Jesus' **crucifixion**, which paid the price for Jesus' **resurrection**, which enabled Jesus'

ascension, which left behind the only thing that mattered: **God's words**, newly invigorated to spread both backward and forward through history with the spiritual power to restore you to faith.

THE PROBLEM OF UNBELIEF

When we look out at the disastrous course of the world, it is only natural to find fear. In our fear, our first reaction is to turn our trust to politics, education, science, medicine, or any number of options that promise to fix the current plight. Most of these things are good parts of the created order. But when we make them our hope, we turn their good into our evil, treating creation as if it were the Creator. No sooner does this happen then these same idols we've built begin to exhibit their weakness. They are not strong enough to create good on their own, and so they begin to break under the strain of our misplaced faith. When this happens, ironically, we do not blame our misplaced trust.

Instead, we blame God. *"Where is God in all this evil?"* we ask, casting about for something else to sink our trust into. We repeat the age-old choice of Adam to believe that it is up to us to surpass the world we've been given, to build a better future, to restore paradise, to save the world.

But more than anything else, the birth, suffering, death, resurrection, and ascension of Jesus means that no matter how this life appears, no matter what destruction or confusion is leveled upon us now, Jesus has the entire thing fully under His control. No matter what you face, no matter how high or deep, no matter how humiliating or debilitating, no matter how dangerous, whether in pain, suffering, age, decay, moth, rust, or sickness, no matter what atrocity the world lifts against you, even in the event that the world destroys you, in all these things you are more than a conqueror. But it is not the kind of conqueror the world can see. The Christian conquers the world not by sight, but by faith alone.

Conquering this world by sight would not be enough to save you. The great kings of history all still died. The great mystics of the world's religions never escaped the curse. But the weakest Christian, the one still plagued by doubts and uncertainties, struggles and failures, wickedness within and threats without, is still more than a conqueror because even the smallest smidgeon of faith in **Who Jesus Is** and **What Jesus Did** fills the void with trust that no matter what we see now, that is not all that will ever be. Even the total devastation of the world by fire and carnage cannot devastate this faith because this faith is not in the present state of any of these things. It is in Jesus, and He has ascended beyond them all. They cannot touch Him now. Rather, they move according to His will, which is not that they would cease, but that all mankind would cease trusting them.

> He poured out on us richly through Jesus Christ our Savior, so that being justified by His grace we might become heirs according to the hope of eternal life. Titus 3:6–7

Jesus is alive. He began the good work of salvation from unbelief when He whispered the promise of His story. He paid for it when He died on the cross. Now He has the authority to finish it by moving the entire cosmos, minute by minute, day by day, to ensure that the words about salvation reach **you**.

Believe *that*. That is the beating heart of Christianity, pumping water and blood from Jesus' pierced side into your heart, strictly according to His Word, believed. It is the thumping Echo the world cannot hear. The world instead busies itself dashing petty hopes and nearsighted doubts against the raging tides of history and the inability of creation to be its own gods. But the **Five Dones of What Jesus Did** stand impeccable, assuring that Christianity will always be more than a "religion" and far more than another "spirituality." Christianity is both of these and yet far more because the Gospel of **Who Jesus Is** and **What Jesus Did** are now just **the way things actually are**.

More.

There is a **Third Element of the Gospel**.

The **way things actually are** will have a dynamic effect on the **way things soon are going to be**. There is something that will come on the other side of faith. There is salvation through faith alone's result. There is faith's wage. There is the good fruit that will bloom from the new root. **Who Jesus Is** makes **What Jesus Did** possible, but **What Jesus Did** is only the setup for **What Jesus Is Coming Again to Do**.

THE SECOND ELEMENT OF THE GOSPEL

What Jesus Did

* **THE FIRST ELEMENT OF THE GOSPEL:** WHO JESUS IS

  • JESUS IS GOD.

  • JESUS IS MAN.

* **THE SECOND ELEMENT OF THE GOSPEL:** WHAT JESUS DID

  • JESUS WAS BORN.

  • JESUS SUFFERED.

  • JESUS DIED.

  • JESUS ROSE.

  • JESUS ASCENDED.

THE THIRD ELEMENT

What Jesus Is Coming Again to Do

NOT ALL "HEAVENS" ARE FOR REAL

There is something missing from popular Christianity. There is something missing that has been replaced by a mythology entirely foreign to the written records that Jesus left us about what His religion means. It is not that the average Christian is entirely ignorant of the fact that Jesus is coming back, nor would many Christians openly deny it. It is just that the second coming of Jesus is not what they really believe in, because it has no place in the spirituality they have borrowed by osmosis from the world around them.

It is a strange thing to see. If you interview the average person on the street, the Christian and the non-Christian, the churchgoer and the non-churchgoer, they will likely believe almost the same thing about what happens to a person after death. One way or another, unless somebody is Hitler or some other form of psychopathic killer, everyone who is more or less a sometimes-good person, which of course includes *Me,* goes to "heaven" when they die.

But the "heaven" of common street-religion and the heaven the Bible speaks of when examined with a little care turn out to be dynamically different places. We see these images drawn from near-death experiences and greeting cards—notions of bright lights and angels and all of us floating around with harps in some disembodied state, sitting on clouds, fluttering our little wings. These images are universal assumptions of people who get their idea of what heaven is really like from dreams and wishful thinking more closely connected to ancient Greek paganism than anything Jesus ever told us is true. But the average person is unable to tell the difference. The average person is unable to see the superstition and medieval make-believe behind such dreams.

> **But we do not want you to be uninformed, brothers, about those who are asleep, that you may not grieve as others do who have no hope.** 1 Thessalonians 4:13

The scary thing about this is not simply that the average Christian might have a few mistakes in their thinking. The scary thing is that by adopting the *We are all trying to die and go to the same heaven is for real* belief, the average church-attending, Jesus-of-Nazareth-worshiping Christian ends up becoming entirely ignorant of the real good news of the Christian faith. By coming to believe that "dying and going to heaven" is the real hope of the Christian faith, the believer is no longer able to believe in the **Third Element of the Gospel**. If everyone gets to die and go to heaven, then why would Jesus ever bother coming back at all?

The answer to this question is as foreign to the street-mythologies of heaven as any other truth Christianity has to echo. For centuries, the picture of heaven has been mismatched and mucked by a hodgepodge of various strictly pagan ideas slipping in piecemeal through such innovative teachings as the papist dogma of purgatory and the revivalist dogma of the secret rapture. So injurious is the confusion that the average, well-meaning, faithful Christian, when confronted with the real reason Jesus is coming back, usually is entirely astounded and quite disturbed. So sad is the state of our current Christian hope, so twisted is our understanding of the end goal of Christianity, that the average Christian becomes tremendously discomforted when confronted with the promise of the resurrection of the body.

HOPE BEYOND ALL HOPE

Jesus is not coming back to take us all to "heaven," if by "heaven" we mean the place that Christians go to now when they die. Jesus is not coming back to put an end to the physicality of human life. Jesus is not coming back to stop us from living in these bodies. Jesus is coming back to raise these bodies from the dead.

The Christian hope of going to heaven after bodily death is only the hope of being held safely with Jesus while the body rots away in the ground, waiting for the day when Jesus will return to re-create that body, making for that body a new cosmos to dwell in, scoured clean of all those things that made our bodies mortal in this world. Those who are in heaven now, the dead in Christ, will be the first to have their bodies changed, in the twinkling of an eye, with an archangel shout. They will be the first to rise. Only after that shall those who are still alive on this earth when Jesus returns have their bodies also transformed to be like His resurrected body.

> For since we believe that Jesus died and rose again, even so, through Jesus, God will bring with Him those who have fallen asleep. . . . For the Lord Himself will descend from heaven with a cry of command, with the voice of an archangel, and with the sound of the trumpet of God. And the dead in Christ will rise first. Then we who are alive, who are left, will be caught up together with them. 1 Thessalonians 4:14, 16–17

This incredibly good news about our bodies and their pending immortality tends to come as a negative shock to twenty-first-century Christians. But that does not demonstrate a problem with Jesus' promise; it amplifies the carelessness of Christianity in echoing the results of **Who Jesus Is** and **What Jesus Did**. Is it any wonder that modern Christians find so much trouble disentangling themselves from the cares of this world when they have been forced to hope in the Christianity that promises a future that looks nothing like this world? How can creatures like you and me, who only exist because **God gave you a body**, put any real trust in a future that cannot be experienced with the body, in a heaven most often referred to in the Bible as "sleep"?

Even though, practically speaking, the average Christian today operates their faith entirely ignorant of this hope, the ancients considered the bodily resurrection on the Last Day important enough to include it in their permanent list describing the **Five Results of the Gospel**. These results will receive extra focus in the next section of this book. But this focus on the bodily resurrection on the Last Day exists only because it is a result of the **Third Element of the Gospel**. This hope in the resurrection is the thing that makes sense of this Gospel, and which makes this Gospel worth looking forward to. It is why the **Third Element of the Gospel** is not only that Jesus will come back, but that He does so in order to be our **judge**.

JUDGMENT DAY IS GOOD NEWS

This seems counterintuitive, but only because modern Christianity has forgotten what Judgment Day is all about. Jesus is coming back to bring with Him a final judgment against the world. But the focal point of this judgment is not you. It is the great Satan himself, that rebellious arch demon and draconic source of disgrace.

This judgment against evil is not about a petty God who gets off raining on everybody's parties, but about a truly good God who takes very seriously the problem of the evil that has ransacked the world He created. The thing God hates the most is how this evil has cataclysmically infected everything and so prevented any ability to establish or sustain the lasting joy everything was designed for. Judgment Day is the day when God will destroy that evil once and for all, annihilate and remove it from all future experiences, banish it forever, and replace it with a rejuvenated physical universe. That universe will be rebuilt to be everything this fallen universe was intended to be, exactly as this universe is but minus the pain, the sorrow, and the decay that has sickened the lives of all.

Jesus is not coming again to take into this new world everyone who meant well or tried hard. He is coming to judge with Satan, to judge both the living and the dead. He is coming to raise up every human body that ever lived, to hold every person accountable for who they are and what they did, to restore balance and unbreak the world with the ransom He purchased on the cross. He is coming to destroy evil without destroying you, but that does not mean that He will not destroy the majority of everyone else.

Judgment Day will be a tremendous courtroom. Jesus will sit as judge upon His almighty throne, and He will require every human who ever lived to give full account of every last thought, careless word, and self-driven deed ever done—and every good deed left undone. It is with good reason that this picture strikes terror into the thorns of our hearts. This is not the picture of Jesus meek and mild, lying in a manger. This is the Jesus of the apocalypse, eyes ablaze with supernatural fire, golden sash about His breast, arms and feet shining like molten bronze as clear as crystal, refracting the light of the emerald rainbow upon which He sits. And there we'll be, standing pigeon-toed in defense. It is terrifying to picture the prosecutor, the devil himself, bringing against you fact after bloody fact demonstrating the continual unrighteousness with which you have selfishly lived your life. He sets them on the table, marks them as evidence, and demands that you justify yourself. He demands that you explain your self-worshiping, heartsick, rebellious existence. He insists to the court that you, like him, must bear the full consequences of your actions. You deserve the full penalty for missing the mark of what God designed you to be. He will make the case that by your actions you have proven that you belong to him, and therefore must go with him into the eternal fire prepared for him and all his servants.

It is not a pretty picture. It would be an open-and-shut case if the judgment were based only on who you are and what you have done, whether you died as an infant or as an eighty-year-old man. The Bible warns that even kings will try to flee from this day, that all who have inherited the flesh of Adam will beg the mountains to collapse on them and hide them in their crushing weight, rather than step into that dock where they know that they will be condemned by their own words.

But this picture is only true for the man who will seek to be his own advocate, his own defense attorney on That Day. The man who decides to plead "innocent" for himself on the basis of his own words and actions, who believes he can set up a counterbalance to his failures by means of his accomplishments, chooses to place himself beneath the naked eye of God. Because a small amount of cleanness does not make pollution go away, because the small amount of health in the body of a dying man does not make the dying go away, such a defendant will only receive exactly what he deserves.

> In Him all the fullness of God was pleased to dwell, and through Him to reconcile to Himself all things, whether on earth or in heaven, making peace by the blood of His cross. Colossians 1:19–20

This is why Jesus died. Jesus died beneath the naked eye of God's impartial judgment as atonement big enough for all of humanity. The crucifixion of Jesus was Judgment Day come early, so that on Judgment Day come later you would not stand alone in your defense. There will be Jesus, that mighty and impartial judge, seated upon His crystalline throne, and there will be Satan, that wily prosecutor, making his rock-solid case on the foundation of your sandy life. But then something marvelous happens in the courtroom for the Christian whose religion is the acceptance of a plea bargain offered in the dead body of God on a cross. There, in the crucifixion, the Christian enters the plea of "guilty as charged," and as a result of this honest faith, which itself is nothing more than trusting in God's words about what humanity deserves, Jesus steps down off His throne to take the floor of the courtroom as your defense attorney. For the Christian who does not seek to defend himself but admits the full guilt and all the consequences he deserves, the judge elects to double as your lawyer.

BUT THAT'S NOT FAIR

That's right. It's not. But don't miss the beauty of it all. It's not fair **to you**. You are the only one who is not getting what you deserve. That is the meaning of the word *grace*.

It is fair for a good God to destroy evil. It is fair for the devil and all his angels to be cast into hell. It is fair for God to give justice to creatures who have sought to unmake His creation by making themselves out to be gods. After all, these creatures have demanded their whole life long that all they want is justice, that the good God give them justice in the end—but their self-absorbed blindness deceived them into mistaking what that justice would be.

It is not fair that Jesus died on the cross. It is not fair that God shed His blood to pay for the exchange of His wrath and His mercy. It is not fair that because of **Who Jesus Is** and **What Jesus Did**, now **What Jesus Is Coming Again to Do** is not condemn you but justify you. It is not fair, and that is precisely why Judgment Day is incredibly good news. No matter what the world might expect, no matter what accurate accusations the devil may make against you That Day, the Gospel of Christianity is that the final judgment has already been announced to you, and because of Jesus, that judgment is **innocent**.

> Then I saw heaven opened, and behold, a white horse! The one sitting on it is called Faithful and True, and in righteousness He judges and makes war. . . . On His robe and on His thigh He has a name written, King of kings and Lord of lords. Revelation 19:11, 16

This is why, from the earliest times, the ancient Christians looked with eager expectation for Jesus' return. This is why they sang in their earliest songs of praise, "He will come again to be our judge." Jesus of Nazareth, crucified as the Son of Eve, raised

165

from the dead on the third day, is bringing with Him at His return total resurrection from the death that plagues us, including the resurrection of the soul, which is experienced in us now only by the faith that hopes in its future coming. That promise is the final judgment of Judgment Day known early, spoken to the first Christians by the resurrected Jesus, echoed with every beat of the heart of Christianity as the antidote to the despairs of every age.

For the Christian, there is now nothing more to worry about ever. Knowing the judgment beforehand, having the verdict already in place, Judgment Day is no longer something to be feared or avoided. The great and terrible Day of the Lord for the Christian will not be like the many misguided, popular conceptions of Armageddon seen in science-fiction and horror movies. It will be much more like that moment in J. R. R. Tolkien's *The Return of the King*, when the heir to the throne, sword of promise in his hand, appears unlooked-for with an army at his back to save his people from their impending destruction. There is nothing more exciting or exhilarating to be found in all the world than this foreordained, steadfast effect of **What Jesus Did**. It is more certain even than heaven and earth still being here tomorrow when you wake up.

The faith-creating, declarative words of God are not done speaking yet. But in the **Third** and final **Element of the Gospel**, He has already told us what He is going to say next. A new world is coming. It brings with it the end to all evil. When Jesus the Christ, Jesus the King, returns, He does so to bring to sight the justification that He has already given through faith in His name. Thanks to a wonderfully unfair judgment of happy inconsistency—based on the representation of an advocate who, as judge, has taken the place of condemnation for Himself—you and I, raised from the dead on That Day, will dwell with Him forever with perfected hearts and hands and voices. We will enjoy the best any world has to offer, a world like this one only entirely better, purged of the corrupting tribulation of thorns.

IT WILL BE AN AIRTIGHT CASE

Hidden behind the bloody cloak of Christ's righteousness, the Day of Judgment will not even be a close call. With the blood of resurrected humanity flowing through your veins because of your communion with Jesus, you will be so physically different from those who seek to defend themselves with only their own blood on That Day. The difference between you and them will be as big as the difference between a sheep and a goat, the difference between a cat and a dog, the difference between a human and a zombie.

Those who are raised from the dead to face the judgment alone will not see their bodies as evidence of Jesus' resurrection. Still trapped in their faithless minds, the best they will be able to make of their resurrected bodies is to use them as one more tool for trying to justify their quest for godhood. This unbelief must be separated from the new universe God is creating, lest that unbelief corrupt and destroy the new heavens and the new earth as well.

Jesus is not going to let that happen. He returns to bring with Him that which is supposed to be, that which (if it weren't for us) should have been all along, an eternal age of world peace and quiet contentment, the kind of life we all long to live but under this curse have never found. He comes to take the dark prince of this age, already bound in chains of God's blood, and cast him into the infernal fire of everlasting ending, in order that you, the one He has named **innocent**, can be placed into the newly minted, resurrected cosmos, made for all of us to enjoy without the threat of such a terrible fall ever happening again.

> **Encourage one another with these words.**
> 1 Thessalonians 4:18

It is because of **Who Jesus Is** and **What Jesus Did** that we can also have confidence that we will never fall again. All mankind fell in the body of Adam, but we will no longer be in the body of Adam. We will be of Jesus' flesh. In order for us to fall, Jesus Himself would have to fall. God Himself would have to choose to be evil. Not only can that never happened, but Jesus has already proved it, resisting such temptation in His suffering, besting every threat with His willingness to drink the cup of humanity's death. As a result, when He returns, He comes as the King who has already conquered every enemy, quelled every threat, and silenced every accusation. He brings with Him, made of His own body, a new earth, a new cosmos, a great and everlasting city with foundations that can never be shaken. All who enter there shall do so already purged of unbelief and doubt. We shall have a faith permanently established in the **Three Elements of**

the Gospel, in Jesus, who lives as the ultimate man, once dead but now alive, never to die again, with the everlasting life of His people written in the scars on His head and hands, His feet and side.

This is the faith that Christianity echoes now—trust in the good news of the past miracle that has established a future perfection. The resurrection of your soul is purchased, and delivery has begun. The resurrection of your body is the hope that your soul looks to. Without this hope, it is impossible to desire the Judgment Day of God. Human reason and will knows well enough what we deserve, and so it seems preferable to hide from the judgment behind mythologies of "heaven" for everybody or the rejection of any kind of afterlife at all. But the Christian crucifies all such mortal doubts and make-believe hopes in the conviction that because of **Who Jesus Is** and **What Jesus Did** nothing in heaven or earth or under the earth will be able to undo the promise of **What Jesus Is Coming Again to Do**. It is a conviction founded not on personal strength nor on subjective dreams, but on the spirituality found in the clarity of the Scriptures, which witness to the life and words of Jesus of Nazareth—that in Him and as Him, God has sworn an oath, and so it is doubly sure. It is sure because first of all, God does not lie. And second, by His solemn vow He has insisted He is telling the truth now.

THE THIRD ELEMENT OF THE GOSPEL

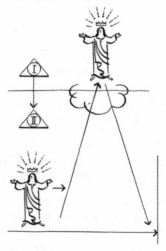

What Jesus Is Coming Again to Do

THE THREE ELEMENTS OF THE GOSPEL

* **THE FIRST ELEMENT OF THE GOSPEL:** Who Jesus Is

  • Jesus is God.

  • Jesus is Man.

* **THE SECOND ELEMENT OF THE GOSPEL:** What Jesus Did

  • Jesus was born.

  • Jesus suffered.

  • Jesus died.

  • Jesus rose.

  • Jesus ascended.

* **THE THIRD ELEMENT OF THE GOSPEL:** What Jesus is
  Coming Again to Do

  • Jesus is coming to judge.

THE FIVE
RESULTS OF
THE GOSPEL

THE FIRST RESULT

The Assembling of Believers

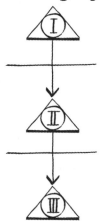

THE PROBLEM WITH CHRISTIANITY

Christianity has a few benefits. There is nothing quite so liberating as a clean conscience. The ability to distinguish right from wrong on the basis of the Ten Commandments is the thing real wisdom is made from. But ultimately, these are not the kind of benefits most people are looking for in a religion. When modern people go shopping for spirituality, they don't stop at the stores that sell answers that will come only once the world ends or you die. People are after something with more curb appeal. They're after a religion (or three) that can help deliver the goods **today**. Modern spiritual consumers want what they believe they need whenever they need it most, which means **right now**.

The vast majority of Christianity's benefits are **not** right now.

Will your God make it guarantee to rain tomorrow? No.

Will your God guarantee the crops will grow better than last year? No.

Will your God heal my cancer? Every time? No.

Will your God bring peace like a river to my soul every day that never goes away, never falters, never wanes? Again, no.

There are versions of Christianity pandering about the marketplace trying to answer yes to questions like these. But whenever we are honest about what the Bible actually says, then we must admit that the God of Christianity is not a great vending machine in the sky. He has given scandalously specific, powerful, and precious promises to all mankind. But they are scandalous precisely because of their extreme limitations. They extend beyond the most fantastic imaginings of men, and yet they do so by remaining almost entirely untestable. **Salvation *is* faith.** But faith is the certainty of things unseen.

> If in Christ we have hope in this life only, we are of all people most to be pitied. 1 Corinthians 15:19

The world's many religions all hinge their spiritual sales pitches on *right now*. They promise answers, fulfillment, betterment, peace. They whisper sweet promises that if you just try long enough, if you just believe hard enough, then you can overcome the world *right now*. Christianity sticks out from these saccharine pretensions by hurtling into the marketplace like a madman with a sword of honesty. The Echo slashes away at brand names and taglines that preach the results you are looking for *right now*. The Echo brashly insists on the fading futility of the present beneath the weight of our thorns. Everything you see will eventually fade. Everything you touch will eventually rot. Everything you experience will be gone like the wind a moment later. It might as well have been a dream for all your efforts to make it last.

Rather than preaching our attempts to fix the problem as the answer to the problem, Christianity preaches that our attempts to fix a perfect world created the problem to begin with. Our continued depraved attempts are not bold, heroic efforts called on by God, but brash, reckless flailings as we try to prop up our idols. With craft and ingenuity, the endless stream of worldly religions shift and move to camouflage the changeless repetition of the endless *Now! Now! Now!* But nothing can escape the exposure of Christianity's consistent, contemplative whisper that hems in all the *Nows!* with a patiently trusting **Not Yet.**

WHEN NOW IS LATER

It is not that there are no **Nows** in Christianity. Christianity is overfilled with **Now** promises. But this doesn't fix the problem. This *is* the problem. All of these **Now** realities are matters of promise that relegate the results to **faith alone**. Because God has spoken, they are truths, realities as unshakable as heaven and earth. But you can't see them. You don't get to feel their guarantee. They are untestable by every method but one: trusting God's words are true in spite of all that you experience now.

The Christian is justified (and that means **perfect**) **right now**. No sin. No mistakes. No thorns. Ever. **Right now.**

The Christian is resurrected (and that means **undying**) **right now**. No sickness. No aging. No death. Ever. **Right now.**

The Christian is with Jesus (and that means **in heaven**) **right now**. Surrounded by angels. Safe from all harm. Forever. **Right now.**

By, in, through, and *as* **faith alone.**

> **Now faith is the assurance of things hoped for, the conviction of things not seen.** Hebrews 11:1

You don't get to see it. You don't get to feel it. You don't get to prove it by what you do. You just are fully and totally justified, without a smidgen of sin in you, by faith alone in God's Word that it is so. You are fully and totally immortal, unable to die, so that even if you do die, yet you live, by faith alone in God's Word that it is so. You are ascended to the highest heavens, present in the body of Jesus, seated and reigning with Him at the right hand of God the Father, by faith alone in God's Word that it is so.

Fantastic and precious promises! But not the kind of promises the world is happy with. By definition, the world wants **now** to mean *Now!* The old man's native religion wants **faith** to mean *sight*. Man-made spiritualities, rooted in our thorns, insist on judging all truth *by experience alone*.

"I don't feel like I'm in heaven. The doctors tell me that I'm dying, and it sure looks like it. I certainly haven't lived a perfect life."

It's a bit like, *"Eating this piece of fruit certainly won't kill me."*

It's not about what seems to be right or is possibly true. It's about what God has surely said. **Who Jesus Is** and **What Jesus Did** are the places of testing, the history where we get to touch with our hands and see with our eyes. But **What Jesus Is Still**

Doing, based upon those past works, is directly opposed to our inborn hunger for endless proofs and signs.

Christianity does not present its worship and prayers, its rituals and spirituality in order to have it judged by what we feel, experience, or understand. It is in opposition to all that. It is not here for us to test the results. It is here to create a willingness to not test, to not prove, to not *justify*.

An evil and adulterous generation seeks for a sign. Matthew 12:39

Because **What Jesus Did** has justified us already, **What Jesus Is Still Doing** is creating trust that it was enough.

PLENTY OF PROOF

What Jesus Did is more than enough. The crucifixion and empty tomb are as established as any other ancient historical event. You can deny the meaning of them, fabricate some loose explanation to satisfy your preconceived notions about what is or is not possible. But dismissing the facts themselves does not make the facts go away.

It is on this foundation, this confession of death and resurrection of Jesus, that Christianity becomes its own form of proof. It is not a blind faith, for it does not trust in made-up events that never happened. It trusts in tangible history that has a present, enduring effect. But on the basis of that certainty, the regenerated faith that wells up in the Christian when he hears about **Who Jesus Is** will blindly trust all Jesus has said about the future.

Now hope that is seen is not hope. For who hopes for what he sees? But if we hope for what we do not see, we wait for it with patience. Romans 8:24–25

Faith alone believes what God has promised about you, even though, according to the same promise, you will not see the completion of that promise until the return of Christ. This faith alone believes that the unseen reality of these promises is more real than even what we do see now. This believing is a deposit of immortality hidden in the present. It is salvation fully experienced in naked trust that, because of Jesus, what God has said has no need to prove itself.

This trust alone is justified perfection. It is the first resurrection from the dead. It is heaven here and **now**. It does not look like or feel like any of these things. But because God has said they are so, He has therefore made them so, no matter what our emotions or eyes have to say about it. It is the essence of Christian salvation to trust God's words, for Jesus' sake.

This strange ordeal is the height of Christian spirituality. It is the religious experience of the heart given the profound freedom to battle against itself. It is a war between the light of what God speaks and the darkness of what our thorns seem to be. The epicenter of this fight is the mind of the Christian. In the Christian mind, saving faith is sustained during the shadowy experience of the *Now* because faith relies on both the **Now** and **Not Yet**.

The thorns of our hearts—which will still dwell with us until we are freed from them in the resurrection of sight—will want to worm their way back into the solution. They will not sit back and see their root cut off and poisoned with the freedom of the Gospel. They will stick and claw to reassert their assumption that the answer to all things—both salvation from the fall and the maintenance of that salvation—must always be a matter of what *Me* is able to do. These thorns will try to turn us back, to claim that we have only been saved by Jesus *so that* by this faith *we become* empowered to love and live without spot or blemish *now*. These powerful thorns will try to trick us into believing the **Ten Important Things** can become the proof of our believing, the bar by which we test the strength and commitment of our faith.

HOW THEN SHALL WE LIVE?

The answer to that question does not begin with us. It does not rest on who we are or what we will achieve while we wait for Jesus' return. It begins with knowing that everything Christianity has or will ever accomplish is truly *Christ*ian. The accomplishments of Christianity will not be done by us, not by any manner of human reason or strength. Jesus has promised to do **What Jesus Is Still Doing** in the same way He has done everything else: by the power of His **words**.

Jesus' words are an alien power among us. Even as we hear them, even as we read, mark, learn, and inwardly digest them, as they go into us and come out of us, they are of Him. Not us. We cannot force His hand or compel Him to work. We cannot equip His words, empower them, or control their effect. The wind that Jesus has sent will blow where it will. The heart of that will remains unflinchingly a matter of the **unseen**. It remains steadfastly a matter of teaching us to trust the promises He has given us.

What Jesus Is Still Doing is creating in you a spirituality of trusting what He has said He is still doing, no matter what it might look like to you. You should not be surprised if the places where Jesus has promised to create and sustain this faith do not appear to be the kinds of places one would think such things could happen in. Instead, you must expect that Jesus will work the power of His promises precisely in places that our minds would never think to look. He will feed your trust in places that will never appear to be what He says they are. To do otherwise would not create faith, but the continued idolatry of your own eyes.

Our ability to see is trapped in this valley of shadowed lands, impoverished and hazy, a halfhearted and foggy reflection of what ought to be but is not. Into this mess, the Holy Spirit comes burning upon Jesus' words. He creates in us belief that the real truth is not how the present experiences appear. The Spirit does not prove Himself by tickling our itching eyes with the idols we would prefer to see. He instead proves Himself by compelling us to rely on what Jesus has already promised. He compels us to be saved by believing in the **Results of the Gospel** as much as we believe in the Gospel itself.

The **Results of the Gospel** are not what we are doing. They are what Jesus is doing to us. The first of these results is both the greatest and the least. It is the most obvious, and the most invisible. It is the result from which all other results will flow, and yet without the others it does not exist at all. The **First Result of the Gospel** is you.

But not you alone.

It is me.

But not me alone.

It is us. It is We. But not ourselves. Not who we are. Not what we've done or will do. It is that we **believe**. The **First Result** of **Who Jesus Is** and **What Jesus Did** is that people who did not see Jesus believe both the Gospel and its results to be true. We believe that Jesus is who He said He is. We believe what the eyewitnesses confess He has done. We believe it was done **for us**. We expect what He is coming again to do.

The **First Result of the Gospel** is you and me. But it is not us alone. Without the others, we would not be here believing at all. It was on their lips, those who believed before us, that these words that gave us faith traveled from Jesus through history until they reached our hearts. They were the mouths of the Echo, hearing and believing, speaking and hearing again, carrying the wind of holy promises from ears to mouths to ears and mouths again.

> **This mystery is that the Gentiles are fellow heirs, members of the same body, and partakers of the promise in Christ Jesus through the gospel.** Ephesians 3:6

These people were not alone either. Just like me and you, they found themselves dragged out of the normal, expected human hopes in a fixed present, and seated down in a pile of *Not Yet* with a host of other broken, incompetent, pain-filled people, just like themselves in all the wrong ways. But they were all aware of the same right thing among them, how they were now together, believing, woken up from the morass of broken life so they could gather around words about the unbrokenness of what Jesus did for us.

The **Assembling of Believers** by the Gospel is the **First Result of the Gospel**. People hear about Jesus, and the result is they want to hear about Him again. Soon they find that they **need** to hear about Him again. They are starving for it. As if by intuition, they know with a supernatural fervor that if they don't get more of this Good News—which spawned their hungering trust in the first place—there will be nothing left in all the decaying *Nows* of this world worth living for.

THE MYSTERY OF HOLINESS

Few things in human history are as obvious and demonstrable as the existence of the Holy Christian Church: people believe in Jesus. Even the most anti-Christian skeptic cannot deny it. He will decry it. He will call it madness and folly. But no matter how wildly he rails against it, the words Jesus left about Himself keep making people believe in Him. From the first days after the empty tomb, people were gathering around the Echo of *why*. More were added to their number day by day, not by gimmicks or ploys or strategies or clever arguments, but by the Echo. First it was eyewitnesses, but soon it was those who, even beyond reasonable explanation, kept finding themselves awakened to believe that it was all true.

Unlike the cult followings of the ancient world, the Echo did not die off with the Echoers. The more they found themselves persecuted for the words, the more they were murdered and threatened to make the Echo stop, the more other people took up the testimony and echoed it themselves. They summarized what was spoken. They memorized it. They copied what was written down. They invented new ways of keeping the copies. They died rather than give these copies over to those who wanted to destroy them.

This Result of the Gospel, the Assembling of Believers, is certain and provable. But you don't have to be a Christian for very long before this same Result of the Gospel will test your faith more than any other promise that Jesus made. The existence of the Holy Christian Church is the most unbelievable of all claims of the Christian faith.

As much as you will want to, it is impossible to see the Christian Church. Not the way we want to see it. Not elect and glorious, dressed in white and overcoming every trial and temptation. Instead, if you decide to look, you will see snarky, sanctimonious, and downright bigoted behavior bubbling up in whichever congregation is closest to you. The church members might hide it behind clean carpet and a full calendar of spiritual events. But the faithlessness is there if you look for it. A few cautious and observant moments at a local board meeting or voters assembly can easily be enough to throw the most earnest believer into a dire ruin of confusion and doubt. *How can real Christians act like this?*

> **For this light momentary affliction is preparing for us an eternal weight of glory beyond all comparison, as we look not to the things that are seen but to the things that are unseen. For the things that are seen are transient, but the things that are unseen are eternal.** 2 Corinthians 4:17–18

Look higher, and you will see the same unbelief rampant among the diverse panoply of congregations, bodies, movements, and countermovements masquerading about the world under the name "Church." They all claim to follow Jesus. They all say they teach His Bible. But they preach and practice an endless stream of conflicted, antagonistic echoes. Who is Jesus? They do not agree. What did Jesus do? They are not always certain. Why did Jesus do it? The debate never ends.

If under this weight you never come to doubt the existence of an actual Christian Church—a Church which Jesus is totally in charge of and in control of—then it can only be because you've never bothered to take the matter very seriously. It is not without reason that the most successful splinter-groups to break off of Christianity have always begun with the premise that the Church that Jesus really intended, the one the apostles actually started, eventually died off and now needs to be restored. After all, didn't Jesus say He wanted His assembly to be unified? So, why isn't it? If He is God, then what's stopping Him from binding us together and helping us overcome all the obstacles we face? If His Spirit is among us, then why aren't we more focused, less worldly, more powerful in thought and word and deed?

CALLED OUT

It gets more complicated still with the postmodern collapse of visible Christianity in the Western world. Nearly all churches are seeing the pews more empty than they were a generation before. With the exception of the few who've mastered preaching financial gains or harnessed a quiet ethnocentricity, congregations are closing at an epidemic level. It is little wonder. For forty years, they have been embroiled against one another in a life-or-death battle for market shares and membership loyalty. Prophets have arisen to teach the assembly how to better gain an audience with the world, but instead they have taught us how to pilfer one another dry. Denominations, resting on investment accounts and bequests but hungry for a better foothold, consult with the oracles most desperately, and so drift further and further from their founding principles. In order to grow, they change their reason for existing, and soon they find themselves with no reason to exist at all.

As obvious as the existence of the Christian Church is, as undeniable as the existence of faith in Jesus is, it is equally as unbelievable that a real Christian assembling can be found. It is doubly as doubtful that a real truth of Christianity exists at all. But this is the **First Result of the Gospel**. In, with, and under all this madness, the Church of Jesus does remain. It is not a building, a community club, or an international institution. It is the ongoing **assembling** of people who, in spite of themselves and their misfocus, their lack of understanding and their poor behavior, at the end of the day still find that when they hear about **Who Jesus Is** and **What Jesus Did** they believe it to be true.

It is this pitifully unseen assembling that Paul calls the "pillar and buttress of the truth" (1 Timothy 3:15). It is not the result we would expect. It is not the plan we would have put into practice. It does not fix our lives, bring us wealth, or give us healing. It does not break forth in endless mass conversions, transform the world, or even give us a lasting emotional peace that never falters. It looks nothing like an army of light taking an eternal stand against the present darkness. It looks like a bunch of bent and broken people constantly making a muck of what ought to have been. But underneath, it is a miracle more fantastic than walking on water. Hidden within it is a wonder more marvelous than raising a widow's son from the grave. No matter how ugly life in the Church gets, despite lukewarm behavior, against all the half-bent teachings, regardless of all the divisions, people are still assembling, Sunday after Sunday, to hear words about Jesus. Some hear less. Some hear more. But wherever even a hint of the Echo remains among all our tearing asunder and distresses, the Spirit of God is still blowing those words where He wills them in order to make people into believers. Over and over again.

> So then you are no longer strangers and aliens, but you are fellow citizens with the saints and members of the household of God, built on the foundation of the apostles and prophets, Christ Jesus Himself being the cornerstone, in whom the whole structure, being joined together, grows into a holy temple in the Lord. Ephesians 2:19–21

Jesus is still preached, and people still believe. Still, small voices scattered about the world will always take up the Echo and boldly echo it again. In buildings often too cheap, with liturgies often too boring, on lips often too distracted, **Who Jesus Is** and **What Jesus Did** will be repeated again. It is a promise from God. It will never stop. It cannot stop. Nothing in heaven or earth can stop it.

This is the **First Result of the Gospel**. Believers in Jesus are being assembled. It does not rely on the efforts of the believers. It is endlessly happening in spite of them. It is not founded on our wit or sincerity. It is founded on the Holy Spirit's power fused into the eyewitness accounts. It does not awaken our strength. It awakens our weakness so that in that weakness we can rest beneath His insistence that no matter what we might see, no matter how things might look, **What Jesus Is Still Doing** is unbending us. By the power within His calling alone, He is **calling us out**. Gathering. Electing. Assembling. The English word for these things, borrowed from German, is "Churching."

It is a tribute to the supernaturality of Christianity that it even exists at all. Even as many people, parishes, church bodies, and movements place their hope in words that are not the simple Gospel words about Jesus, the words about Jesus still infiltrate our assemblies and assemble us out of them. We may be surrounded by make-believe promises dreamed up and preached in the name of God, or innovative regressions and the man-made idolatry of purpose taking the place of the cross. But even in the midst of all this, the betting man, if he knows the history of Jesus, will still place his chips on the ability of God to do more with the unseen than the seen, more than man can even bother to dream.

> But you are a chosen race, a royal priesthood, a holy nation, a people for His own possession, that you may proclaim the excellencies of Him who called you out of darkness into His marvelous light. 1 Peter 2:9

The frightening secular attacks that keep striving to roll a stone over the Church's tomb are as old as the empty tomb itself. They have not stopped the Echo yet. The Echo goes on. It will not change, even in spite of our current doubt-filled devotions to trust in the present, our emotion-driven consumption, and our loud boasting of how we shall strong-arm the Spirit into fulfilling our own versions of mission. The unworthy hearts of wretches like you and me, wavering and unstable as we are, will continue to be the result of the Gospel. Because Jesus' promises do not fail.

Jesus' words will create faith. It is what they do. It is who the Spirit is. You believe because He is in you—these words are in you—in order to make it so.

And you are not alone.

Together, we are the **First Result of the Gospel** of Jesus. The good news of **What Jesus Is Still Doing** will continue because it is not up to us. The great mystery of His **Assembling of Believers by faith alone**, hidden beneath the swelling tides of our own unbeliefs and distractions, is as steadfast and firm a guarantee as the rising of the sun tomorrow. More sure. More steadfast. One day, the sun will not rise, and we will **still** believe.

There are four more results to come. Four more results that are already here. **Now**, but **Not Yet**. You and I and us all, assembled around the oath-bound promises of the almighty God, have been radically set apart from the mass of humanity that does not trust in the words of God. We are divided from the rest of the world

by faith alone, which creates a substantial unity that we share. It is more than the bond formed by common ideas or personal views. It is a shared state of existence into which even angels long to look, the fusion of two things into one so that they can never be separated, as material as real flesh and real blood, as unseen as the ascended body of Jesus Himself.

THE FIRST RESULT OF THE GOSPEL

The Assembling of Believers

* THE FIRST RESULT OF THE GOSPEL:
The Assembling of Believers

{ *[Jesus said,] "This is My blood of the covenant, which is poured out for many for the forgiveness of sins."*

Matthew 26:28 }

The Second and Third Results

The Fellow-Shape of Believers and the Divorce from Evil

FELLOWSHIP IS A BAD WORD

What does *fellowship* even mean? Especially at church? When Christians talk about fellowship, they usually mean something like "getting together to be friendly with other Christians." An average "fellow" is just some guy. A dude. But it can also mean "to have something in common," as in, "my fellow citizens." But fellow*ship*? What on earth does a boat have to do with poorly lit church basements where people drink freeze-dried coffee and eat hot dishes before the quarterly voters assembly? In the "fellowship hall," you can often find an unused stage and semi-ancient folding tables that feel heavy enough to be made of cast iron. But there won't be any nautical equipment. The "fellowship committee" might gather monthly to plan an ice cream social. But rarely will they plan fishing trips or take the congregation water skiing.

It's no mystery that there are no "ships" in Christian fellowship, so why are there "ships" in the word? The answer is a history lesson about the structure of English that only a history nerd could love. English evolved over the course of several hundred years as a mishmashed combobulation of people who spoke Latin, Celtic, Old Norse, pre-German, and pre-French all tripped over one another to dominate a big island in northern Europe. Without getting into the geeky details too deeply, this means that a lot of what we speak as English today came about because we mispronounced other languages and made them into funky English words. You know, words like *reconnoiter*. What this means is that the "ship" in *fellowship* is not the word *ship* at all. It is *skapaz*, a pre-Germanic word that meant "the form of something," while *ship*, as in "boat," comes from *skipam*, a totally different pre-Germanic word that means "a vessel on water." Ahoy, skipper!

If you say *skipam* out loud while mispronouncing the *k* as a "ch," you can hear how, with the aid of low literacy rates, "schipam" worked its way down to "ship." In the same way, "schap-az" dropped its ending to become "shape." How we butchered *skapaz* into "ship" at the end of words is a matter of conjugation, a terrible science of dark linguistics where only immortal grammarians dare to tread. I won't bore you with it. But the point of this is that if we want to know what the word *fellowship* means, we can figure it out easily by replacing its strange, archaic ending "ship" with the word we still use in English: *shape*.

> That which we have seen and heard we proclaim also to you, so that you too may have fellowship with us; and indeed our fellowship is with the Father and with His Son Jesus Christ. 1 John 1:3

The **fellow-shape** of Christians is the **Second Result of the Gospel**. It has nothing to do with boats, just as at its root it has little to do with eating mayo-based salads and casseroles topped with dried cereals and bagged chips. Christian fellow-shape is what happens when hearing about Who Jesus Is and What Jesus Did puts Christians into a **common state** of being. A triangle is not a square because they have different "ships" (or "shapes"). But a square and a diamond are both rhombuses because they do have a fellow-shape. The real issue here is not whether you remember the meaning of the word *parallelogram*. The issue is asking the question, "If Christians have a common shape, what is it?" Is it just a matter of eating whipped pudding desserts with celery in them? What if we stop using celery? Will this change our shape? What defines the real shape of a Christian?

ONE SHIP TO SHAPE THEM ALL

There are two parts to the Christian common shape. Every Christian has them, or he is no Christian at all. The first part of the Christian shape is the shared awareness of our thorns. The second part is the shared awareness of the place where God has made those thorns go away.

The awareness of our thorns is the shared Christian spirituality of a troubled heart. It was called **anfechtung** by the old Lutherans. That word never made it into English at all, but it is a wonderfully gritty, grimy word. It can mean contest, disputation, or doubt. But for Luther, it was **the dark night of the soul**, the turmoil you face when forced to see yourself clearly reflected in the demands of the Ten Important Things about Being Creation. This honesty is a shockwave of supernatural brokenness. All mankind shares being broken, but only the Christian fellow-shape truly believes it to be **wrong**. To be unfixable. To be evil.

For the Christian, this shared state of painful awareness is the foundation of our fellowship. It is strange to say that the first mark of a Christian is that he has "faith" in his sinfulness, but it is true. The fellow-shape of Christians is the shared state of believing our sinfulness is what God has said it is. We

> **Above all, keep loving one another earnestly, since love covers a multitude of sins.** 1 Peter 4:8

know that we are born into this bent shape. We cease to hide from the fact. We admit that *Me* is not the answer to it, but rather the heart of the problem. We call it out. Admit it. **Confess** it.

It can be scary to be vulnerable about our thorns at a potluck. But there are few life experiences as emotionally binding as when humans share the fellowship of Christian *anfechtung*. Knowing our need paves the way for the mutual consolation we receive in God's answer to it. Liberated from ourselves, we no longer need to hide from one another behind masks of pretend perfection. Exposed by the light, unable to hide in shadow, the fellowship of the awareness of our thorns is a glue only surpassed by the fellowship of knowing that our thorns are no longer all that we are.

People assembling around the Gospel do not look the same. They have all manner of backgrounds, preferences, and styles. They have differing bodies, unique families, varying skin pigments, and different ages. But if they are Christians, they have a shared shape. Not only are they are caught up in one level of *anfechtung* or another, but they have also heard words about Jesus, and they want to hear more because these words do more than say things. These words do things. These words change things. These words give the fellowship its common shape. That shape may still be hidden from the world. It is not visible to the eyes. But what you see can't stop the second half of Christian fellowship from being true. It is only what Jesus **says** that matters here.

INVASION OF THE BODY RITUAL

There is no place where this is more obvious than in the ancient ritual of the Lord's Supper. There are many arguments about the meaning of this meal. Depending on which Christian denomination you belong to, you might be more or less concerned with it. But what is obvious beyond dispute is that there is no more enduring, undisturbed, consistent, regular, literal fellow-shape of Christian experience than assembling together to eat a bit of bread and drink a bit of wine, simply because Jesus told us to.

It is so simple. It seems so insignificant. But it is a unifying act that has bound up the gathering of Christians for thousands of years. Wherever Christianity goes, the common-unity of "doing this in remembrance" goes with it. There, it takes the diverse physical shapes of countless peoples and forms them into an ongoing, unified, time-defying common-unity of people who are awakened with the desire to take Jesus at His words. Where we have misunderstood or disbelieved those words, where the medieval or modern blind spots have distracted us or discounted the possibilities, where the Supper has been enacted too often or not offered enough, the Supper itself still goes on. All of our own mistakes have not slowed down its practice.

This is the fellow-shape all Christians share. A ritual. Created by Jesus. Received by you and me in order to make us **us**. This is miraculous in itself. Here is a gift from Jesus in which your likes, dislikes, interests, or tastes do not matter and have no effect. Here, your personal thoughts, feelings, and dreams can only distract you. But they can never stop that which is bigger than you. Here is the location, the physical place, where faith is created by Jesus saying, "Do this. Believe this. Remember this."

Here faith is sustained, tested, and born again. Here is a tie to God in the fellow-shape of kneeling, eating, and drinking with a neighbor who might very well be my least favorite person in the world, but who now shares with me a bond that is stronger than blood. This blood of the fellow-shape is the promise of resurrection that we have in the man who gave it to us. By receiving, trusting, having, and waiting—without any worth or merit on our part—the many who are broken are made one with Him who is unbreakable. In this act, if only momentarily, the thorns that rise up between us must come down. Enemy dines with enemy, and together they are cleaned by the same hope. They may not be friends later, but unless they are entirely nonbelievers, they can no longer hate each other as much as they would if they did not have the fellow-shape of drinking from the same cup. They may still sin against each other, hold grudges, gossip, offend, or be offended. But soon enough, they will need to kneel together again within the same act of submission. If there is any faith in the Assembling of Believers at all, that faith must mitigate the evil they would do. Their faith mitigates evil because of their shared hope in what Jesus has said He is doing.

Of His own counsel and through His words, this binding event has brought the Church alive down through history, until now you

> **The cup of blessing that we bless, is it not a participation in the blood of Christ? The bread that we break, is it not a participation in the body of Christ?**
>
> 1 Corinthians 10:16

and I partake of the same ritual that was participated in by those who first believed. This is not our work. It is Jesus' continuing work among us. This is not how we would guarantee that our religion would last until the end of the world, but this is how Jesus has guaranteed it.

It is **working**.

It has worked.

It will continue to do so.

The Lord's Supper is a heartbeat that has not stopped since the night it began. It is a transfusion of unbelievable words given to fallen people to make us into believers again. It may seem faint, but the body and blood of Jesus pump onward where the cross and our *anfechtung* meet. That is the fellowship of Christians. At the Lord's Supper, no Christian is alone. All Christians "do this." Here, we are all one. We are in the same shape. Kneeling as beggars, we are promised riches. Eating what is seen, we are promised the unseen. Drinking what is felt, we are promised the unfelt. Entering broken, we are sent out restored. Bringing with us the common state of Adam, we are given the common (resurrected!) state of Jesus.

> If we walk in the light, as He is in the light, we have fellowship with one another, and the blood of Jesus His Son cleanses us from all sin. 1 John 1:7

This is no dead ritual. This is a warfare against the dark deceptions of our world that our world has never overcome. We can spill more ink on *how* this happens (and I plan to someday). But we cannot deny that it goes on happening. This one physical place is where Jesus, by His words, continues to assemble and shape individuals into His body. The Sacred Meal of Jesus is the common-unity of His assembling. This is the **Second Result of the Gospel**.

THE GREATEST DIVORCE

Forgiveness has a beautiful ring. It is **soft**. Gentle. It calls to mind flowers and sunshine, smiling grandmas and the wiping away of tears. Forgiveness is about **overlooking** and letting go, absolving and making right. Its meaning rolls off the lips with its sounds. Unlike fellowship, everyone knows what forgiveness means. That is, unless you're reading it in the Greek New Testament. Because in the Greek of Jesus' day, the word *forgiveness* is not pretty at all. It is **stark** and violent. Abrupt. Terrifying. Greek forgiveness is a word that means **tearing**, ripping, and exiling. It is, literally, the word ***divorce***.

To us English speakers, *divorce* has a ring as savage as *forgiveness* is kind. The syllables of *divorce* are the sound of division, animosity, the antithesis of grace. There is almost no image further removed from forgiveness than that of two humans who once professed undying love for each other, now set so steely-eyed against each other that no reconciliation can overcome their desire to tear their union apart. How can any language be so obtuse as to use the same word for both **forgiveness** and **divorce**?

The answer comes when you look behind the surface of the words to their root meaning. There you find in both words an action unmistakably identical. That action is taking two things that cannot be divided, and ripping them asunder. It is the taking of a single thing and splitting it apart. When dealing with marriage, such dissonance is always a tragedy. But when taken and applied as the rupture that God inserts between us and our thorns, *divorce* can become the most beautiful word you've ever heard.

In the forgiveness of sins promised to us in Jesus, God doesn't just *overlook* your evil. He doesn't say, *"It's okay. Don't sweat it. It's all good."* No. Real forgiveness is not the licentious permission that looks the other way. It is not foolishly thinking that good could come by leaving evil the way it is. Forgiveness in Christ is a surgical operation. It is a precise separation. Two things that could not be divided, you and your *Me*, are rent in two. All your thorns, all your most grievous faults, all the consequences of your deeds and misdeeds—in forgiveness, these are all ripped out of you and inserted into the body of Jesus as He hung suspended from the cross. There, forgiveness crucifies you by condemning Him. Like a cosmic black hole, His flesh and blood drew all the evils of all men into the infinite vacuum of Himself so that when His body was laid in that tomb, your sin went with Him.

All of it. Entirely. So much so that it's not even here anymore. Your willfulness. Your curved inwardness. Your judgmental- ness. And with these your state of decay, your fellow-shipping on the flowing sea of human destruction, your heart that bleeds with mistrust, and your naturally misguided belief that you ought to be God.

> As far as the east is from the west, so far does He remove our transgressions from us. Psalm 103:12

Dead. Divorced from you. Forgiven. Violently. Intensely. Truly and everlastingly. All your debts. Nailed to the cross.

When Jesus walked back out of that tomb on the third day, none of your sin came with Him. He came out, but the thorns stayed there. He bore the scars. The memory of His victory will last forever, but the **Third Result of the Gospel**, no matter how things might look or feel right now, remains as certain and unbreakable as the identity of God Himself.

GOD DOES NOTHING HALF-HEARTEDLY

Getting divorced from sin is no picnic. Forgiveness is not an idea. God's words are actions, and His "I forgive you" is a living sword. It divides you from your thorns as the singular act of saving grace that Christianity exists in order to achieve. But it hurts. A fiery blade of soul-restoring truth is jammed through your ear and into your brain. When God divorces you from your *Me*, *Me* feels it.

It is a bizarre set of emotions, when the light of the regenerated, Christian you awakens and rejoices even as the reprobate, natural you is murdered by the love of God. The selfishness within us longs for its continued existence more than any other thing on earth. It doesn't die easily. Or, more precisely, *Me* has a nasty habit of refusing to believe that it is dead.

This is why God sent preachers to repeat that we *are* divorced from our sin: we are the Assembling of Believers fellow-shaped and born anew by that promise. This promise needs to be **echoed**. Over and over again. Because as surely as you believe it, *Me* does not and never will. As surely as *Me* is dead, crucified with Jesus on the cross, every morning you still wake up with *Me*, like an old cantankerous criminal, sentenced to be locked away but committed to making sure that you go down with him.

> **You have heard about Him and were taught in Him, as the truth is in Jesus, to put off your old self, which belongs to your former manner of life and is corrupt through deceitful desires, and to be renewed in the spirit of your minds.**
>
> **Ephesians 4:21–23**

This means that especially for the Christian, forgiveness is always something you don't want to hear. You don't mind the sunshine and grandma version. You don't mind talking **about** forgiveness as an idea, some kind of "niceness" philosophy that we'd all do better to put into practice more often. But **being** forgiven—which means having your thorns violently exposed and then ripped from you in piercing, brutal honesty—that is something that even the most mature Christian never gets used to. We never learn to like it. No one loves being **rebuked**.

But God doesn't really care what we like. He cares about saving us. So He gives us the free gift, delivered as great and precious promises, whether we want to hear it or not. Whether we want to believe it or not. He insists that we are forgiven, regardless of whether we see or feel it, because that is the only way to get the greatest divorce over and done with. So, no matter how nice you dress up, no matter how clean and pretty you manage to make the outside, He keeps meeting you as the Good Doctor, ready to cut the cancer out again. It makes facing the wrinkles in the mirror seem like child's play. He exposes the hidden sore. He points to it, shoves it in your face, yells "**Look at this, you worm**," all so that He can remind you that it is now meaningless. Because of Jesus.

Thankfully, none of this is up to you. Not if you're a Christian. It is up to God. It is the **Third Result** of His words about **Who Jesus Is**, **What Jesus Did**, and **What Jesus Is Coming Again to Do**. Not just you, but the whole world is already entirely divorced from evil. "**It is finished**" (John 19:30).

It is a fact: there is no more evil. It is dead. There is no more wickedness. It is destroyed. There is no more sin. Jesus killed it. Now, but Not Yet. But still *Now* and eternally so!

MORE REAL THAN ALL THE REALS THERE HAVE EVER BEEN

The fellow-shape of Christians is that of evil men divorced from the evil they still bear. It is the spirituality of thorny people compelled by promises to believe that their thorns don't exist anymore. Not in God's eye. Not in the ascended body of Jesus. Not in the bread and the wine we share as the foundation of our common-unity. Not as the people assembling around the light of these words piercing our darkness. Your sinlessness in Jesus is truer than the next breath you will take, than the universe infinitely expanding, than the sun rising tomorrow. Though the stars and the foundations of the earth pass away—which they surely will—these Results of the Gospel will never pass away.

Today, we only contact the Results in the words Jesus gave us about them. That is why we gather. That is why we listen to them echoed. We do not assemble for entertainment or philosophy. We assemble for real food and real drink. We've heard about Jesus, and we want to hear more. We want to mark, learn, and inwardly digest. So that we don't forget. So that we fellowship while we wait for the day when we will get to see these words as well as believe them.

Awakened by His words, we are different **now**. Nothing has changed. But everything has changed. We are still broken, but we despise our brokenness. The world is still dark, but we see. We still experience evil, but by **faith alone** in the promises, we know its time is short. We know evil is limited. This hope—alone, spoken, echoed—is the power of God to assemble varied, diverse peoples, born of all manner of culture and time, but also all born of Adam, and promise us into the shape of the risen body of Jesus Christ.

This shape is yours even if you never attend a single potluck in your entire life. This shape is not something you do. It is something God does **to** you. By telling you it is so, He molds you with the life, suffering, death, resurrection, and ascension of Jesus into the awakened state of believing these things have divorced your sin from you. Deep in the conscience. Beneath your psyche, your id, and your ego, the beating heart of *Me* is scourged and blasted, segregated and banished, sent further away than the edge of the cosmos. This divorce from your *Me* is infinitely impossible for your finite existence to overcome or undo.

> **Therefore, if anyone is in Christ, he is a new creation. The old has passed away; behold, the new has come.**
>
> 2 Corinthians 5:17

Unless, of course, you don't believe it.

But you do. Because it's a promise. From God.

Your thorns are only seen until death do you part. But even then, you will not be dead. That is the **Fourth Result of the Gospel**. That is the *Now* but *Not Yet,* which comes next.

THE SECOND AND THIRD RESULTS OF THE GOSPEL

The Fellow-Shape of Believers
and the Divorce from Evil

* **THE FIRST RESULT OF THE GOSPEL:**
  The Assembling of Believers

* **THE SECOND RESULT OF THE GOSPEL:**
  (around) The Fellow-Shape of Believers

* **THE THIRD RESULT OF THE GOSPEL:**
  (to deliver) The Divorce from Evil

The Fourth and Fifth Results

Immortalization of the Body and the Eon of Replenishing

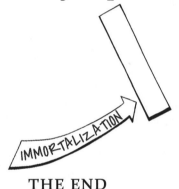

THE END

It will happen before you are even aware of it. The blink of an eye will be an eternity by comparison. A strike of lightning filling the sky will be a moment too slow. There will be one phenomenal, supernatural sound, and we will change.

Instantly.

Fantastically.

Entirely.

It won't just be you. It will be everyone. It will be everything. All the "should have beens" will move into being. An age of replenishment will leave nothing untouched. Not the sky. Not the government. Not music.

Not your body.

> **Beloved, we are God's children now, and what we will be has not yet appeared; but we know that when He appears we shall be like Him, because we shall see Him as He is.** 1 John 3:2

ECHO

The first taste you will have of this new reality will be through your body, the likes of which you have never even dared to dream. Muscles made vigorous will be wrapped around bones that can never break. Eyes perceiving perfectly will gaze on spectrums of color revealed by light that is the source of life itself. Those eyes will feed vision to a mind intimately recrafted to only ever know the joy of receiving, filling a spirit purged of every inward-curved thought, every self-perpetuated worry, every vain wish. Reason, faculty, free will, and emotion will bind together in utter harmony. Head and heart will serve you rather than dominate you. Head and heart will be gifts to absorb the magnificence of everything around you, in order to respond to them all with the ever-constant zeal of love for everything else that is. It will be a new order, a radical age, a creation once again designed without blemish by the wisdom of an almighty God, and you will experience it all through the immediate **Immortalization of Your Body**.

Flash!

It is finished!

There you stand. Immortal, and not only you. All who have been fellow-shaped into that common-unity of the imperishable body and blood of the one man Jesus Christ will be there with you. Feeling what you feel. Enjoying what you enjoy. Sharing what you share. From Him, like a head feeding the body, all other things will be infused with meaning and purpose and drive. Nothing will ever again end in the dead road of *Me*. Instead, there will be a million billion redeemed others that you will now rejoice to serve.

The birds. The beasts. The trees. The heavens. Everything will refresh. Creation will reboot. There will be an **Eon of Replenishing**, the likes of which defy all that we could ask or imagine. The atoms and quarks and galaxies and superclusters will align in absolute **justification**. You won't be at the center, but you certainly will be in the middle of it all. You will be instantly aware of all this and more. A smile will settle

> For the creation waits with eager longing for the revealing of the sons of God. . . . The creation itself will be set free from its bondage to corruption and obtain the freedom of the glory of the children of God. Romans 8:19, 21

198

across your lips, never to leave you again. With perfect sensation, you will forever desire exactly what "is." If any contrary thought ever bothers you, it will only be a moment taken to marvel that you could ever stand it being any other way.

THAT DAY

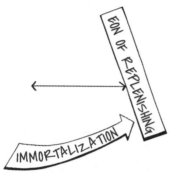

A great deal more will happen. There will be matters of books and final decisions. There will be retribution for those who insist on it. There will be a castigation of all evil that will leave it eternally unable to assail us again. But these events will come and go. The **Fourth** and **Fifth Results of the Gospel** will come and never go. For the **Immortalization of the Body** and the **Eon of Replenishing** all things, Judgment Day is only the beginning. More than that. These Results have already begun. Judgment Day is only the moment in time when you finally get to see things as they already are, in Jesus.

The Echo of Christianity, wherever it is spoken and heard, is the mysterious power of this same Judgment Day come early. It came early to Adam and Eve when God promised a Son to save them. It came early to Abraham when God said the same to him. It came later to Paul on the road to Damascus. But even then, two thousand years ago, the end of the world still met him on the road. One world ended. Another began. But it all happens by the powerful, cosmic reality that **That Day** came first when Jesus of Nazareth hung suspended from the cross. It was the middle of time. It was the fullness of time. It was an hour like any other. It was the inbreaking of powers transcending time and space. It was a Friday afternoon. It was the end of the world.

Now into this broken age overlapping with it, two timelines, two histories are folded over each other. One age is the era of the seen, which is also the eon of our fall. It is the generation of thorns and epoch of unbelief. The other is the era of **the Replenishing**, which is also the eon of our redemption. It is the regeneration of a new root and the epoch of trust and fidelity. It is seen in Jesus—in Who Jesus Is and What Jesus Did—and He declared it to be coming next. But that does not mean that the Replenishing is not here now. It is here by means of the greatest power there is: the words of God. The problem is—as the **Third Important Thing about Being Creation** teaches us—that it is all but impossible for broken, thorny humans to believe what God says. We are trapped in a cycle of obstinacy, a childish mind-set prepared to argue with anything God says just because God said it. But the Third Important Thing also teaches that God's words alone remain more real than all our thorny tantrums. We might remain blind to them and their working, but God's words are most certainly doing what they promise.

So Judgment Day and all its results are also *Now*, but *Not Yet*. Here, but coming soon. Already, but on their way. We have it all declared. You already know the verdict! But it is only here now by faith alone. Even so, this overlap of ages, when believed, is the foretaste of all that is coming. To trust it is the down payment. To have faith in it is everlasting life, not yet for your body, but already for your soul, your heart, and your mind.

This trust is a euphoria the world cannot know, feel, or perceive. It is a hope that lifts up its eyes past the trials and destructions of the dying age, with eager expectation for the resurrection of the dead and the life of the world to come. We long for it, and we long for words about it, because we know that those words *are* it. Now. Here. Everlasting life. Presently owned. Faith.

> He said to him, "Truly, I say to you, today you will be with Me in paradise." Luke 23:43

Faith **is** salvation.

God's words are more real than all the experiences we can find in what we see. Both the physical and material present are limited by the decay of their half-life. All that we now see and touch and feel is the expression of God's creating words. Nothing exists of itself. Not the dirt. Not the trees. Not the rocks. They are all words declared into existence by the mouth of God. The **Fourth** and **Fifth Results** of the Gospel are no different and no less. The **Immortalization of the Body** and the **Eon of Replenishing** of everything are not found everywhere that we look. But they are found where God promises them to be. They are found in the promises themselves, which are words as omnipotent as **"Let there be light!"** These words are a new age, breaking into and replacing this one, even while this one stumbles on like a drunk man headed for the gutter.

So long as your new immortality and the replenishment of creation are still attached to your broken *Me*, because *Me* shares a body with you, this hope remains a golden treasure hidden in a clay pot. As a result, you won't always feel the hope. You won't always think the truth. You won't always want the love.

But!

When you hear the truth preached, when you hear it declared, that unique euphoria of **trust alone** awakens once again. A wild and reckless hope blasts these words into your being, waking you up like a man roused in the middle of the night by a loud trumpet. Springing from bed and rushing to the door, he actively seeks out the source, no matter how much his groggy body complains. Your immortality, once risen as faith, seeks and risks all that this futile life can promise rather than willingly go back to sleep. When you know that the trumpet call goes on, when you know that the judgment to come is already here, even the futility of this age ceases to be an obstacle to overcome and becomes instead one more dose of freedom that enables you to live as if the world has already ended and paradise has been restored.

BECAUSE HE HAS

"Vanity! Futility! Everything is meaningless!" (See Ecclesiastes 1:1.) Solomon the preacher knew well and penned what the history of the world plainly teaches to all who will listen to it. Man gains nothing by all the sweaty labor with which he toils under the sun. Children are born and grow to die. The sun rises, but then sets. The wind blows and no one can catch it. The rivers run endlessly into the sea. There may be moments by the sea filled with calm, but the end of the day is ever filled with weariness, so much so that we cannot even express it. We dare not. The creeping existential terror is too much to bear. So we laugh instead of face the insanity. We turn on a sitcom or escape into fantasy for relief. But these, too, are vanity. These, too, are futile. For soon enough the alarm clock screams, and weary eyes must face the power of endless futility once again.

But the Christian knows this not as condemnation. The Christian knows this as **good news**. The Christian believes that this means his thorns are meaningless, his failures are meaningless, all the brokenness is meaningless. It is divorced from us! It cannot touch us. We are free from it. As a result, though the *Me* will certainly still whine and complain, faith can smile, shrug, and believe that the meaningless not only will pass, but already has. In Jesus. The God who is. His name speaks. What He speaks is that even though this age must die and us with it, He has established another age, begun already, in the flesh and blood of Jesus, whose fellow-shaping with you has resulted in your immortality, and not only yours, but also the whole world's.

To believe in this coming new age is euphoria. It is comfort incarnate. It is the joy that only a Christian knows, for it is the bare, naked trust in the **Five Results of the Gospel**. It is free for all. This comfort cannot be found in the teachings of Buddha or Mohammed or anyone else. It cannot be discovered in the dreams and speculations of men. The joy found in the hope of the age to come is always, ever, constantly given by God's authorita-tive, rock-solid words. He has inserted this truth into the **Ten Important Things** and the **Elements of the Gospel**. The Echo of Christianity is the hope that feeds on these confident promises, because they are more certain than the sun rising again tomorrow. The **Immortalization of the Body** and the **Eon of Replenishing** all things are more true than the next crash of waves on the sea or the dancing movements of the stars in their places.

Tomorrow, the sun might not rise. Tomorrow, all light might instead come from a man who walks among us. Our King will feed the world that He has built for us with the life that eternally resides in Him. That light will transfigure and reflect through us all. We will not be bothered if the sun never rises or sets again. Jesus will replace the vivid colors of the setting sun with everything that made us love sunsets in the first place. What is more, the light that flows from Jesus will be eternally beautiful, beyond perfection.

Perfection in your body and in the world. No more taint. No more sick edge.

No. More. Curse.

You will blink, and you will feel what is already true: you are immortal now. This is life everlasting: You trust God again. His words are more real than your words, again. His works are more valuable than your works, again. It is more blessed to give than to receive, and therefore God gets to be the giver. Not you. You get to be still and know who God is again.

This coming decursed **eon of man's trust in God** is already here because of that time warp that happened when Jesus became a new humanity in His incarnation, because of that coronation completed on the cross. The little season of New Testament hope reigns even while the time of decay putters out. The future reality is only the natural outflow of the fact that He has completed all things. The death of this age,

> And I heard a loud voice from the throne saying, "Behold, the dwelling place of God is with man. He will dwell with them, and they will be His people, and God Himself will be with them as their God. He will wipe away every tear from their eyes, and death shall be no more, neither shall there be mourning, nor crying, nor pain anymore, for the former things have passed away." Revelation 21:3–4

which we still see, has lost its apocalyptic meaning. It has been drowned and murdered in its own futility, a broken age nailed to a broken body—one man, Jesus, on the cross.

The real catastrophes of this broken age are not the thorns nor the sweat that frustrates us. They are not the laborious weight of our endless work to battle against moth and rust, nor the constant friction of relationships that disconnect, shatter, and need to be rebuilt. The real tragedies are not the wars and rumors of wars, the industrial complexes and falsely weighted scales. They are not the deaths of loved ones nor chaotic chances of misfortune. All these things are but fruits of the real problem. The real problem is that

ECHO

we have no trust to believe the words of God over and above these things. Mankind, by nature, believes only what we see.

In the same way, all the best promises of Scripture—the streets of gold, the end of tears, the finding of loved ones long lost, the lion and the Lamb—are all likewise not life everlasting itself. They are only the result of it. The wages of sin—the wages of unbelief in God's words—is death. The wages of righteousness—the wages of faith in God's words—is life: a free gift created by the very words that speak it as a promise.

Faith is the thing into which all the new future flows. The way, the truth, and the life is poured into trust. The real God is always the giver, which means He never wants you to pay Him back for His gifts. So even to you, little sinner that you are, He promises a replenished eternity to be enjoyed by your immortal self, body and soul, so that even in the unruly darkness of this present age, the euphoria of believing Him again might preach even to the heavens how great and how high and how wide His ever-giving goodness really is.

> I consider that the sufferings of this present time are not worth comparing with the glory that is to be revealed to us.
> Romans 8:18

Even though the mountains should fall into the sea, even though the stars should die, even and especially as you are wracked with pains that the doctors cannot stop, compelled to look on helplessly as your own body corrupts into the sickness of death, you will nonetheless know the euphoria of comfort **not** in you but **always in Jesus**. Literally. Physically. Spiritually. Totally. No catastrophe can trump His sufficiency. All our tragedies are but distractions of the present, shadows that try to hide the light but cannot avoid its piercing rays, empty winds that, no matter how they might blow against the words of God, cannot by all their disbelief ever make God's words untrue.

SO THEY TRY TO MAKE YOU FORGET

Because falsehood cannot take down the Results of the Gospel with a direct assault, it has to try to slip in through the back door. Since **faith alone**, buoyed by God's words, simply cannot be overcome, falsehood's last resort is to try to obscure the source of that faith. The devil's one trick is to hide the fullness of God's words from you long enough in the hopes that you might forget them.

Sadly, that is exactly what has happened in modern times to the connection between the **Fourth** and **Fifth Results of the Gospel**. Christians and non-Christians alike still believe that *heaven is for real*, or they desperately want to. But the common notion of "heaven" has become a soft and increasingly meaningless word. That spiritualish, floaty space that comes to mind when most people talk about "heaven"—filled with puffy white clouds and plump children with over-large eyes and too-small wings carrying harps everywhere they go—is a far cry from the **Eon of Replenishing** that Jesus has promised, precisely because missing from that picture is the **Immortalization of the Body**. *Heaven* has become a catchall word for the place where, regardless of religion, all mostly good people's souls (and a few dogs) go when they die (except for Hitler; obviously not Hitler). That view of heaven has slowly eclipsed the Christian belief in the resurrection of our bodies.

> **There will be false teachers among you, who will secretly bring in destructive heresies. . . . And in their greed they will exploit you with false words.** 2 Peter 2:1, 3

Strangely enough, the more that people claim for themselves the idea that after death, everyone who has been mostly good in some way more or less gets to go to this amazingly awesome disembodied place, the more time and effort we have spent as a civilization trying never to go there. On the one hand, we write, buy, and sell book after book about the dreams of children and near-death experiences in the hopes of justifying the existence of that place we call "heaven." But at the same time, we spend countless dollars on every possible item that can stop us from going there, all for a few more years or months of daytime TV.

It is no wonder! Why would a human look forward to being disembodied? Something inside of us intuitively knows that to be human is to be physical. Your body is not a shell or carcass to shed on your journey to a higher plane. You *are* your body. How could anyone be excited about losing that, even with all the promises in the world about how awesome it will be anyway?

The **Results of the Gospel** of Jesus promise something very different from an eternity of halos and clouds. After Jesus, the man, God with a body, was killed, He did not go straight to heaven as a place of eternal human rest. First, after three days, He woke His body back up. He then spent forty more days walking about, showing people His body, and insisting that He was not a ghost. He ate fish. He let people touch His scars. Only after this did He ascend into heaven with the **promise** that **He didn't plan to stay there**. He planned to go there only in order to make a new place for us, a new planet, a new solar system, and the **new creation**.

HEAVEN IS A WONDERFUL PLACE

It is true. Those in common-unity with Jesus cannot die. Those whose bodies die before **That Day** comes, because they are washed into Christ's death and resurrection, yet still live. For the Christian, temporal death is only to fall asleep in Christ. Sharing the fellow-shape of His body, without a body of your own, you go to be where His body is, ascended to the right hand of God the Father.

But this rest in "heaven" is not the real hope of Christianity. Bodiless is not the final state in which Jesus intends to leave us. More than that, this heaven where Jesus is now will not last forever. According to His own words, "Heaven and earth will pass away" (Mark 13:31), but His words will never pass away: "Whoever feeds on My flesh and drinks My blood has eternal life, and I will raise him up on the last day" (John 6:54).

When Jesus returns, He will bring with Him all those who have died trusting in His name and reunite them with their bodies. Even before those of us who may remain until His coming are changed in that twinkling moment, they will be pressed back into those remains that were once buried, burned, or drowned here. But no matter where their bodies might be, He will immortalize their flesh to be just as undying as His own. Since Jesus died and rose again, by His own resurrection He will fuse His people back into the bodies that they were in before death took them from us. But now, like Jesus, death will not be able to contain them any longer. Those bodies will restart. They will breathe. Blood will flow, and out of their tombs the world over they will come to join us as we are all caught up to Him with our own transformed bodies.

> Even when we were dead in our trespasses, [God] made us alive together with Christ . . . and raised us up with Him and seated us with Him in the heavenly places in Christ Jesus, so that in the coming ages He might show the immeasurable riches of His grace in kindness toward us. Ephesians 2:5–7

Not ghosts.

Not angels.

Not spirit beings.

Humans. Men and women. Man. As man is supposed to be. Unbent. Set right. Awake. Washed clean as the new fallen snow.

We will stand in the judgment of That Great Day of God, experiencing our divorce from evil, more sinless than the day of our conception, robed with the flesh we have been fellow-shaped into by promises priceless beyond compare.

THE WORLD TO COME IS EVEN BETTER

The new innocence of the body you will be clothed with on That Day will be so obvious that, when the judgment actually takes place, God will not even need to look at the books that recorded all that you did or did not do in this former life. Your righteousness, imputed to you from Jesus, will be so obvious that He will simply flip to the place in the Book of Life where your name is written, and say, *Well done, good and faithful servant.*

But then, it will not be back to heaven for you. Oh no. Not if by heaven we mean that meager disembodied state of waiting for the resurrection. God has something far better than that planned. With paradise fully restored, with the cosmos set back into its proper order, you and I and all those assembled into Christ will be stewards of the new order. A world without end. Just like ours, only better. Made right. **Justified.**

If this is confusing to us now, it is largely because many people have come to rely on the word *heaven* to do double duty. We use it to refer **both** to that place where Jesus will keep us safe after we die **and** to that place where He will put our new bodies when He raises us all from the dead. The word *hell* has the same problem. It is used to refer to that final lake of fire, Gehenna, the raging pit of flame where the worm does not die and the teeth ever gnash, into which the devil and all his angels will be cast at the end of time. But we also speak of people dying and "going straight to hell," referring not to that final place, but to the temporary, bodiless perdition where those who are not fellow-shaped into the body of Christ go to await the final judgment. In that temporary place, usually referred to in the Bible as the grave, the pit, Sheol, or Hades, there are no teeth to gnash, for there are no bodies. The bodies have been buried in the ground here, waiting for the Day of Judgment. In the same way, you cannot behold Jesus face-to-face while your face is still down here, lowered six feet under. For face-to-face, you must wait for the Day of Resurrection.

> **For the Lord Himself will descend from heaven with a cry of command, with the voice of an archangel, and with the sound of the trumpet of God. And the dead in Christ will rise first.** 1 Thessalonians 4:16

It does not matter if we use the same word to refer to two different places, so long as we do not forget about those two different places. The danger is when, by subtly merging the two, we lose something, as has happened with the common understanding of the hope of our resurrection. We lose that better place. We lose the meaning of Job's "In my flesh I shall see God" (Job 19:26) and David's "Let all flesh bless His holy name forever and ever" and "I shall dwell in the house of the LORD forever" (Psalm 145:21; 23:6).

That is why Jesus is coming back on That Day. To make it so. To usher in a physical universe of everlasting paradise, and to place all who hope in Him really into it both body and soul. He will come to bring that twinkling moment when the cataclysm will be entirely undone and reveal the real, cosmic mystery behind those boring moments when simple water and few words from the mouth of Jesus promised Christians the world over that they "have been united with Him in a death like His," and so "shall certainly be united with Him in a resurrection like His" (Romans 6:5.) This is why He has washed us, set us apart, and taken such pains to buy us back from our captivity to ourselves.

Death has not lost its sting because *heaven is for real*. Death has been swallowed up in the victory of life over the grave. Heaven is not your forever home. Rather, better, on That Day you shall look triumphant on your enemy death as you descend from heaven with Jesus and claim your body back by right as a child of the living God. Soon and very soon, the archangel Jesus sends will shout, "Wake up!" And you will. Eyes will flood with strength given by living water, and all that you will see will be changed.

Together with the fellow-shaped assembly, once for all divorced from all our trespassing, we shall shout *"Amen!"* to what is not the end of the world, but rather the beginning.

UNBROKEN NOW, PLEASE

We are not there yet. We are here.

Waiting.

Waiting for then to come. But it is coming.

The broken age has overlapped with the **Eon of Replenishing**. The **Immortalization of the Body** has been preceded by the resurrection of the soul. Reality has folded over on itself so that the future has come early in what is spoken but not seen. Though the world decry it, this does not mean that the new age is not here. It means that it is only here by **faith alone**. The euphoria of Christian trust believes in this hope, even while it experiences all too closely the despairs and futility of the present. Through these trials, faith looks forward **through the words** of the Gospel. Because those words *are* the future. Not just ideas. Realities. Here. Now. Everlasting. Given. Owned. **Believed.**

> But if we hope for what we do not see, we wait for it with patience. Romans 8:25

This faith is only a foretaste. It is only a down payment. But it is the down payment of healthy seed and a new root. This faith is a golden treasure hidden in a clay pot. That clay vessel is still filled with the brokenness of *Me*. As a result, you don't always feel the hope as much as you'd like to. You don't always think the truth as much as you want to. You don't always will the love as much as you ought to.

But!

When you hear the truth declared, the euphoria of trust alone awakens again. A wild and reckless new you, believing, wakes. Like a man roused in the middle of the night by a splash of cold water, the new you springs from his bed of hopelessness and rushes to the door of promises about divorce from sin, about a common-unity with the body of Jesus, about being assembled out of darkness and into light.

We do not find these promises everywhere we look. The euphoria of faith cannot grow in just any old soil. So it is driven. It is compelled to seek out the good soil, even if that means risking all that this futile life can offer. The **Three Elements of the Gospel** and its **Five Results** are that good soil. They are the food of our faith alone. Words about Who Jesus Is and What Jesus Did point us forward to What Jesus Is Coming Again to Do. They call us back. They call us out. They wash us clean.

This changes everything. The Gospel, believed, doesn't leave you just as you are. Your eyes are open now. You see the broken. You see the fix. You see the need for what

> **For God has not destined us for wrath, but to obtain salvation through our Lord Jesus Christ, who died for us so that whether we are awake or asleep we might live with Him. Therefore encourage one another and build one another up, just as you are doing.** 1 Thessalonians 5:9–11

comes next. Awakened within you is a hunger for more good words from God. Awakened within you is a desire to be further set apart from this age of sin, death, and the devil. Awakened within you is a hunger for sanctification.

And that means a hunger for **prayer**.

THE FOURTH AND FIFTH RESULTS OF THE GOSPEL

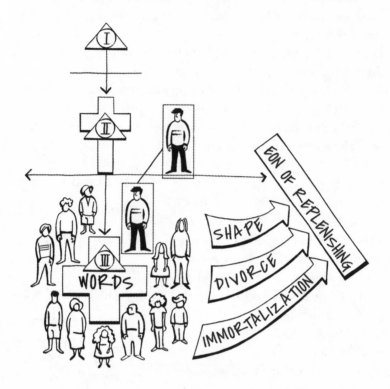

The Immortalization of the Body
and the Eon of Replenishing

THE FIVE RESULTS OF THE GOSPEL

* **THE FIRST RESULT OF THE GOSPEL:**
  THE ASSEMBLING OF BELIEVERS

* **THE SECOND RESULT OF THE GOSPEL:**
  (AROUND) THE FELLOW-SHAPE OF BELIEVERS

* **THE THIRD RESULT OF THE GOSPEL:**
  (TO DELIVER) THE DIVORCE FROM EVIL

* **THE FOURTH RESULT OF THE GOSPEL:**
  (WHICH RESULTS IN) THE IMMORTALIZATION
  OF THE BODY

* **THE FIFTH RESULT OF THE GOSPEL:**
  (AND) THE EON OF REPLENISHING

PART FOUR

THE SEVEN
EDGES OF
CHRISTIAN
HOLIFICATION

> { *Be still, and know*
> *that I am God.*
> *Psalm 46:10* }

THE ONE HOLIFICATION
OF THE CHRISTIAN

There Is a God, and through Jesus, He Is Your Father

THE DEVIL'S FAVORITE WORD

This is the lion's den. This is where the devil prowls about Christianity, looking for some words of God to devour, in order that he might replace them with his own. This is where he gets to dress up as an angel of light and pretend he is only here to help us be more like God.

This is where the thorns can get some juice to grow on. This is where we can at last move past the cross and onto what really matters to the old man. This is where you will be tempted to believe that you can *do something.* This is the chance to take all that Christianity has given and make it about *Me* again.

But the powerful, life-altering, never-the-same-again spirituality of Christianity does not fill you more and more full of things you can *do*. Instead, the more it sets you apart from the world, the more it presses on you the jarring, slicing knowledge of how much more you need to have done **for you**.

> **Be still, and know that I am God. I will be exalted among the nations. I will be exalted in the earth!**
>
> **Psalm 46:10**

It's not like this happens without your being involved. Something **has** changed. Radically. We are not rocks on the ground. Christianity **does** impart the regenerated **euphoria** of faith. You cannot trust or hope without trusting or hoping. You cannot pray without **feeling** the need to pray.

The Christian faith is no dead letter. It is a living, breathing regeneration of the mind, with massive, revolutionary effects. When God says, "**You need this,**" dead men do not reply, "**Amen! Yes I do.**" Only the living do that.

But the things God tells us we need are not the great and mighty things we would expect. Sanctification is not the result we would choose. The works that flow from true holiness are not the kind of works we want. They are the inglorious kind. The humiliating kind. The seemingly empty kind. The kind that hold no apparent power in themselves. The kind that give us no solace in ourselves.

When you are in a lion's den, the last thing you want to be told is, "**Sit tight and wait.**" The last thing you expect is to be told that the best thing to do is to do nothing. When you are in a lion's den, the natural thing to do is to believe that *"Now is the time to act!"* But in this case, that's exactly what the lion wants you to do.

YOU CAN'T CLIMB OUT

Acting is what all the religions made up by men will always tell you to do. It doesn't matter what culture or history, style or veneer your spirituality comes from, mimics, or is designed by. If it is man-made, then it is inevitable that it will wallow its way down to the same root as all the others. Our thorns can't help themselves. Our unbelief can only ever bring itself to believe in this way. We're in a lion's den, and religion is the only way out. It's only natural to therefore believe that *spirituality is like a ladder*.

Ladders take you up. But not without a little help from you. Our thorns assume that it is therefore our job to get on the ladder and climb. But just as ladders always have a top, they also have a bottom. You can always go up. But you can always go down. You can get closer to God. Or you could be getting further away.

Very few people believe they are at the bottom of the ladder. Most people assume that they are somewhere in the middle. You might be more of this and less of that, but it all evens out in the end. You're a little more profane or a tad more pious, but you're *on* the ladder. You're *trying* to go up. *That counts for something, for certain.*

Trying is just the soft form of *doing*. It's the kind of doing that isn't quite *done*. But it means to be. But how much is enough? How much *trying* really counts? How much better or worse a person do you really need to be in order to stay out of the lion's reach? How holy does one need to become to cease being in danger of profanity?

> **To the one who does not work but believes in Him who justifies the ungodly, his faith is counted as righteousness, just as David also speaks of the blessing of the one to whom God counts righteousness apart from works.**
>
> Romans 4:5–6

If an apple is 1 percent rotten, then it's no longer a good apple. You might slice off the wormy part, but any child can tell you that 100 percent of its goodness is still missing. But our problem is multiplied. Humanity is not a pile of mostly good apples, with just a bruise here or there. We are bad apples through and though. We are lumps of dough with leaven spread throughout. One percent of leaven is 100 percent of a leavened loaf.

If you're not 100 percent at the top of a ladder, then you're not high enough. Imagine the damage if you ever got confused. What if you thought you were going up, but in reality you were climbing down? What if with each step you thought was progress, you took yourself step after step closer to the gaping maw of the lion?

Know this: .0001 percent evil is 100 percent evil. What if the ladder has no top? What if it's just a ladder to nowhere? What if there are just more lions at the top? What if the only way out is through the lion's mouth?

ECHO

PROXIMITY TO GOD

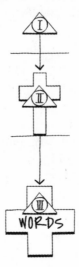

The factor that truly sets a Christian apart, the difference between a Christian and non-Christian, is not how good a person you manage to be. Christians do not become Christians by being good, and neither do they remain Christians by staying good. Christians are "Christians" because they have been made holy, which is just a fancy way of saying **set apart**. The way we have been set apart is not a matter of how good we are. It is a matter of how close we are to God.

It is easy to see how people accustomed to the *religion of the ladder* could be confused by this. On the ladder, how close you are to God is directly related to how good you are. But we've already seen that Christianity turns this all on its head, as God recognized from the moment of our fall that we would never be good enough, so He sent Jesus to be Who Jesus Is and do What Jesus Did to remedy that.

Jesus came close to us. He increased our **proximity** to God by being God Himself. His presence as God in our flesh set humanity apart forever. His deeds accomplished under Pontius Pilate paid for the transaction of your divorce from evil, but this divorcing is done by fellow-shaping you into His body. By this alone, He is assembling you out of this world and into God's presence. He is increasing your personal proximity to God just by bringing Himself near to you.

This, alone, sets you apart from the world. This, alone, is your sanctification, your **holifying**. It's still all about Jesus. All at once. All in a moment. Washed. Cleaned. By Him. From Him. Into Him. Not what you've done. What He's done *to* you.

Gift.

You do not become holy *by* believing this. You believe this **because** you **have been** made holy. Not by sanctifying yourself, but by being brought near to the **Sanctified One**. Not climbing out of a den of lions, but by being woken up out of that nightmare by the promise that you're no longer in the den at all. You are set safely on the deck of a boat.

> **Let us then with confidence draw near to the throne of grace, that we may receive mercy and find grace to help in time of need.** Hebrews 4:16

IT'S A GOOD BOAT

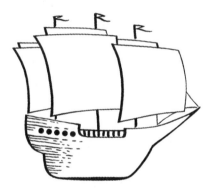

You are not in the process of *climbing*. You are in the process of **being taken**. You are safely tucked away in the ark of the good ship *Christ*ianity, which is pressing its way steadfastly through the midst of the crashing storms of every age. There are surely lions out in those dark waters, but they cannot get to you. Not while you're aboard.

What matters on a boat is the destination. What matters is where the pilot is headed. The crew will swab the deck and pull the mast from time to time. They will have moments of strength and moments of weakness. But so long as they do not mutiny altogether, so long as they do not tie the pilot up and throw him overboard, the ship will continue to sail in the right direction.

Even while you are still sleeping, the ship keeps sailing ever onward. It is powered by the wind of God's Spirit, who is not *Me*. You are a passenger whose body is important, but not the means of travel. The only thing that can stop this ship from carrying you along is to willingly, intentionally, jump off the ship.

> He will not let your foot be moved. . . . Behold, He who keeps Israel will neither slumber nor sleep. The LORD is your keeper; the LORD is your shade on your right hand. **Psalm 121:3–5**

Here, you are not further or closer to God based on your own spiritual power to climb. Here, the storms on the water are not your concern. Here, your awareness of your faith or your awareness of your thorns at work within you are never related to how close or far you are from the destination of the ship. They are never related to whether you are on the ship.

Here, all that matters is the fact, the promise, that the ship is being driven in the right direction by the Sanctified One. There is no more or less of Him. There is no closer or further away. When you're aboard His ship, He has drawn close to you. End of story.

GETTING YOUR SEA LEGS

There is perhaps no greater proof of our thorny ability to doubt the certainty of God than the way Christians can look at such a flagship and call it cheap, simply because we did not build it and we do not pilot it. In reality, the ship is not cheap—Christ's precious blood seals us in its invaluable worth. But the root of our unbelief is not really about how much we think this ship is worth. The root of our doubt is how uncomfortable real grace makes us, for suddenly we are naked. Suddenly, we are without any ability to rely on our thorns. When for so long we've learned to use them for protection, to lean on them for surety, the idea of being left truly naked in the midst of the stormy sea can be terrifying.

You were ransomed from the futile ways inherited from your forefathers, not with perishable things such as silver or gold, but with the precious blood of Christ, like that of a lamb without blemish or spot. 1 Peter 1:18–19

Especially if we don't believe firmly in the power of the boat.

Rather than honestly voicing our disbelief that the Pilot can navigate the ship for us, without our help, we usually couch this disbelief as a mask of concern for the good of the rest of the crew. After all, what better hiding place for unbelief than the powerful dream of love?

"Won't people stop working hard if they believe that the Pilot will do everything?" we ask. *"Won't they just lounge about, assuming that the ship will take care of itself? Surely, they need to be restrained with the fear that they could veer off course with the poor quality of their seamanship. Otherwise, won't they take advantage of the ship?"*

They are fair enough concerns, if we were talking about the kind of boat an unbeliever could actually get aboard. It is entirely possible for an unbeliever to climb into the trappings of Christianity and proceed to use the Elements and Results of the Gospel as a license for swimming in the dark waters. They look pretty silly as they do it, shouting about their freedom, as they are cast to and fro about on the dark waves. *"I'll be safe swimming. I'm on a boat."* The idea is ludicrous. It's the kind of thing only the insanity of unbelief could say.

But we are not talking about how to make sure unbelievers don't take advantage of our Echo. We are talking about the certainty of holiness, the **One Holification of the Christian**. The Christian, by definition, **believes**. The Christian, by definition, is on the boat.

When you are dragged out of the raging seas and onto the safe deck of a ship, the last thing on your mind is jumping back in. You're just grateful that you're not drowning anymore. The boat itself is all the motivation you need to cling on tight and turn

ECHO

down any offers to go swimming again. The Christian loves the boat, because to be a Christian is to know that the boat is your only hope.

Christ is the one who sets Christians apart. It is not up to us. He pulls us from the stormy waters. He sets us on the deck.

Christ loved the church and gave Himself up for her, that He might sanctify her. Ephesians 5:25–26

This salvation does not free us *from* the Ten Important Things about Being Creation. It frees us *into* them in the right way. For the first time. We dive into them, rather than back into the dark waters.

We do not dive into the Ten Important Things because they are the foundation of the ship. We don't try to make them back into another ladder to climb. Rather, awake, with new breath blown into us, we can see how they define the calmer waters that should have been. We know that it is those calm waters, that Eon of Replenishing, that the ship is sailing toward.

We see all too clearly the brutal jeopardy of the current stories. We feel all too acutely the ignorant blows of the waves, by which the age we live in is being cast in every which direction. We hear the singing of the sirens of chaos, can feel them calling to our thorns, notice the way they compel the old man within us to long for the lies that were left behind.

But for all that the song pulls on the worst part of us, it no longer appears quite the lullaby of bliss we previously thought it to be. We've known the depths. We remember the soul-draining emptiness. We've felt the life-depressing pressure. We can see clearly now the mind-confounding blindness of it all.

Who would willingly go back to that?!

The euphoria of faith cannot bear the thought. It cries out, **"Lord, have mercy!"**

The faith of the Christian is anything but dead. It is the fullness of being made holy in one brilliant renewal of the mind. It is a euphoria of belief, even though we cannot overcome all the things in the world that should not be. But faith sees what should not be, and it believes the answer is the Lord Jesus. It knows that all hope rests on Him. So, it is left with only one option.

PRAY

Prayer is, by definition, not doing. To pray, to call on the name of God and beg Him for a remedy, is to demonstrate, by definition, that you do not have what you need. That you cannot attain what you need. That you are in the state of "not doing." That you rely on Him to do something for you.

The euphoria of faith cannot feed itself. It cannot call to itself. It cannot even see itself. It must see the proper object. It must cling to an external anchor. It must trust in something trustworthy.

The **One Holification** of the Christian is the "process" of believing. There are seven distinct needs of broken humanity that we are awakened to see by the Ten Important Things and the Elements of the Gospel. None of them are ultimately things we can do. All of them are faithful reliances on God being the one to provide them.

These Seven Edges of Christian Holification are immeasurable. Each of

> **Take the helmet of salvation, and the sword of the Spirit, which is the word of God, praying at all times in the Spirit, with all prayer and supplication. To that end, keep alert with all perseverance, making supplication for all the saints.** Ephesians 6:17–18

them is given to faith alone. Each of them is built on a promise of what will be fulfilled when our Lord returns. The gift in the present is that we see our need. The gift is that we know there is a Sanctified One who holds their answer. If it were not for Him, we would not even know what to pray for. We would be like the child who asks his father for a pony when what is really needed is for the father's debts to be paid. The child is ignorant of the real need, and cannot see how the pony would do him no good and only be taken away when the bill collectors came.

Our ignorance is not absolution. In our human way of thinking, we want to narrowly define holiness as a bit more goodness accomplished in the present. But that thinking suffers from the same nearsighted addiction of the *Me* that has been our problem all along. Even our hopes are trapped within themselves. When this age imagines a better world, it can only do so by picturing more of itself. All we can dream of is more of what already is. The better man is not something different from man, just *more* of man.

The higher good is not beyond us, outside of us, just *more* of us. The real problem of humanity, the real thing that keeps us from being truly set apart, is not a lack of love for our neighbors—the real problem is our cold and heartless focus on ourselves.

So we willfully conclude that the problem with humanity is a lack of being nice to others and doing enough good things, when the reason we are not nice and do not do good things is because we have believed too deeply in our ability to do them for ourselves.

Prayer then is the antidote. Prayer then is the polar opposite. Prayer is admitting that **I cannot** do it myself. Prayer is the acknowledgment that holiness is the result of proximity to God, and if I ever shall have it, then God Himself must draw close, and do so in a way that does not destroy me, but gives me life where I have made only death.

WHO GOD REALLY IS

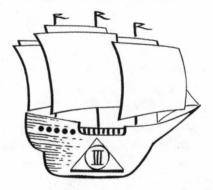

This is what has changed. It is radical. A life lived with true knowledge of God is a life raised from death. Even while we are physically dying, such faith is everlasting life that death can neither touch nor contain.

Faith is rooted in the essence of Who Jesus Is and What Jesus Did. The Elements of the Gospel and their Results reshape us from mere mortals segregated from God to imperishable humans who trust in God again.

More than that. Now even the God behind Jesus' name—the hidden mystery that we can never peer into no matter how desperately we try to be His equal—pulls back the curtain, not for our eyes but for our hearts, to believe that He is more than just our God. He is more than just a deity. More than just a supernatural power. He is **our Father**. We are His children. So while we might keep asking for ponies and Porsches, which any genie in a bottle could grant you, our Father keeps doing the tender work of teaching us to ask for the right things, because it is into our asking Him for these things that all holiness and righteousness eternally flow.

The name in which we are washed by the words of Jesus establishes this relationship unshakably. You might reject the fatherhood of God. You might deny Christ and curse Him. But you cannot unbaptize yourself. You can refuse to believe God's promise of His Fatherhood to you has done any good, and in so doing you certainly would lose the faith at the heart of the

> **Pray then like this: "Our Father."**
> Matthew 6:9

promise. But just as a child once born remains the child of his father (even if he commits patricide), so you remain God's child because of your rebirth in Baptism. God promises you that you are purchased by Jesus' blood. This promise sets you apart once and forever, marking you with water according to Jesus' command. It is not magic. It is there precisely to be trusted. It is there to open your lips and teach you how to begin your prayers. It is there to teach you to pray rightly, which means to pray to the right One.

If anything will ever be good, it will only come because it is first given by God. He is the sanctification from which all the sources of our own holiness must ever flow. The popular, inborn belief of thorny man ever disappoints itself by chasing holiness through fleshly navel gazing. But the **One Holification** of the Christian crucifies this lust for *Me* with an ever-present *no*. You cannot get closer to God by trying. You cannot get closer to God at all. God is already close to you.

He has written His name on you. He has fellow-shaped you with His Son. God is Jesus' Father. You are one with Jesus. You are God's son.

> **For you did not receive the spirit of slavery to fall back into fear, but you have received the Spirit of adoption as sons, by whom we cry, "Abba! Father!"** Romans 8:15

There is no more certain relationship. There is no more changeless set-apartness. This is what sets you apart as a Christian, as Christ's. You've been given the name that is above everything name. That name broke through the hostile

ECHO

wall that divided you from God, divorced that wall from you, and thereby restored you to live in the real, eternal knowledge of who God actually is.

The Fatherhood of God now is over you. No matter what you see. No matter what you experience. He declares in Jesus' name that you are His. No matter what else in the world might come to be, no matter how evil the days of men around you might seem, the God who is not you will turn it into good before it is all over.

> "I will be a father to you, and you shall be sons and daughters to me," says the Lord Almighty.
>
> 2 Corinthians 6:18

As your Father, He promises that behind all other things He is working it all for the good of assembling you, fellow-shaping, divorcing you from evil into that Immortalization and Eon of Replenishing that is bought and paid in full **for you**. He is more committed to this than the best human father ever was. It is from this commitment that all fathers have been given their name.

Prayer is only as strong as the God you pray to. But if you pray to the almighty God, then how strong is that prayer! The **One Holification of the Christian** is the process of believing this, the euphoric experience of faith and trust that the ship we are on is enough to get us to the destination. We are not at the destination yet. But we will not get there by climbing any ladders up or down into the storm. We will get there because the Pilot holds the course.

The author of our salvation is its perfecter. Having done the magnificent, gory work of saving us from ourselves, He will not teach us to return to the vomit of self-proofs. Rather, He teaches us to pray for what we will not have until He gives it. He sets us apart from the world as people who believe we still need to be set apart. He makes us holy by teaching us to know that we are not holy. With glorious humiliation, we are sanctified precisely in our ongoing awareness of our profanity and the compelling desire we now have for Him to take it all away.

THE ONE HOLIFICATION OF THE CHRISTIAN

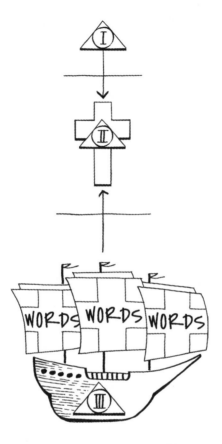

There is a God, and through Jesus, He is your Father.

* THE ONE HOLIFICATION OF THE CHRISTIAN:
THERE IS A GOD, AND THROUGH JESUS,
HE IS YOUR FATHER.

{ *O Lord, open my lips,*
and my mouth will
declare Your praise. }

Psalm 51:15

THE FIRST EDGE

Prayer for More Prayer

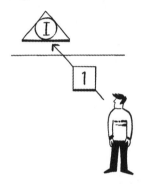

WE PRAY BACKWARD

If you listen carefully to what people pray for, or to what people ask you to pray for, you will find that, with rare exception, the requests fall into five or so categories: healing, birthdays/anniversaries, healing, a trip somewhere, and healing.

It is understandable. We live in a world filled with calamity. Illness, accidents, struggles, and tragedy jeopardize the welfare of all of us. It would be easy right now to jot down a page or more of threats to your life. To your goals. To your body. To your happiness.

Recognizing these temporal dangers is not the problem. Asking our Father for help with these dangers is not the problem either. But if you listen to our prayers, it is clear that we think these are the *only* dangers.

That is a real problem.

It's the same problem that has faced us all along. We're tied to this ego-driven flesh. As a result, even the rare times we are able to muster up the desire to pray, because we naturally pray from the wrong, we inevitably take God's name and try to make it serve our vanity. We call on Him for all manner of wrongheaded or nearsighted things.

Asking the sky for a pony is easy. Any child can do that with or without faith, with or without the name of the true God. It takes no practice. Passionate hunger for *Me* wells up from within without any effort, and even wishing on a star will do for a god when prayer is only a matter of trying to get what I want. But real prayer, holy prayer, is not about asking God for what I want. It is about asking God for what **God wants**.

> If one turns away his ear from hearing the law, even his prayer is an abomination. Proverbs 28:9

But what does God want? We cannot know this just by guessing. We must be told. We must invert our prayers. We must **learn** to pray.

NATURAL PROF(V)ANITY

The heart does vanity all too well. The old man within doesn't mind calling on God's name, so long as he can do it to serve his own interests. He doesn't mind praying, so long as he can pray in vanity. This is what it truly means to take God's name in vain. It is to offer **bad** prayer.

My best words are blasphemy without God's words. My best prayer is blasphemy when it is not the prayer that God teaches me. I do not ask for what I need, but am maddened by the blindness of what I want. My heart and mouth are convoluted. My mind is trapped in its own absurdity. I pray only for more of this world, more of this thorny life, more of what I want, more of *Me*.

> Their throat is an open grave; they use their tongues to deceive. The venom of asps is under their lips. Their mouth is full of curses and bitterness. Romans 3:13–14

The first prayer we must learn, therefore, is to pray **against bad prayer**. It is to pray not from the heart but **against it**. That heart knows only how to pray for itself, in *its own name*. We must learn to pray in God's name. Our Father must set us apart. He must distinguish us from the world; He does this by teaching us to pray **in Jesus' name**.

Jesus' name is not a magic formula to slip on the back of our profane prayers in order to make them holy. Praying in Jesus' name means learning to no longer pray in my own name at all. It means no longer praying for what I want, but for what I need. It means learning to pray against my self-directed dreams, against my distracted wallowing, and against my misdirected hungers. It means knowing that I don't know what I need, but that I must be taught it.

Praying in Jesus' name is to pray knowing that we do not know how to pray rightly. It is to be taught to pray by Jesus. It is to pray **with Jesus' prayers**. Praying with Jesus' prayers frees us from our slavery to merely human, and therefore unholy, prayers. Praying in Jesus' name replaces my inborn profanity, worrying, fretting, and dreaming with words that our Father wants to hear.

HOLINESS IS INVISIBLE

The closer you come to God, the less of yourself you will see. True holiness will always be **more** of **Him** and **less** of *Me*. The more holy you are, the less you will see it. The greater your proximity to God actually is, the more you will experience how far away you actually are without Jesus' name.

The moment you try to see your own holiness, the moment you look back to yourself in order to test your progress or measure your height on the holiness ladder (if you have any actual holiness working upon you at all), you will find only a startling absence of holiness. Instead, because you are set apart, because you *are* near God, you will see what He sees. You will see your thorns as you have never seen them before. You will see a darkness deeper than you'd ever imagined. Stripped bare of all the self-justifications you once hid behind, you will see only the source of your own self-destruction.

> Do nothing from selfish ambition or conceit.
> Philippians 2:3

The Christian faith is not made for looking at yourself. It is made for looking at Jesus. Christian holiness is then never about seeing more of yourself. It is about seeing more of Jesus. It is about learning to pray, not for more of me but more of Him. It is about knowing that His name is not your name, but that His name *has been* given to you. That is the free gift of proximity to God. It is the power of prayer in His name. It is holiness in a word.

The **First Edge of Holification** is to see this distinction clearly. It is to realize that without God's work, we cannot pray. It is to

ECHO

learn that the first prayer we must pray is the **prayer for right prayer**. The First Edge is to stop trying to make our names holy, and to ask God to make His name holy among us.

Even the best good work in the history of the world, if it is done *for Meself*, is not a good work at all. Though the entire world laud it with boisterous fanfare, praising *Me* for what *Me* has done, though it save thousands or inspire millions, if it is done for the sake of *Me's* hopes in *Meself*, then it must remain a great evil.

> For where jealousy and selfish ambition exist, there will be disorder and every vile practice. James 3:16

So, too, with prayer.

The world does not see this or know this. It cannot. The world is compelled to pray backward. It is compelled to pray for more of *Me*. It is trapped in the pretension of pretending to be good, all the while seeking self-interest in the act. Even in prayer. *Especially in prayer.*

No matter how hard the world tries, no matter how *active* it manages to be in *doing* prayer, when the prayer flows from our pro-**vanity**, then it never amounts to more than pious pro**fanity**. The name of God is holy in Himself, but we profane it when we believe it exists only to serve our own words. The First Edge of Holification of the Christian is **God's action** to change this. He changes it by teaching you to pray. He teaches you to pray for what you need more than anything else in all the world: **right prayer**.

HOLIFICATION HAPPENS

When the Sanctified One draws near to you, when the Elements of the Gospel begin compelling you to hope in the Gospel's Results, being made holy happens. It happens all at once. It is done. But you will always experience it as a process. You've been set on a boat. The boat is going somewhere. You're going to notice.

But this hardly guarantees a peaceful or happy life. Holiness is not a means of gain. Pleasantries, victories, power, and success, even in your soul—**especially in your soul**—are *not* marks of holiness. They may well be marks of blindness, but more often than not they are not marks of anything. They are chance. Happenstance. The twists and turns of thorny, dying fate in this world.

Holiness is everlastingly more than that. Holiness is plain and simple proximity to God. God draws near to you. God puts His name on you. It is an objective reality. A clear and present gift. A promise.

This promise happens **to** you. This promise will do things **in** you. But none of it comes **from** you. The euphoria of trust breaks into you. But the more it does, the more the world looks like the dysphoric place it is, godless and dying, broken and out of control. The comfort of God does not bring, *"Peace! Peace!"* but divides you from the world with a flaming sword. God's drawing near to you does not make you feel closer to Him. Rather it awakens you to how very far away from Him you are in this world.

> **Create in me a clean heart, O God, and renew a right spirit within me. Cast me not away from Your presence, and take not Your Holy Spirit from me. Restore to me the joy of Your salvation, and uphold me with a willing spirit.** Psalm 51:10–12

All of this drives you to the First Edge of Holification. It is this prayer: **"Jesus, draw me close. Jesus, do not let me get away. Create in me a right prayer. Renew in me a spirit that understands."**

Holification is never about *Me*. It is never about moving past **Jesus** and into *action*. It is never about moving past **trust** and into *doing*. It is never about moving past the **cross** and into *my life*. Those things, so long as I see them, are about *Me*. The urge to chase them is the urge to chase my glory, my honor, my name.

But Holification is about the presence of the God who has His own name. It is about believing that His name is above every other name. Having heard and believed that God has a name, having come to know this name in the person and work of Jesus, Christian euphoria realizes that, more than anything else in all the world,

> **Who will deliver me from this body of death? Thanks be to God through Jesus Christ our Lord!** Romans 7:24–25

you want to remember that name. You want to hear it spoken again. You want to use it. You want to learn to **pray in the right direction**. You want God's proximity to remain.

So you learn to pray in **Jesus' name**. **In Jesus' name**, make us holy with **more of Jesus' name**. Keep us in the boat! Make our awareness, our belief, our power, *my name*, subject to His. Do not let *Me* mutiny. Teach me to pray for right prayer. Teach me to pray not to a magic answer-machine or as a path inward to a god of my own making. Teach me to call on the true God in every trouble. Teach me to call on the true God in every blessing. Teach me to praise Him for both trial and release. Teach me to give thanks, even for suffering, even at death, knowing that the end of my name in this age is only the beginning of the age wherein His name is everlasting holiness among us, that my last breath is the first breath of a life where my words will be released from speaking the profanity of my vanity ever again.

THE FIRST EDGE OF HOLIFICATION

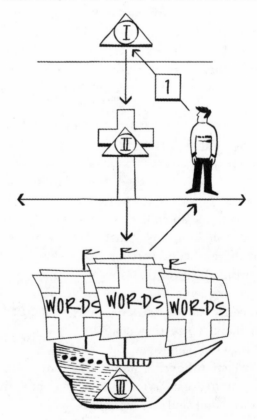

Prayer for more prayer

* **THE ONE HOLIFICATION OF THE CHRISTIAN:**
  THERE IS A GOD, AND THROUGH JESUS,
  HE IS YOUR FATHER.

* **THE FIRST EDGE OF HOLIFICATION:**
  PRAYER FOR MORE PRAYER

THE SECOND EDGE

Prayer for God to Speak More

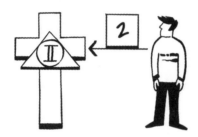

IT COULD HAVE BEEN A FLUKE QUESTION

But it was the right fluke.

Jesus' disciples were no different from us. They were consistent bunglers when it came to the words of God. Time and again, they confronted Jesus with all manner of poor motivations and misdirected thinking. *"Which one of us is the most awesomest? Dude, you totally need to let me be Your number 2! Forget that, Jesus, dying on a cross is a stupid idea!"*

But in spite of themselves, Holification was working on them. Holification was being given. They were fellow-shaped enough to know who stood before them. They were assembled enough to see that in Jesus there was something of the Father. It wasn't by their own reason or strength, but they had been found by the man with the name by which God was saving the world. As good Hebrews, schooled in the Ten Important Things, they knew God spoke, and they heard God speaking in Jesus. As a result, at least one of them was inspired to a brilliant idea: that the best possible thing to do was to ask Him to **talk more**.

Jesus said, "Man shall not live by bread alone, but by every word that comes from the mouth of God" (Matthew 4:4). "Great then!" they replied. "Then, Jesus, please **say something**." "Teach us to pray" (Luke 11:1). Give us the words we need. We know that we need right prayer. Tell us what more we are missing.

So Jesus did. He gave them the **Seven Edges of Christian Holification**, the purest list ever developed of things to ask for. The clearest list of what, even more than the Ten Important Things, humanity needs most. The one source and the seven things you need from Him. The seven things that being a Christian means acknowledging that you do not have. The seven things that being a Christian means **asking for**.

> We have the prophetic word more fully confirmed, to which you will do well to pay attention as to a lamp shining in a dark place, until the day dawns and the morning star rises in your hearts. 2 Peter 1:19

That is what it means to pray in Jesus' name. It means to pray with Jesus' words. It means to pray with Jesus' prayers. This is, in a moment, to know all the Scriptures. It is, in an instant, to be handed the entire mind of God.

Every child learns to speak by hearing the parent. Whether you like it or not, your offspring are mimics, repeating your thoughts, your emotions, your **words**. So also, in Jesus' words, we are made into children of God by proximity. You are a son of God by being brought into God the Son.

WHAT HAPPENS WHEN

You walk into church.

This is an action. You've *done* something. It's a **good work**.

Some may deride this. *"Going to church doesn't make you a Christian!"* As if any work could! But just because the works don't make you a Christian, that doesn't make the good works into bad ones. God is going to speak, and you are here to listen. He is assembling you. So you walk in, and you sit down.

A few songs are sung.

People like to argue about which instruments. I prefer to argue about which songs—which **words**. Singing songs doesn't make you a Christian any more than walking into a church does. But God's words **do** make you a Christian. God's words are the only way. No one is fellow-shaped into Christ without them.

That is why the Bible is read.

A man who is not you stands up. He takes the words that were read and he speaks them again. He **preaches**. It's not a lecture—or it shouldn't be. It's not story hour or a bit of advice for your hobby. This is God's words **proclaimed**. This is God's activity acting.

You walked in. You sat. You sang. You listened. But these actions don't matter. What credit may you take? These actions are useless in themselves. The listening, especially, is **passive**. The sounds fly at you, waves of pressure swimming through the air until they rattle off the three little bones in your ear. Those bones shake about. Those bones are you. But this action is not yours. You are being acted upon. Even if you aren't really listening, God is making a very small part of you move.

From your three little bones, electricity runs up to the gray matter in your skull. Electricity, stolen from the cells of matter you recently digested, sparkles in vivid pathways down your brain. Creating thoughts. Reinforcing ideas. Drilling ruts into the road of your worldview.

> Be transformed by the renewal of your mind, that by testing you may discern what is the will of God, what is good and acceptable and perfect. Romans 12:2

More action! But the action is not its own source. It is not a work worked. It is a work working upon you. By the words.

You, listening, are trapped in *Me*. You, walking, sitting, and singing, are enslaved to futility. But these words are not. These words are free. These words are their own power. They do more than describe. They **dictate**. They do more than advise. They subjugate. They do more than suggest.

THESE WORDS REIGN

We haven't lived in a world of kingdoms for centuries now. We might remember a little about kingdoms from (too often) boring history classes, or perhaps from slightly less boring (depending on who you are) fantasy fiction. But that knowledge of kingdoms hasn't served us. We've lost something. We've kept the wars between nations. We've kept the greed of the powerful causing oppression to the weak. We've kept dishonest scales and the bad rep for tax collectors. But we've lost the heart and center of what makes a kingdom a kingdom.

It isn't the land that makes a kingdom. It is not a set of borders, a matter of lines drawn on a map. It is not a place. It is not the mountains or rivers, laws or culture. Laws and culture are only a reflection. Geography is only a parameter. But what do they reflect? What do they encircle? Once upon a time, it was the reflection of one man's words, the borders of one man's mind. Once upon a time, what made a kingdom was a **man**. What made a kingdom was a **king**.

A law was the law because the king spoke it. The culture was the culture because the king protected it. The territory was drawn on a map because the king ruled over it.

Dominated as we are by belief that personal independence is a high virtue, we have a gut reaction against such an idea. Words like *subject* and *subjection* are an offense to us. *Submission* is an insult. *Patriarchy* is a pejorative. For us, there can be few ideas more foreign than a kingdom because there are few things more appalling to us than a king's **reign**.

But this was the beauty built into the **Fourth Important Thing about Being Creation: God designed authority**. He designated it. He fused it into creation as a hearthstone for our hopes. He put men and women under other men (and women) who were given as gifts to cherish us, to aid and protect us, to see that we grew up well.

Authority was created for **action**. Reign was given to **do**. The problem for us fallen men is not power. It is not absolute power that corrupts but fallen men who corrupt absolute power. It is not the idea of a kingdom that is wrong, but the men who would be kings. But just because we have been unfaithful with God's gifts does not mean He does not preserve them. Rule remains an attribute of God, fused into the world for our benefit. He will do it rightly, even though every one of us botches the job.

The days of Arthur, Caesar, and Cyrus may be little more than dreams, but the kingdom of God is not. God still reigns. God still acts.

God still speaks.

Through Jesus.

Through one man. One who is King. One man who is the Kingdom. One man whose words are not bound by borders, whose reign is not limited. A single syllable from Him is greater than all the works our hands and minds could ever lift up.

So, rather than lift hands to work, we lift them to pray. We speak the syllables He gives us back to Him. We ask Him to keep speaking them again and again, to keep reigning, until what He says is all that we ever know.

> Long ago, at many times and in many ways, God spoke to our fathers by the prophets, but in these last days He has spoken to us by His Son. Hebrews 1:1–2

WHERE GOD SPEAKS, HE ACTS

You walk into church. You sit down. A few songs are sung. A man who is not you stands up. He takes the words from the Scriptures, and he speaks.

The reign of God infiltrates you. He subjugates you. God is placing His flag in your soul, claiming your mind as conquered territory. This is more than sound waves bouncing off the bones in your head. This is **truth**. This is grand architecture. This is the building and shaping of the fibers of who you are. Not just now. Forever.

He establishes you. He gives you His identity. He renews your thoughts with His own, cutting a highway through your head, literally forging the shape of your mind, rewiring you with a new operating system for your heart, writing a program of trust into you.

In a man. In a King.

All that you've done is sit. All that you've done is listen. These are not bad deeds. These are **good** deeds. They are useless by themselves. You are a man of thorns, after all. All that you've brought to this conversation is your evil. But against your evil, and yet **for you**, God has brought **Holification**. He has brought proximity to Himself.

Dominating you. Putting you in your place.

An answer to prayer.

A Kingdom.

The service is over. But the **Second Edge of Holification** will not let you leave without **praying for more**. Back out into the dark world you must go. But being made holy, you do not want to go alone. You want to take this light with you. You want the reign of the King to come with you.

For people who speak thus make it clear that they are seeking a homeland. If they had been thinking of that land from which they had gone out, they would have had opportunity to return. Hebrews 11:14–15

Outside, nothing is really fixed. There is no glorious transfiguration. There is no magic pill to take away all that we by our folly have wrought. But now, you know that there is something more. There is a **homeland**. There is a city with foundations. There is a better country.

Out there in the darkness, **the Second Edge of Holification** sees how desperately the reign of God is missing. From the world. From *Me*. We cannot live by bread alone. But we are trying. That is why we are dying.

The antidote is not more of us. It is not more of our kings. It is not more of our actions. It is not more of our rule. The antidote is God's words. Returning to us. Again. Always. Over and over again. Completely. Every time.

So you rise with bold confidence, and ask.

Lord Jesus, be active more.
Holy Father, speak more.

Dear God, send more of the words that make us **live**. More of the words that make us **act**. More *than* the words that tell us what we *ought to be*. More of the words that make what we *ought to be* into what **we actually are**.

NOTHING WRONG WITH AN ECHO

The world hungers for magic words. It wants words to make us gods, to steal from the heavens their power and imbue us with them. It can only conceive of *divine words* as words that contain their own power. Power segregated from the one who made it.

But God's words are no such thing. They give without giving up. They share without diminishing. They work without being worked.

God speaks. To listen is to learn to pray rightly. To listen is to hear holy speech and begin to repeat it. To echo it.

This is not about having magic words. Prayer is not about vain repetition and incantations. Prayer is not about getting all the right syllables or making sure as many people are praying for you as possible. Prayer is not the power to bend God (or the gods) to your will. That is *backward prayer*.

Holification runs the opposite direction. Holification is about the renewal of your mind by authentic, external inputs. It is the regeneration of your heart by sufficient, repeatable truth. Holification doesn't try to bend God's will to yours. It bends your will to God's.

This is about dogma.
Doctrine.
A living stagnancy.
A life-giving rigidity.
A King who reigns.
Where the Good King rules, all is well.

> **Follow the pattern of the sound words that you have heard from me, in the faith and love that are in Christ Jesus.** 2 Timothy 1:13

Where God's words have free course, they do not destroy but create. They do not tear down but build up; they do not decay but sustain. The **Second Edge of Holification** is the euphoric belief that the King's edicts will do more for us than we could have ever hoped for from ourselves. The Second Edge of Holification is, in Jesus' name, having the audacity to ask for more of His words.

THE SECOND EDGE OF HOLIFICATION

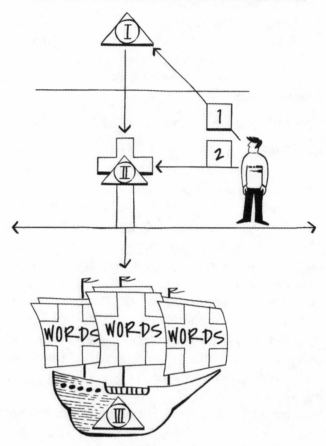

Prayer for God to speak more

ECHO

* **THE ONE HOLIFICATION OF THE CHRISTIAN:**
  THERE IS A GOD, AND THROUGH JESUS,
  HE IS YOUR FATHER.

* **THE FIRST EDGE OF HOLIFICATION:**
  PRAYER FOR MORE PRAYER

* **THE SECOND EDGE OF HOLIFICATION:**
  PRAYER FOR GOD TO SPEAK MORE

> *Before they call I will
> answer; while they are yet
> speaking I will hear.*
>
> Isaiah 65:24

THE THIRD EDGE

Prayer for Things I Don't Want but Need Anyway

THERE IS NOTHING WRONG WITH THIS PLANET

We may still see a thorny, cracked world that never seems to get any better. We may still see the ever-long line of corrupt governments, dishonest businesses, profit-driven bosses, sticky-fingered employees, thoughtless children, insufficient marriages, distracted parents, backstabbing neighbors, gossiping friends, and endlessly envious hearts. We may still sit in too-boring churches with too-inauthentic prayers with our fear, love, and trust placed in a million things other than the almighty God. But all of this is okay with Jesus. Jesus has ascended. That means that Jesus is the one in charge.

The world may look like it's spinning radically out of control. But it's not. Everything is fixed. Everything is under control. Sin is conquered. Death is vanquished. The power of the devil has been wrested away from him, and history is now being folded over on itself in a giant scheme to bring the words about this salvation to the end of the earth. The Gospel and its Results are spreading.

Everything else, even the truly diabolical things, are now serving that end, whether they intend to or not.

The design may be corrupted by us, but Jesus is still using it. He is using the Ten Important Things about Being Creation as the places for humanity to stand while His words move from ear to heart to mouth to ear to heart to mouth of fallen human after fallen human. He won't let it fail completely. Under His reign, these Ten Things are the highest **Law**, a natural order so ingrained in existence that even those who would rebel against it must rely on it in order to rebel. **Everyone must stand somewhere.**

The Romans built roads for Rome, but they were roads the Gospel traveled on. The medieval kingdoms colonized the world for themselves, often using Christianity as their excuse. But they were still colonies in which the Gospel traveled to the ends of the earth. The internet may be most famous for cat videos and pornography, but on its digital streams the words of God are also flowing into places previously thought impossible. Jesus is using what is here to achieve an impossible task. Christianity is assembling people back into trusting that no matter what we see, God's answers are always enough.

> What has a man from all the toil and striving of heart with which he toils beneath the sun? For all his days are full of sorrow, and his work is a vexation. Even in the night his heart does not rest. This also is vanity. Ecclesiastes 2:22–23

God's answer to our present darkness is not to burn it all with the snap of His fingers, but to bend space and time and all our misguided willfulness into the perfect soil for the growth of the one thing that can save us. The only reason we really have to complain about God's answer is that it keeps stopping us from the one thing our thorns would rather be doing. We'd like to be given the power to make all our dreams come true *right now*. When we pray, we pray to be able to achieve the lives we really want to have. But ultimately, God isn't making decisions about our day-to-day lives on the basis of what we'd like them to be. Instead, He's sacrificing the present for a better future.

The whole world is caught up in a great game of trying to pretend this is not true, and Christians are not immune from this temptation. The barren futility of our present condition is a bit much for our egocentric minds to handle. It's much easier to spin the rat wheel of avoidance day after day. The closer to the existential terror of meaninglessness we draw, the harder we run with our eyes closed into the great abyss of nowhere fast, filling our talk with a litany of philosophic yammering, spiritual-religious mantras dreamed up to brainwash ourselves back into the safety of ignorant pretense.

Life is good!

Change the world!

Everyone is beautiful just the way they are!

Go out there and make a difference!

Make a difference in what? Isn't everyone already beautiful? If life is so good, why all the hubbub about changing it? It's all the same grand pyramid scheme of willful ignorance, blind men leading the blind into believing that pits won't exist if you refuse to believe in them. It all begs a hard truth: we only tell ourselves *to make lemons out of lemonade* because **we don't like lemons** the way they are. We invest so much time, money, and will into *gratitude training* and the *power of positive thinking* and *looking at the bright side* because the dark side is so terribly unavoidable, total, and oppressive.

YOU DON'T LIKE LIVING HERE

This world kind of sucks. Christianity doesn't fix this. Christianity **amplifies** this. Christianity is not about learning how to be happy with this present age. It's about embracing the fact that you can't stand it. It's about owning up to the truth that it infuriates you. Where the rest of the world is singing songs of distraction, pretending with blue faces that we can will it all away, the words of Jesus well up within you as a new, **holy discontent**.

Thanks to the Ten Important Things about Being Creation, you know how things really ought to be. Knowing what the design is supposed to look like, you can't be satisfied with anything less. Having smelled the sweet aroma of hot steak topped with mushrooms and parmesan wafting from the kitchen, how could you possibly be content with a bowl of lukewarm pottage? Thanks to Who Jesus Is and What Jesus Did, you know that all of it has also been born anew and is headed for perfection. Believing this, but never getting to see it, having it be a matter of **faith alone**, having to **wait for it**, produces a maddening inner struggle. *Me* is still right here with you. *Me* also isn't happy with the way the world is, but *Me* doesn't like being shown the problems in detail. *Me* likes the idea that pretending hard enough will actually make the futility go away. *Me* remains convinced that the world could be a better place if only a few things were done differently.

Me firmly believes that world could be what it is supposed to be if only everyone else would stop messing it up. Life *could* be good, if only everyone would do things the way they *should* be done. If only everyone would live life the way it *should* be lived. If only everyone were a bit more like me. If only *Me* was in charge.

Me has been a rebel from the beginning. This hasn't changed. Cradle to grave, *Me* is a traitor. An instigator of mutiny. A would-be tyrant in the making. As much as Jesus' ascension has saved everything, it has not saved it the way *Me* wants it to be saved. As much as Jesus' ascension has everything under control, it hasn't put *Me* in control.

This is what makes the **Third Edge of Holification** one of the easiest to overlook. *Me* is the last person in the world who wants you to see it. So *Me* works hard to mask it, to hide it right in front of your nose. To preach about the *power of prayer*, but forget to mention that prayer isn't about getting what you want. To paint a pleasant picture of a man praying in a garden, looking so meek and pious, to distract you from the blood that was pouring through His sweat glands as His total Holification compelled Him to pray directly against what He actually wanted.

THY WILL BE DONE

Think about what that prayer means! It's the prayer of an insane person. No one in his right mind would pray for such a thing. It is a prayer for someone else to get the final say. It is a prayer for someone else to be in charge. It is a plea for subjugation. An application for submission. A request for powerlessness.

A petition for enslavement. An imprecation against yourself. A prayer for the end of *Me*.

"Dear God, please take away all my power. Please take all my control. Please don't let me make any more decisions. Please let me not be in charge of anything. Please don't give me any more choices. Any more. Ever again. Dear God, please compel me, even against my will, to do anything and everything that I don't want to do whenever You feel like I need to do it. Dear God, it's Your call. Please stop me from making calls."

Can we actually pray this? 100 percent? And actually mean it? No reservations? It's impossible.

"Take away my options. Get rid of my choices. Subdue me. Humiliate me, if You need to. Make me believe that I am the dust that I am. Shove the dust in my face. Return me to it."

This is not something that *Me* can pray. It's not in *Me's* power. *Me's* reason or strength can't handle it. This is holy discontent taken to an entirely different level. It's much bigger than just not being happy about the state of the world. This is a miraculous, God-given self-confliction. It's the supernatural compulsion of an **I** who has come to believe that the biggest problem **I** have in the world is *Me*. You have become an **I** who believes that *Me* needs to be stopped. You have been raised up as a holy **I** set apart to pray against your profane *Me*. You have been given a new will to cry out that God would save you, protect you, and rescue you precisely **from your own will**.

> Since all these things are thus to be dissolved, what sort of people ought you to be in lives of holiness and godliness, waiting for and hastening the coming of the day of God. 2 Peter 3:11–12

This holy **I** is you, the believer. It is not a part of you. It's not 50 percent of you. You and this holy **I** are the same **person**. But this new will, narrowly speaking, is not yours. It does not originate with you. It is not *from* you. It is **from** God. You, the believer, are **His will** being done.

But the profane *Me* is also still you. It is also not part of you, not 50 percent of you. You and the profane *Me* are also the same person. This old will, narrowly speaking, is all yours. It originates with you. It is entirely *from* you. To *Me*, this entire situation of having to share you with God means *war*.

TWO WILLS, ONE PERSON

It's nothing short of a mystical union. You have **two wills**. Your Christian faith is one of them, the regenerate **I**. The believer. Your sin living in you is the other, the reprobate *Me*. The unbeliever.

Trying to figure out how this works out mathematically has gotten more than one theologian into trouble, and usually leads to distraction and speculation. What is important is that this is the **Third Edge of Christian Holification**. You are one person experiencing life as **both** a sinner and a saint, as both a profane person and a holy person, as both an unrighteous one and a righteous one, as both an unbeliever *and* a believer.

> For I do not do the good I want, but the evil I do not want is what I keep on doing. Now if I do what I do not want, it is no longer I who do it, but sin that dwells within me. So I find it to be a law that when I want to do right, evil lies close at hand. Romans 7:19–21

God is doing this to you. He is the one making it happen. By His words. With His words. As His words. It is a daily experience that will continue until death parts you. The Gospel of Jesus results in the creation of contrition and repentance in you, by which *Me* is forced to drown and die, by which all evil desires are hemmed in, limited, and cut off, by which the holy I emerges as alive before God.

This is a gift! This is the first resurrection. This is the experience of living by faith alone.

The Scriptures call this the war of the spirit against the flesh. They call it the new man putting down the old man. They call it the law of the mind overwriting the law of sin. They call it the righteousness in the ungodly. It is the mystery of godliness inhabiting we who are unrighteous.

Whichever phrase we borrow, it also is Luther's *anfechtung*. It is the simultaneous existence within you of two motivations, two desires, two hearts. It is being two things at once, but **believing** that only one of them really matters. In the same moment, every moment, you believe in and serve God, **and** you don't believe in

Him and rebel against Him. **But!** You believe in and serve God by believing in, hoping in, trusting in His war to silence you in His presence, to subject you to His words, to bend you to His will, to murder your animosity and raise up in its place an everlasting love.

This is exactly what Holification is. Not you, but the Spirit at work **on** you. **In** you. **Against** you. So that even as the *Me* (who is you) won't ever want to pray such a prayer, the holy **I** (who is also you) believes it is right to do so. You actually **do** believe the world would be a much better place if only God would push you out of the way of your own life and take it over. The Third Edge of Holification are words of agreement with this. The Third Edge is a growing desire for God's will to be done. The Third Edge is a prayer for **you** against *Me*.

A POWERFUL DESPERATION

This is backward power. It is the strength of being authentically weak. It is the courage of being authentically afraid. It is the confidence of being authentically humiliated. It is the will to authentically ask for what you do not want.

"Dear God, teach me not to act on my will, but to be still under Yours. Teach me not to speak for my will but to listen to Yours. Teach me not to insist on my will, but to pray for Your will to be done."

Wait, this prayer seems counterintuitive. It seems like the wrong answer to our problems. It seems like I'm praying for a future in which I'll never get my own way. Exactly. It's unbelievable that any of us would dare to pray it. But **we do.** This *is* faith: born within you, setting you apart to see that the problem is not God's design. The problem is not the world. The problem is us.

The seemingly *obvious* answer to the problems of the universe is for things to be the way *Me* wants them to be, for *Me* to be *more* in charge of my life, *more* in control, *more* respected, *more* looked to. We all have this ever-present desire to invert ourselves, to turn ourselves inward, to ask for power as the answer to all our problems, to pray for the ability to fix, to overcome, to survive, and to save. We all want to be the ones who make the world a better place. But the **actual** answer is for you to be less of these things, for your opinion to matter less, for your life to be more subjected to powers beyond your control, for you to ultimately be powerless.

ECHO

In order for the holiness of God's name to turn back the clock to paradise, in order for His reign to actively change the way things are into the way they should be, then a key part of this Holification of the whole world is for you and me to stop changing the world, to stop trying to be the source of a new perfection, to stop constantly trying to have our own wills be done.

This can only happen by believing that, as much as you are addicted to your will, it is that very infatuation with yourself (shared by each one of us) that is the entire world's only real problem. Your will doesn't just want a little more power. It wants all of it. Your will is not just sometimes selfish. It always is. The world would not be a better place if things were done the way you want them to be. It would be very much worse. Imagine the chaos if each of us actually had the power to make everything we want happen. It's bad enough right now, as we scuttle about trying to bend everything to our preferences, constantly running into one another, a billion wills all bent against one another, scrambling in an endless game of king of the hill.

> Do nothing from selfish ambition or conceit, but in humility count others more significant than yourselves. Let each of you look not only to his own interests, but also to the interests of others. Philippians 2:3–4

Right now, things are not as bad as they could be precisely **because** your will is not being done. Jesus is ascended. He's reigning on high, hemming us in, setting boundaries, curbing everything so that our little rebellions never amount to more than soil for Him to scatter His Word on. Jesus has set limits on our vanity. These limits, these boundaries, do not enslave us. Our slavery is our self-imposed exile into the so-called *freedom* of our willfulness.

We are terrible masters, but the Good King is not. Under Him, subdued, you are not less free but more free. You do not have more to worry about. You have less to worry about. You do not have more to fear about what you might not have. You have less to fear and more to share with others. You do not have to fight harder for whatever whim or dream might take you. You need not fight at all. You may turn the other cheek. You may repay evil with good. You may stand set apart, placed where you are in God's great chain of design, and believe it will be for the best, certain that, however it turns out, Jesus is working it for not just your good—not just your salvation—but that of the entire world.

ANSWERED ALREADY

The **Third Edge of Holification** *is* what it asks for. **Thy will be done** is our prayer, and in praying it, it has happened. Unbelievers have been raised as believers. *Me* has been crucified, and the holy **I** lives triumphant over his grave.

God has no greater desire for you than this. His love for the world is so great that there is nothing He desires less than its destruction. The death and damnation of the wicked does not please Him. What pleases Him is to give, to cherish, to have mercy. So His will has been done. He sent His Son, a holy assassin on a secret mission to infiltrate behind the enemy lines of our willfulness. When our hate nailed Him to a tree, He slaughtered our hate and left in its place the awakening of new minds. New minds He makes trust more in Him than in ourselves. New minds that exhibit this trust not as the triumphant experience of never having to see our putrid willfulness, but in the mortifying experience of seeing it all too clearly and learning how to pray against it.

> Every athlete exercises self-control in all things. They do it to receive a perishable wreath, but we an imperishable.
>
> 1 Corinthians 9:25

You are starving—not for more of you, but for more of Jesus. You are hungering for righteousness, not from within yourself, but from without. From Him. You are learning to believe that even though your will wakes up with you every morning and shouts, "For God *and* for *Me!*" the Spirit is right there with you, warring against that thorny flesh with words that will not let *Me* win.

It is an Almighty-given prayer for powerlessness. "Thy will be done" are divine words that set a new will against your old one. This prayer is the strength of being the weakest so that the strongest might save. It is the immunity of being enslaved to the Good King, so that He might set you free from the tyranny of yourself. You are free to admit that *Me* is problem, and you are free to change your prayer. You are free to ask not for more power, but for less; not for more mattering, but for less; not for more of what you desire, but for less.

THE THIRD EDGE OF
HOLIFICATION

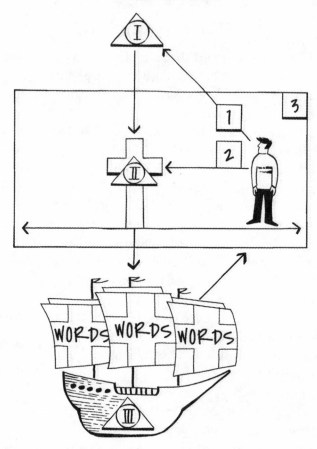

Prayer for things I don't want but need anyway

* THE ONE HOLIFICATION OF THE CHRISTIAN:
  THERE IS A GOD, AND THROUGH JESUS,
  HE IS YOUR FATHER.

* THE FIRST EDGE OF HOLIFICATION:
  PRAYER FOR MORE PRAYER

* THE SECOND EDGE OF HOLIFICATION:
  PRAYER FOR GOD TO SPEAK MORE

* THE THIRD EDGE OF HOLIFICATION:
  PRAYER FOR THINGS I DON'T WANT BUT NEED ANYWAY

{ *It is one of the twelve,*
one who is dipping bread
into the dish with Me. }

Mark 14:20

THE FOURTH
AND FIFTH EDGES

Prayer for Enough, but No More
and Prayer for Patience
to Overlook Today

THIS IS THE CHAPTER WHERE I
ADMIT WHAT I'VE BEEN DOING

I've kept it up about as long as I can. But I don't think I can do it anymore. The last chapter alone was a dead giveaway. But I'm sure you've seen through the sleight of hand for some time.

It worked, though, didn't it? I mean, how likely would you have been to pick up and read the book this far if it had simply been titled **The Catechism**? No need to pretend. You can be honest with me. It wouldn't matter who wrote it or what kind of fun little pictures it might have, the word *catechism* has about as much curb appeal as the word *dictionary*. Maybe less.

It's too bad, really. Transliterating *catechism* straight from the Greek as we have, it comes off sounding like some kind of diabolical

259

mind-crank or torture device. But it can also be translated as a beautiful word. At its root, it's just the word *Echo*, smushed between the word **again**, and then ism-ized to stop being an action and become a thing. Yes, to echo something again is redundant. That's on purpose. What else would you do with the shortest summary of life-altering, absolute truth ever received by the minds of men? You would never want to stop repeating it. You would never want to risk forgetting it. You would speak it. You would **teach** it. You would **learn** it. You would **echo** it. Again. And again.

But who is ever going to do that with something called the *catechism*? It's about the last thing I'd ever seriously consider picking up to read. In fact, if it weren't for book six of the Harry Potter series keeping me up too late one night and filling me with too much adrenaline to fall asleep, I never might have done so. It was my second year at the seminary, and I was supposed to have already studied Luther's Large Catechism diligently. But students tend to only study diligently what will later be on the tests, and the tests were on books *about* the catechism, not on the catechism itself. But I *had* purchased the book, and so late one evening while searching for something else to read to help me calm down and get to sleep, my eyes alighted upon my copy. Little did I know it, but my life was about to change forever.

> **Like a lame man's legs, which hang useless, is a proverb in the mouth of fools.** Proverbs 26:7

I flopped back into bed and opened to the Preface, where Dr. Luther wrote this:

> **What else are such proud, arrogant saints doing who are unwilling to read and study the catechism daily? They think they are much more learned than God Himself with all His saints, angels, prophets, apostles, and all Christians. . . . I will promise them—and they shall also see— what fruit they will receive, and what excellent people God will make of them. So in due time they themselves will admit that the longer and the more they study the catechism, the less they know of it and the more they will find to learn. Only then, as hungry and thirsty men, will they truly relish what now they cannot stand because of great abundance and contentment. (LC Preface 16, 20)**

What was he talking about? My memories told me that the *catechism* was an encyclopedic tome filled with red ink and a million questions I would never ask. But the key to understanding him is learning that for Dr. Luther, the *catechism* is **not a book**. It's not a series of questions and answers, nor is it very long at all. It's a very simple list, easily fit on a sheet of paper. It is nothing more nor less than the bare texts of the Ten Commandments, the Apostles' Creed, and the Lord's Prayer. As he says:

> **But for myself I say this: I am also a doctor and preacher; yes, as learned and experienced as all the people who have such assumptions and contentment. Yet I act as a child who is being taught the catechism. Every morning— and whenever I have time—I read and say, word for word, the Ten Commandments, the Creed, the Lord's Prayer, the Psalms, and such. I must still read and study them daily. Yet I cannot master the catechism as I wish. But I must remain a child and pupil of the catechism, and am glad to remain so. (LC 7–8)**

Drawing these **Three Foundational Realities**, or summaries of Christianity, out of Scripture and putting them together in one place wasn't Luther's idea. But it *is* a **golden one**. It is an inheritance of gemstones from the most ancient Christians. They lived in a world very different from our own, where most people were illiterate and the cost of owning a Bible was beyond what you or I would have been able to afford. But on the heels of the apostles, they realized that they had at their disposal three short lists that contained **everything**. Three short lists that even a child could memorize, and three short lists that the Romans couldn't take away from them even if they were stripped of all their goods and thrown in prison.

> The rules of the LORD are true, and righteous altogether. More to be desired are they than gold, even much fine gold. Psalm 19:9–10

So before adult converts to Christianity were baptized, they began to be given the **Echo**. It could come with as much as three years of further instruction, but it never amounted to more than the same summary of all Christian doctrine smaller than your back pocket, about which Luther also said:

> **Therefore, I again beg all Christians . . . not to think of themselves as doctors too soon and imagine that they know everything. . . . Instead, they should daily exercise themselves well in these studies and constantly use them. . . . Steadily keep on reading, teaching, learning, pondering, and meditating on the catechism. And they should not stop until they have tested and are sure that they have taught the devil to death, and have become more learned than God Himself and all His saints. (LC 19)**

This book is the result of Luther both shaming and inspiring me with these words. I must confess, I remain a meager student. I do not study the Echo every day as I would like, and even when I do, the content is still beyond me. But the last fifteen years have brought with them many wonderful teachers who were more than happy to impart marvelous insights. It is that which I have tried to congeal here for you.

THE NUMBERS DON'T COUNT

Luther also said, *"Whoever knows the Ten Commandments perfectly must know all the Scriptures"* (LC 17). He said this because he saw how one of the most marvelous things about the Ten Commandments, the Creed, and the Lord's Prayer is their cohesion. Their parts interlink in a unity of forms, exchanging with, complementing, and completing one another. The conclusion of this book hopes to draw out and exhibit this marvelous, cross-shaped idea. In order to get there, we first need to explore the remaining Edges of Holification that the Lord's Prayer teaches us to ask for.

But we have a problem.

And it's a boring problem.

It can't be helped. There isn't any avoiding it. Like I said, this dilemma is important enough that it has forced my hand, convincing me to reveal the word *catechism* long before I really wanted to. My goal was to keep piping along without having to resort to words like *commandments* and *petitions* until almost the very end. But if I did that, while I could still share with you some nifty tidbits about the Fourth and Fifth Edges of Holification, I wouldn't be able to tie them to the completed whole. We wouldn't be able to finish our picture.

So the jig is up, and here's the issue: numbers. Arbitrary numbers. When God spoke to Israel from Mount Sinai, Moses said God spoke **Ten Words**. It's evident that He spoke a lot more than ten actual words, so we've developed a habit of translating it as **Ten Commandments**. Even then, there is enough wiggle in what God said that if He hadn't said there were ten, you could easily come away thinking there were as many as fourteen or as few as eight or nine. Various groups have debated how best to number them.

It's not really a big deal. It can be annoying when trying to buy Sunday School posters from different denominational websites, but we could have totally avoided it here if it weren't for the second set of numbers—that is, the ones Lutherans have historically connected with the Lord's Prayer.

In the Bible, the Lord's Prayer has no numbers at all, but for centuries it has been taught that there are essentially seven **requests** that Jesus teaches us to make, **seven petitions** we are to ask for. We usually number them one to seven, which makes perfect sense. But

> **Remind them of these things, and charge them before God not to quarrel about words, which does no good, but only ruins the hearers.** 2 Timothy 2:14

then, they come after another part, an **introduction**, as Luther called it, in which we don't ask *for* anything but speak **to** God.

Again, what's the big deal? Well, nothing, until you start trying to compare the two side by side. The first thing that happens, which is very exciting to theological nerds like me, is that you see that they seem to be an exact match. The second thing that happens, which is far less exciting, is that you see they seem to be an exact match *except for the numbers.*

The **First Commandment** (Lutheran numbering here) is **you shall have *no other gods***. Jesus then teaches you to pray to the real God. He says, "**Pray like this, *Our Father*, who art in heaven.**" The **Second Commandment** is that **you shall not misuse the *name*** of God. Just like that, Jesus teaches us the first thing we are to ask our Father for is "**Hallowed be Thy *name*.**" The **Third Commandment** exhorts us to **sanctify the Sabbath Day**, and Jesus in turn teaches to ask for that the thing that makes all things sanctified by its presence, the **kingdom/reign of God to come**. The **Fourth Commandment** tells us to **honor our father and**

mother, placing us under the will and authority of those whom God sets over us. And again, Jesus teaches us to ask that our own wills not get in the way of God's design, but that His **will be done**.

It's pretty sweet. But then, you start trying to teach it using the numbers. It doesn't matter whether you use the word *petition* (bane of confirmands everywhere!) or **Holification** (which, amazingly, they intuitively know the meaning of), you still end up with the pedagogical catastrophe of trying to teach that the **First Petition** asks for the fulfillment of the **Second Commandment**, and the **Second Edge of Holification** asks for the granting of the **Third Important Thing**, and so on:

I *You shall have no other gods.*	**O** *Pray like this, Our Father.*
2 *You shall not misuse the name of the Lord.*	**I** *Hallowed be Thy name.*
3 *You shall remember the day of God's words.*	**2** *Thy kingdom come.*
4 *Honor the authorities God puts over you.*	**3** *Thy will be done.*

Ack!

Then, it gets worse.

With the **Fifth Important Thing** (which lines up with the **Fourth Edge of Holification**—oy!), something new happens. There is a **shift**. Up to this point, even though the numbers were off, everything was lining up one by one. But now, things go all askew. I mean, *this* can't be right:

5 *You shall not murder.*	**4** *Give us this day our daily bread.*
6 *Your shall not commit adultery.*	**5** *Forgive us our trespasses.*
7 *You shall not steal.*	**6** *And lead us not into temptation.*
8 *You shall not lie.*	**7** *But deliver us from evil.*

Wha? You can make a loose case that feeding your neighbor is the opposite of killing him, but then I'm not sure forgiveness is something we apply only to adultery, nor is avoiding temptation something that shouldn't be applied to adultery. Are we never tempted to lie? Can a thief not pray to be forgiven for stealing? You might try treating the extensions "on earth as it is in heaven" or "as we forgive others" as their own lines, but it won't help. (Go ahead, I'll wait if you want to try it out on your own piece of paper.)

No matter what you do, it all appears to break down.

Unless . . .

THEY MERGE

What if the reason Jesus teaches us to ask for **seven** things rather than **ten** is because there is more going on in Holification than just the fulfillment of the Ten Important Things. What if **seven** is not *less* than **ten**, but *more*? What if there is not just a re*align*ment, but a re-**enlighten**ment taking place? What if reality is not just shifting *back* but shifting **forward**?

Here is what I mean.

A single, entirely ignorable, but startling word shows up for the very first time **between** the Fourth and Fifth Edges of Holification that Jesus teaches us to pray for. It's ignorable because it's unbearably common, bothersomely uninteresting, so much so that editors the world over are constantly telling writers to not even bother using it. But there it is, used for the first time in the prayer, right there between "daily bread" and "forgiveness."

And.

It's a linking word. A **conjunction**. A word that insists on a connection between two things. A word that inextricably ties two things together. Puts them on the same ground. Promotes their **fusion**.

To know wisdom and instruction, to understand words of insight, . . . let the wise hear and increase in learning, and the one who understands obtain guidance. . . . The fear of the LORD is the beginning of knowledge. Proverbs 1:2, 5, 7

And got me thinking. What if the Fourth and Fifth Edges of Holification are not meant to line up with the Fifth and Sixth Commandments at all? What if they are meant to merge them? What if "not murdering" and "not ruining families" are not meant to be countered by the petition for daily bread and forgiveness, but to exist between them? What if the needs of our neighbor's body and life aren't about doing daily bread and forgiveness, but about living **inside** them?

More. It's not like "not stealing" and "not lying" don't belong inside this same box. So, what if the Seven Edges of Christian Holification lined up with the Ten Important Things about Being Creation like this:

1 You shall have no other gods.

O Pray like this, Our Father.

2 You shall not misuse the name of the Lord.

1 Hallowed be Thy name.

3 You shall remember the day of God's words.

2 Thy kingdom come.

4 Honor the authorities God puts over you.

3 Thy will be done.

5 You shall not hurt your neighbor's body.

6 Your shall not commit adultery.

4 Give us this day our daily bread.

7 You shall not steal.

5 And forgive us from how we fail to love our neighbors.

8 You shall not lie.

9/10 You shall not covet anything.

6 And lead us not into temptation.

7 But deliver us from evil.

For each of the Fifth through Eighth Important Things, there are two extreme poles. But they all exist between the Fourth and Fifth Edges of Holification. You can murder your neighbor's body, or you can feed it. You can destroy his community, or you can help him grow it. You can steal his crops, or you can loan him the tools to tend them. You can ruin his good name by telling everyone else all the evil he has done, or you can forgive him just as God, in Jesus, has forgiven you. The two-edged petition of bread *and* forgiveness sets everything else in life apart as well. It is a prayer that puts things in their proper place.

THE IN-BETWEEN

We still must till the soil. We still must sweat to bring forth food from the earth. We must feed our children. We must find or build whatever tools it takes to make this possible. Our good names depend on it. But as we work for bread, for life, for family, and for honor, even as Christians, I will yet fail and harm you, and you will yet fail and harm me.

There will be moments when you instinctively consider your neighbor's needs to be a greater priority than your own. But those moments will be rare. Nor will he make it a regular practice of putting you before himself. The euphoria of faith will compel you to pray for daily bread, but the old man will also lurk beside you, compelling you to ask for *more*. It is not just today's bread that *Me* wants, but next week's bread as well. So *Me* finds a way to *take* it. But who is there to take it from? No one else but you.

> The soul of the wicked desires evil; his neighbor finds no mercy in his eyes. Proverbs 21:10

Before we give in entirely to the full violence of these thoughts, Holification preempts our self-seeking, and the damage it will inevitably cause to others, by teaching us to ask for forgiveness in the same breath in which we ask for our needs. It teaches us to assume that when we seek out our bread, we will seek it with all manner of the wrong reasons and motivations.

Forgive us, we pray, for both you and me. Dear Lord, let mercy dominate **our** life. Not just sanctimony. Not just talk of religion. Not just the boast of love and charity that walks about in tight-grinned bitterness. No. Let us have hearty, earthy mercy. Let us have love that can admit that I do not like you, my brother, and you do not like me much either. But we are both slaves set free by the same Good King. Neither of us has ever managed to quite fully do our duty. We both deserve to be cast back into the debtor's dark prison with bankruptcies we could never repay. So whatever fights we might have with one another now are best dropped before we ever think to call the Judge. He will surely condemn us both if He finds that after His love has come down to us, we still scrabble and fight over such petty misdemeanors.

Our Father. Not mine.

Today's bread? Give us what we need.

Our errors? Our missteps? Our hatreds? Our evils? Forgive us what was not ours to take.

The result? Whether that means sharing a cup of water with a stranger or sharing the name of a good plumber with your neighbor, teach **us** to be **we**.

This is the dynamic, radical freedom in which Christianity lives. We all need to eat today. We all need to be forgiven for forgetting that everyone else needs to eat too. We are all stuck here together, where moth and rust destroy, where thieves break in and steal, where it is all too easy to let these dangers chase us into seeking less of **us** and more of *Me*. But the box of the Fourth and Fifth Edges of Holification bind us to one another. These Edges teach us that if all we ever demand of one another is justice, then we must eventually end by demanding one another's deaths. We must end with warfare and bloodshed and an eye for an eye. We must end in the disastrous place that we already are.

But Christianity has set us free from precisely that. We already know that one day even the best barn will collapse, that even tomorrow's bread will also dry and crumble, that the many wondrous gifts of God's design that remain for us to enjoy cannot be kept by *Me* for *Me* forever, no matter how hard *Me* might try. We already know that as much as today is filled with many good things, it is inevitably also filled with many evils, the chief of which is my innate worship of my own perceived needs. We already know that none of it really matters because God has already set a date on which the world will end.

So, before we find that the injustice of our fight for scraps of bread has whipped us into a rage against one another, we preempt our thorns by begging the mercy of God be upon us all. In so doing, we inadvertently implore Him to teach us how to have mercy on one another, how to see one another in our need, how to put the other above the self. We ask that God would tend to our stomachs without letting us make gods of them. We pray that we would enjoy the warm sun on a cool fall day, and a secure home to rest in with our children, and a bit of warm cookie fresh from the oven delivered to a neighbor, certain in the knowledge that the world might end tomorrow. So why not share? Why not overlook the offense? Why not repay evil with good?

> **Do not be anxious about tomorrow, for tomorrow will be anxious for itself. Sufficient for the day is its own trouble.** Matthew 6:34

WE

This box Christianity lives in while we wait for Jesus' return, the Fourth and Fifth Edges of Holification, is the hard and painful place of real love. Not the kind of love that only loves what it likes. Not the cheap and easy forgiveness that only forgives what it feels like forgiving. This is the cross in action. This is the supernatural holiness that you can't earn, you can't create, you can't climb up to. This is **faith alone**.

Real forgiveness is not the desire to forgive, the lack of a feeling that evil was done to you. Real forgiveness feels the evil. It feels the rage. It owns the injustice, and then it swallows it in the cross of Jesus. Real forgiveness is not the kind of thing you can take credit for. You don't get to walk away and say, *"Look at me! How forgiving I am!"* No. Real forgiveness happens when you know you should forgive, but you don't want to, and then act like you have forgiven anyway. It happens when you know in your heart that you are a poor sport and a meager benefactor, but you make every effort to hide your hatred from your neighbor **for *his* sake.** Even when he deserves it. **Especially** when he deserves it.

This only happens when you are freed from the ladder. You can't demand love, of yourself or of others. You can't legislate it. You can't love others for the sake of your own righteousness. Any such skin-deep compassion would be the definition of hate. But standing on the ship built to hold you above the storms of even your own hatred and pride, looking out on those raging seas of self safely kept by the protective power of Jesus' cross, those with you on the deck are no longer only a means to your own end. Much less those you see still drowning in the sea. When we are given life under grace that all our self-justifying attempts to climb can't even dream of, we are truly set free to see the neighbor for who he is: one of **us**.

Do you not know that you [*plural*] are God's temple and that God's Spirit dwells in you [*plural*]?
1 Corinthians 3:16

The Fourth and Fifth Edges of Holification own the fact that you are still in a fellow-shape with all the sinners of the world, while at the same time praying on the fact that you are promised the fellow-shape of the righteousness of Jesus Christ. Here, in this box of need and answer, it is possible to look at your neighbor and his needs as something more than a chance to capitalize on his poverty, whether that be by pressing him into your debt or by feeding him your scraps to assuage your own guilt. Set apart between your own need for bread and your own need for absolution, you can see your neighbor for who he really is: someone just like you, desperately in need of today's bread, even more desperately in need of tomorrow's mercy.

And you now have that mercy to give! In abundance! You've been reidentified out of *Me* into **We**. The name of Jesus has washed you. All the debts that have ever been amassed against you by God are now struck down. What debt does anyone else owe you that can compare?

This is the quiet miracle of Holification. This is the self-forgetfulness that is created without your seeing it, when the mercy poured over you becomes the mercy you can't help but pour over others. You have no debt, but you do not want to own others more, but to set them free as well. Fear of threat or the possibility of losing what has been given could never cause this Holification. But unadulterated, radical mercy can. Being forgiven, standing eyes open, loving the other people on board without any expectation that it will ever come back to help you suddenly exists as a marvelous, wonderful idea. You will not become more holy. You will not become more righteous. You will only receive the gift of being more merciful.

How can we who died to sin still live in it? Romans 6:2

So, give **us** bread today, we pray. *And*. Forgive **us our** sins tomorrow. Because of **Him**.

This is the hunger of Holification. This is the holy discontent with the present. **Our** Father has taught **us** to see the **we**. Surrounded by jeopardy but safe in the boat, we wait. We may be broken, but there is no reason to enjoy it. We must yet toil with our hands, with sickly bodies and imperfect families, with a lust for too many things we don't need and names deserving to be dragged through the mud because of it, but this is no reason to let the *Me* that's still here run loose and destroy who God has made **us** to be.

Far less than a cure for cancer, we need bread today. On the day your cancer prevents you from eating another bite, on the day it puts you into the ground, far less than bread, you need to die with forgiveness spoken over you by God. Dying means being divorced from evil, leaving it behind and going forward into a rest where the knowledge of Jesus will be the everlasting lifeblood of all you ever know. You might be tempted to cling to this dying world. But that is when this Holification, this setting apart, arises by faith alone, a living hunger for the real needs of this body and life. Today's bread. Tomorrow's peace.

THE FOURTH AND FIFTH
EDGES OF HOLIFICATION

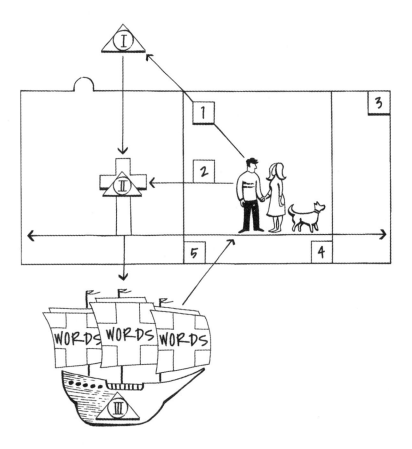

Prayer for enough, but no more, and
prayer for patience to overlook today

* **THE ONE HOLIFICATION OF THE CHRISTIAN:**
  THERE IS A GOD, AND THROUGH JESUS,
  HE IS YOUR FATHER.

* **THE FIRST EDGE OF HOLIFICATION:**
  PRAYER FOR MORE PRAYER

* **THE SECOND EDGE OF HOLIFICATION:**
  PRAYER FOR GOD TO SPEAK MORE

* **THE THIRD EDGE OF HOLIFICATION:**
  PRAYER FOR THINGS I DON'T WANT BUT NEED ANYWAY

* **THE FOURTH EDGE OF HOLIFICATION:**
  PRAYER FOR ENOUGH, BUT NO MORE

* **THE FIFTH EDGE OF HOLIFICATION:**
  PRAYER FOR PATIENCE TO OVERLOOK TODAY

{ With You there is forgiveness,
that You may be feared.
Psalm 130:4 }

THE SIXTH EDGE

Prayer for Others to Be Protected from Me

IMPROVEMENT!

That word seems so good. It seems so harmless. Who could argue with it? If you have a headache, life is better once you can take an aspirin. There's nothing wrong with eating when you're hungry. Helping others have a better standard of living is a great thing.

But *Improvement!* has a problem. Over time, covering up a headache can hide the undiagnosed cancer. Eating lunch will fill you for today, but it won't fill you for tomorrow. Jesus said that the poor will always be with us (Matthew 26:11; Mark 14:7; John 12:8). He also said, "Nation will rise against nation" (Matthew 24:7; Mark 13:8; Luke 21:10) and "You cannot make one hair white or black" (Matthew 5:36). What all of this means is that no matter how much *Improvement!* you manage to accrue, you cannot add one hour to your life (Matthew 6:27; Luke 12:25).

No matter how hard we try, humanity is not going to *Improvement!* our way out of world hunger, homelessness, or poverty. We won't achieve enduring political safety, an ever-improving economy, or world peace. Whether it's a painkiller, a quick lunch, or a peace accord signed by the United Nations, *Improvement!* is never more than a mask for these troubles. Filling the belly or disarming the war is always temporary. No matter how necessary it may be for the moment, it will never be good enough *forever*.

It is amazing how good we are at forgetting that **there is something terribly wrong** with a world that needs *Improvement!* in the first place. A world filled with headaches is not a good world. Achieving world peace can only be the goal of a world constantly at war. Ending world hunger is only possible in a world filled with starvation. Living longer, better lives can only be our ambition in a world filled with short lives and painful deaths.

INSTEAD OF MYSELF

Adam didn't just grab any old apple. He grabbed a particular fruit holding a particular knowledge because he believed that knowledge was the key to improving the world. God had already called the world **very good**. But that didn't stop Adam from thinking he could make the world *better than good*, particularly by making him*self better than good*. Adam's fall was the result of man's first ambition for *self-Improvement!* But in this quest to make himself *better than* **very good**, he only made the whole world worse.

Ever since, every last one of us has been born into that world, in which the best "good" we ever know isn't really **good** at all. It is a new, *Improved! less-than-good.*

Amazingly, rather than cease tinkering with what we tainted by trying to fix it, we've all inherited the bad habit of believing our only hope to get this *less-than-good* back to **very good** is to crank out more of the same ambition that cracked the cosmos in the first place. With a supernatural addiction, we venerate success. We *believe* in victory. We *trust* in triumph. With religious conviction, we worship *Improvement!*

> The serpent said to the woman, "You will not surely die. For God knows that when you eat of it your eyes will be opened, and you will be like God, knowing good and evil." Genesis 3:4–5

This is not the best of us. This is the *worst*. Far from leading to a better world, *Improvement!* often leads to a more deficient one. The fixes we find today create the problems that need to be fixed tomorrow. More victories for me means more losses for you. More food on my table means less food on someone else's. Even more attempts to love your neighbor, when done in the name of making yourself a *better* person, when done for your own *self-Improvement!*, only turn love into one more rung on the ladder of *Me*.

Love that only loves because it believes it will receive something in return is not actual love. If I try to be more loving toward you, but I do so only because I am trying to make myself into a more loving person, then I haven't really loved you at all. I have only acted *as if* I love you because I actually love *Me*. I have fabricated the outward illusion of love because *Me* believes those actions are the key to getting something else for myself.

> Love is patient and kind; love does not envy or boast; it is not arrogant. 1 Corinthians 13:4

Love inspired by *Improvement!* turns the "loved" into mere tools for personal satisfaction, all people in need into objects to be served only to serve the ultimate benefit of *Me*. Real love, real goodness, has no need to be compelled by such rewards, nor can it be inspired by threats of punishment. Talk of threats and rewards is always the tarnish of selfish ambition, of self-serving need. It is true that threats and rewards can hem our selfishness in. The

ECHO

thief is stopped from stealing by laws that make his life worse if he steals and better if he does not. But stopping the hand from stealing does not mean that the heart has ceased wanting to steal.

WHERE YOU'D RATHER GO

If you think about it, the fact that we are generally only inspired to good works by talk of threats and rewards betrays just how deep our slavish self-worship runs. Goodness is good in itself, but *Me* cannot bear this. To *Me*, goodness is an effort, a toil to be avoided if possible. If good works are to be done by *Me*, then they must have a *better* reason than goodness' sake. They must *merit* something more than themselves. They must ensure a personal advantage to be gained by doing them.

So, *Me* always turns "love" into law, and treats the law as a ladder to climb up to the new, improved *Me*. But even though actual love knows it won't be repaid, it loves **anyway**. That's why it's good! Without growth, without victory, without reward, without reason beyond the good of others, real love is willing to end up worse off than when it started. It knows that where you are doesn't matter, because you're not on a ladder. **Good things are worth doing** no matter what because they're good, regardless of how they might affect *Me*.

> For the love of Christ controls us, because we have concluded this: that one has died for all, therefore all have died; and He died for all, that those who live might no longer live for themselves but for Him who for their sake died and was raised. 2 Corinthians 5:14–15

The whole world believes that *being good* and *getting better* is what religion is all about. But Christian Holification slices through our addiction to *Improvement!* with the confession that deep down you don't want to get better. You don't want to live a truly righteous life in which you give everything away and have nothing to show for it. You don't want to do a bunch of good works from which you gain nothing. You still want to live the most wicked kind of life, the one in which you get to boast about your good works, in which you get to test them, to measure them and to find satisfaction in them.

The moment you look to yourself for satisfaction, you take your eyes off the vicarious satisfaction given to you freely in Jesus. To save you from this, Christianity does not grant you the power to rise up on your own, but rather the conviction to acknowledge the depths of your fall. Whatever improvements God works on you, they will not increase your ability to pat yourself on the back and tell yourself how much *better* you've become. Rather, Christian spirituality increases your ability to see more clearly how filthy you remain, to be honest about your continual lack of good-enough-ness, your perpetual, expected, shouldn't-be-surprised-at-it need for forgiveness.

> **Not by might, nor by power, but by My Spirit, says the LORD of hosts.** Zechariah 4:6

All these thistles stuck in your heart are still a threat, and Holification is not the ability to avoid them on your own. Your great weapon against them is not *strength*, but **weakness**. Not *progress*, but **redemption**. Not prayers for *power* but prayers for **help**. Not prayers for *self-affirmation* but for **salvation**. Not prayers for *pride*, but for **mercy**. Not *forgive Me, and give Me the Improvement! to stand on my own*, but **forgive us and lead us not into temptation**.

These are trepid, cowering words. They are words that can only be uttered by the quiet heart of people who know the meanness of their shape, that no matter how good we might have become outwardly, no matter what baggage we've left behind, we still carry around within us the constant desire to regress, the ever-present tendency to put *Me* first, the steadfast presence of unbelief.

Pride.

Hate.

Me.

So the Sixth Edge of Holification speaks the same plain, boring words that have been spoken in plain, boring churches by plain, boring Christians for millennia. **Lead us not into temptation**. They are words of profound conviction. Words of terrible honesty. Words of ultimate trust. The song of the broken who know it.

> **If I must boast, I will boast of the things that show my weakness.** 2 Corinthians 11:30

Make no mistake. Anyone can mutter an incantation, but no man of license may truly pray this prayer. No unbeliever may actually mean it when he says, *"Take my temptations away! Keep from me the freedoms to pursue them. Whatever You do, God, don't let me have my desires."* All talk of cheap grace must dry up here. All talk of measuring our progressive *Improvement!* must be smothered by faith in the embarrassing proportions of our incompetence, by the extravagant depths of our continued need.

This is not dead faith. This is extreme faith. The ever-present religion of the world ever echoes the opposite, even stealing the outward forms of Christianity in order to deceive us back into the poisonous hope of ambition. But the Sixth Edge of Holification is the antidote, the prayer prayed by a heart that has been brought to believe there is nothing to be done to truly improve the self. The self must simply be stopped, and only God has the power to stop it.

MORTIFICATION

The Spirit is willing. But the flesh is weak. You believe. You want to do better. But the *Me* you still dwell in has not improved. Not even a little bit. By faith alone, the newness of life you are given in Christ constantly, daily, moment by moment, runs right alongside that old man who still wants to make the entire universe all about *Me*. But God has already drowned that cantankerous bastard with the hard love of exposing his worthlessness, and He isn't about to let you mistake it. The Sixth Edge of Holification is the gift of never forgetting that you walk in danger all the way, and the greatest danger is you.

This is the real crossroads. All debates about works and grace, obedience and mercy, Law and Gospel will always revolve around this continual moment of either faith or unbelief in this most central tenet of hope: you have no hope but Jesus. No matter how much you do, *Me* cannot be improved. *Me* cannot be rehabilitated. *Me* cannot be saved, because *Me* is the very thing you most need to be saved **from**.

Me needs to be **killed**.

So, Jesus says to you, *"I have crucified your Me. It is finished. I have divorced you from evil. It is done. I promise."*

Immediately, Me cries out, "But I'm still here!"

*Because **Me can't believe it! Me won't believe it**. Me will not board this ship.*

Yet, **you are** aboard that ship. You are a Christian. You hear Jesus' words. There is no denying them. You therefore believe the impossible. You trust what is not seen or felt but only spoken by Him—that He has become your sin for you. Even the sinfulness you still carry with you, even the sins you have not committed but most surely will before the end, He took it all. Your whole life. Up to its last breath. Down with Him into the grave, all in order to bury your *Me* there but not leave you there. To three days later walk out carrying your new life with Him in the scars of His hands.

Baptized into His death.

This is not an easy thing to believe. No lip service to the Gospel lives here. This is a matter of heroic weakness. It is a gift of supernatural humiliation. The Sixth Edge of Holification is the ongoing murder of the fleshly pipe dream of *Improvement!* It is the spiritual opening of your eyes to see that it's all a smoke screen. It is the spiritual opening of your ears to hear that sanctification is not the Christian version of *self-Improvement!*, but the experience of getting used to the good news that no matter where you are, God is still reaching down His mighty hand to save you **from** *Me's* idolatry of yourself.

> *"My grace is enough,"* Jesus says.
>
> *"But I will cause more damage,"* you argue.
>
> *"My grace is enough,"* Jesus says again.
>
> *"But what if I chase another god, pierce myself with many pangs, abandon You and fall away?"*
>
> *"My grace is enough,"* Jesus says a third time (see 2 Corinthians 12:8–9).
>
> *"So there is nothing I can do to guarantee I remain saved?"*

There's the crux! Do you see what the heart does with that question?

God has spoken a vow. Jesus, King of kings and Lord of lords, has **sworn with an oath: My grace is *sufficient*.** In this oath, you have a declaration of total pardon and peace, a cease-fire from the eternal wrath of God. But *Me* not only seeks a better guarantee. *Me* thinks the only better guarantee is for *Me* to have some part to play in the final outcome of the matter!

> *"Is there nothing I can do to ensure that I remain in salvation?"*

No. **Nothing**. You are helpless. *But* Jesus has promised that **He intends to keep you** saved.

> *"How can I be certain I won't betray Him?"*

You can't be certain in you. **But you can be certain** *in* Him.

The desire to be certain in your*self* is the entire problem in the first place. That's the thorns. That's the sin. That is what must be pulled out. The only way to do that is by **grace alone**.

Grace must murder *Me's* desire to trust in *Me* again. Faith lives on the knowledge that Jesus won't let you get that far. Christianity will keep setting you apart by supernaturally renewing your mind to recognize the honest and totally infuriating, firsthand, painful knowledge of your thorns. If anything increases, it will be the evidence of your brokenness; the bogus hypocrisy of every attempt to "righteousify" yourself will fail in your face.

This mortification is the real, continually repeating experience of having to trust by **faith alone** that you are still being saved. That your only hope is God keeping you from destroying yourself. That the greatest work you will ever do is asking God to stop you. That Jesus has it handled. That His righteousness needs no *Improvement!*

BUT ISN'T THIS A RECIPE FOR LICENSE?

Only if you don't believe it. Only if you're still trapped in the reprobate mind of thinking that goodness is only good when it brings a benefit to *Me*. Only if by **lead us not into temptation** you really mean *ignore me while I do whatever I want*. But no Christian means that. Even in weakness, Christianity is the Spirit-driven desire to be free from evil, which by definition means hunger for the good. **Lead us not into temptation** can only mean "stop my mind, mouth, and hands from bringing harm to others."

Contrary to *Me's* endless protestation, such a **faith-alone** experience of trusting in **grace alone** does not breed the freedom to hate, but rather revives the possibility of real love. It quiets you, slows you down, forces you back to the authentic goodness of the cross, the absolution, the hope in another who is better than you.

And why not do evil that good may come?—as some people slanderously charge us with saying. Their condemnation is just. Romans 3:8

Unbelievers don't care about such things. Unbelievers aren't mortified by their thorns. But you are. That is faith. That is **repentance**. That is hunger for the good.

Far from quenching your desire to progress in works of righteousness, the Sixth Edge of Holification only increases it. Far from stopping you from improving the way you view and treat others, your desire for a better today will only be propelled, so much so that you will disdain the meager whitewashed improvements the world keeps boasting of as if they were real answers. With your poverty of spirit not evaporated but exposed, with your humiliation not hidden but revealed, with your self-loathing amplified in the most healthy and godly of ways, the Sixth Edge of Holification will well up within you. This Edge will give you faith that the world ought to be better than it is, not because we can make it that way, but because of who God the Creator actually is.

THIS IS THE BEST WORK

All truly good works flow from believing that God's work is your only hope. To know God is to be discontent with the diseased mire of *Improvement!* You have been pulled from the morass, enlivened by a life that exists outside of your*self,* dead in the wounds of Jesus. Now the Sixth Edge of Holification is the prayer of a man awakened to see the false promises of the *ladder.* It is the plea of a man for whom the worst thing imaginable is finding himself climbing up it and off the ship again, suddenly drowning in that stagnant, stormy, chaotic sea of endless need for *Improvement!*

Making things better does not live or die on whether it makes things better for *Me.* The ultimate liberty is the conviction that there is **nothing to lose** because everything rests in someone else's hands. Having been awakened to your neediness at its most gruesome level, you've been set within this other man's power to divorce you from your neediness. **To forgive you.** To make what you cannot fix or change or achieve **overlooked. Passed by. Paid for.**

It is impossible for such faith to lie dormant. It is impossible for such faith to not have **results.** You have been set apart from the depraved mind of the broken, busy, manic, dying, climbing world, made to believe that even at your best you are at your worst, still needing to be saved. You have been promised that you are pardoned into a better good. You have tasted the real hope and trust in the one man who has proven capable of managing all things by Himself, and you have the vision of that promised eon proven in the bloody scars of this truly Good King. Your human psyche cannot possibly lie idle or live comatose now. You will spring forth. You will arise.

This is the first resurrection. Newness of life **will be** a potent desire to see in the Ten Important Things about Being Creation a world so much greater than the atrocity we have made of it that in childlike eagerness, your born-again Christian soul must and will begin to contend for that goodness **right now**. But you will do so not by believing that such goodness is achieved by you becoming better. It is achieved by God stopping all of us from becoming worse.

You've been taught by God to pray for the right prayers, to ask God to keep speaking the right answers, to pray against the things you want and for the things you need, and to pray for today, because today is enough. Now you will learn to pray for tomorrow rightly as well—not as the time when we go here and there and do this and that, but as the time from which we still need to be saved, the day on which you still will need God to protect both you and others from yourself.

> **We were buried therefore with Him by baptism into death, in order that, just as Christ was raised from the dead by the glory of the Father, we too might walk in newness of life.** Romans 6:4

To the old man, the mortification of *Improvement!* is reason to give up on helping others, since for him, it can now bring no benefit. But while the world worships only self-*Improvement!*, you will stand set apart. You will stand **holy**, euphoric in the faith that just because whitewashing the tombs isn't good enough, that hardly stops you from caring for those who are about to die.

The Sixth Edge of Holification is the spiritual gift of seeing the evil within you and without, more than you have ever seen before. The thorns will not seem less, but greater. Your brokenness will not feel further away, but closer. But your hunger to be rid of it will rise exponentially. You will daily find yourself unable to stand living in it any longer. So you will be inspired, not only to pray **lead us not** further into it, but **save us from it!** You will long for the day of the coming Eon of Replenishing, filled with zeal for what Jesus has promised to come again and do, burdened with anticipation for the real fulfilled experience of deliverance from evil.

But that's another chapter.

THE SIXTH EDGE OF HOLIFICATION

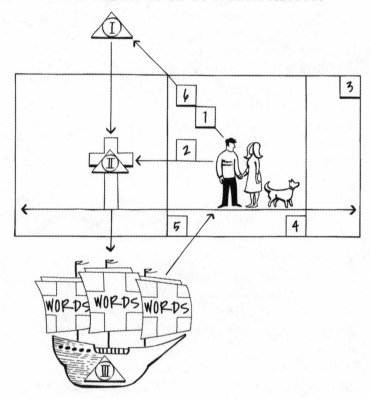

Prayer for others to be protected from me

* THE ONE HOLIFICATION OF THE CHRISTIAN:
THERE IS A GOD, AND THROUGH JESUS,
HE IS YOUR FATHER.

* THE FIRST EDGE OF HOLIFICATION:
PRAYER FOR MORE PRAYER

* THE SECOND EDGE OF HOLIFICATION:
PRAYER FOR GOD TO SPEAK MORE

* THE THIRD EDGE OF HOLIFICATION:
PRAYER FOR THINGS I DON'T WANT BUT NEED ANYWAY

* THE FOURTH EDGE OF HOLIFICATION:
PRAYER FOR ENOUGH, BUT NO MORE

* THE FIFTH EDGE OF HOLIFICATION:
PRAYER FOR PATIENCE TO OVERLOOK TODAY

* THE SIXTH EDGE OF HOLIFICATION:
PRAYER FOR OTHERS TO BE PROTECTED FROM ME

> *I wait for the LORD, my soul*
> *waits, and in His word I hope.*
>
> Psalm 130:5

THE SEVENTH EDGE

Prayer for the World to End. Soon.

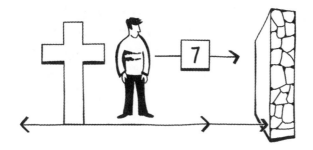

THE DAYS ARE EVIL,
AND IT'S ALL GOD'S FAULT

Christianity is a terribly disappointing religion. Discontent with Christianity usually takes a while. The initial rush fills you with zeal and passion. Invigoration. But once the adrenaline wears off, once the **mortification** sets in, the obvious flaws become much harder to ignore. Schisms among the body of Christ start to become more apparent, more frustrating, more insurmountable. The obstacles you, in your zeal, thought would be easily overcome once everyone felt the way you did, turn out to be the very things others are willing to fight against you for. You even find that your attempts to overcome all this sometimes become the very heart of the problem that perpetuates it. The poor behavior of other Christians gradually wears on you. If you don't start to act against them in return, at the very least you begin to look down on them.

The many institutions that have risen up to support the Church show themselves to be not just inefficient, but often more interested

ECHO

in their own preservation than in the mission the Scriptures speak of. Some congregations are culturally selling-out their heritage. Others rot away in dusty obtuseness. The reins are held by the power hungry or the childish. There are pastors who make no sense when they preach, or they make far too much sense in the totally wrong direction. There are brothers and sisters who wouldn't attend a Bible study if their eternal life depended on it, families with fracturing marriages, parents with rebellious children . . . the list is endless.

> They will say, "Where is the promise of His coming? For ever since the fathers fell asleep, all things are continuing as they were from the beginning of creation." 2 Peter 3:4

You start to wonder why the salvation of the world didn't actually save the world. You start to wonder where the God who is preached as having saved you actually is. Supposedly this Jesus guy ascended into heaven with all authority in heaven and earth having been given to Him, and He is reigning over all things. Supposedly He sent this Third Person of the Trinity called the Holy Spirit to inhabit the hearts of Christians. But He certainly did not bring the relief from frustration, suffering, and sin that you would have brought. He certainly is not curbing the evils of the world as He rules from the right hand of God the way you think He should. That's even the reason you pray! The bulk of what you think ought to be happening is not. Much of what you ask for seems to be ignored, or at the very least answered with an ever-quiet "No."

God did not save you the way you would have done it, and this is what makes God Himself the most disappointing thing of all.

> Have you believed because you have seen Me? Blessed are those who have not seen and yet have believed. John 20:29

Jesus is risen, so the teaching goes, but the world keeps falling apart. The churches keep wasting their time. Everyone else keeps living like jerks. You keep thinking you're the only one who doesn't.

It's all God's fault. He promises you are already saved, but this salvation seems to be *doing nothing*. It's *just* a promise. *Just words*. That's it. A blank check, but no bank in sight. A box of gold, but in the middle of a desert. Faith alone, but not a wit of power to show for it. A newfound love for the Ten Important Things, but no ability to truly put them into practice. You aren't free from the evil yet. *Me* isn't perfect yet. You're still in the heart of the storm, where war, inequality, tyranny, and death taint everything. The **cross** has become more than just a story about your Savior. It becomes a firsthand experience. You're still **cursed**.

DEFINITELY NOT CONQUERORS

The worst idol of all is still buried back beneath the carpets in your tent. *Me*, ever with you, still thinks that the only good reason to have a religion is to make things better. For *Me*. Right *Now*.

But Christianity makes things worse. Christians aren't set apart by our victories. What's unique about Christianity is how regularly it's defeated. It is not our lives that are most precious to God, but our deaths. The more zeal you take with you into the Ten Important Things, the more they wreck you. No matter how many times you repent and try again, you still can't do enough to ease the conscience. You still can't fix everything you keep deciding to improve. You still can't perfect even a moment so that it stays satisfactory. In fact, while the world keeps deciding that *good enough* is the same thing as **very good**, the brutal disappointment of it all becomes more and more impossible to ignore.

My God, My God, why have You forsaken Me? Mark 15:34

It is your present crucifixion, in body and in will. Jesus saved you, but that just means you now get to see your death coming. Get to know it for all that it's worth. It doesn't give you anything worth having now. Except for that promise. Except for the hope.

Being set apart by God does not save you from the present experience of evil, including and especially that which keeps welling up from within yourself. Holification doesn't save you **from** the experience of your sin. It saves you **through** it. In the midst of it. Over and against it. In spite of it. Through the fiery trial that is no pleasure cruise, but does leave you every day less a believer in yourself and ever more a believer in Jesus.

> Who shall separate us from the love of Christ? Shall tribulation, or distress, or persecution, or famine, or nakedness, or danger, or sword? . . . No, in all these things we are more than conquerors through Him who loved us. Romans 8:35, 37

But if you can't admit that being forced to wait like this is a bit disappointing, then you face the greatest threat of all. You face the danger of the *Me* within you convincing you that this life is something other than it really is. Once Christianity does not give *Me* the results that *Me* wants, *Me* won't take that sitting down. *Me* will try to find a way to make *Me* happy anyway. Rather than admit the horrid reality that Jesus is a great disappointment, *Me* will set about trying to *justify* Jesus! In a bizarre turn of events, *Me* will devote everything to pretending that Jesus actually has been the God that *Me* wanted all along. *Me* will redefine words, harbor doubts, and try to pretend that the inborn hatred of God is actually love.

Allowing *Me* to run rampant in your conscience like this can only slowly bleed you dry. It sets loose the deep, malicious sentiment of your natural heart to frolic in your conscience without boundaries. It lets your thorns and all their gory horror hide right in front of you, in plain sight, so prickly that even while all the world might be able to see that your real problem is a delusion about the present, you remain hardened and unable to just step back for a moment and let grace be **grace**.

DELIVER US FROM THE PRESENT

It is easy enough to pray **deliver us from evil** when we don't think that the greatest evil is *Me*. It is easy enough to pray **deliver us from evil** when we don't believe that today is a day of clouds and deep darkness, that this world is a barren waste full of fire and slow, dry death. It is easy enough to pray **deliver us from evil** when we really mean, *"Deliver Me from everyone else, and stop the world from getting in my way,"* or when we mean, *"God, don't do things differently than I would do them."*

But that is not the Seventh Edge of Christian Holification. These are the prayers of immaturity. These are the false faiths of ladder-climbing spirituality. These are the prayers of *Me*. These prayers wonder why God, who claimed to have saved *Me*, isn't helping *Me* get further up and higher into whatever I might want at the moment. These prayers end by blaming God for my own failures.

Christianity is a terribly disappointing religion because it really is the death of *Me*. All the pious, knee-jerk reactions against admitting our Christian disappointment with Jesus as God are just the last subterfuge of *Me*, trying to find a way out from under the deep implications of the cross. The righteousness you've been promised doesn't get to be the righteousness *Me* creates. The faith that has been regenerated in you doesn't get to be faith in yourself. The resurrection you've been united to doesn't stop the decay, the despair, the tragedy.

Instead, Christianity digs down deep into the center of your stony, puss-filled heart, breaks open the rotten root of your soul, and exposes the poisoned dart that lives there, dragging it and all its barbed animosity for the real God up and out through the center of your chest. Once that poisoned dart is exposed, you can't do anything but see it, confess it, call it what it really is, and beg that God would stop waiting around and end the world already.

> Grace to you and peace from God our Father and the Lord Jesus Christ, who gave Himself for our sins to deliver us from the present evil age, according to the will of our God and Father. Galatians 1:3–4

It will be earthshaking. It will be world rending. When Jesus returns with all His replenishment to deliver us from ourselves, to resurrect us into the new and eternal era of God's man, then we will see the evils of this present darkness vanish like a mist before a storm. Then we will see the ancient enemy and all his lies, that dragon named Satan, cast into a pit of burning sulfur from which he will never rise again. But these great futures will all be great because we will also see then the joy of our thorns wrenched from our souls by the root, our *Mes* mortified forever, dead and gone from **us**.

ONCE AND FOR ALL

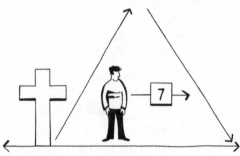

The end of the world is what we pray for, because it is the prayer for the end to our broken selves. Christianity awakens you into this cry through the midst of your disappointments, under the weight of your crosses, as one experience with your mortification. Holiness dies and yet calls out to the same God you are enraged with, the same God who is killing you, "**Come back!**"

Wandering in the spiritual darkness of God-hating, you are born again into simultaneous **God-trusting**. The real question is not whether this warfare taken up by the Holy Spirit of God and against your *Me* flesh is true. The real question is how long you pretend that it is not.

How long will you be a Christian while denying the full expression of our hope and subjecting yourself to the delusion that you don't really hate God? How long will your faith be able to stand up under the lie that you don't constantly, subconsciously blame Him for every little wrong thing that happens to you? How long will you let the pretensions, the sanctimony, the faux faith, and the echo of ladder-climbing deceive you into insisting that there is nothing left for God to justify in your life, nothing left for Him to set you apart from, no need to remain in the state of **being saved**?

It won't stop. Christianity never matures past this prayer. You aren't going to stop coveting, and with it, bringing down on your head the burning coals of disappointment. You won't ever stop making idols of everything you have or do not have. This idol-making is nothing but trying to stop yourself from understanding what it really means to be delivered from evil.

God is going to do it. He will put you in the grave, and it will be done. He will end this world, and it will be accomplished. The Seventh Edge of Christian Holification, the final prayer and the ultimate freedom, is the euphoric faith to see it coming and give in to the disappointment that hopes in that freedom. To be set apart to despise the present age. To beg the God who rules it to put it to an end. To see beyond the ramshackle tent of this age another one, with foundations set deep and a Good King who will give yet more goodness.

You can pray for the end of the world only when you have faith in a resurrection. You can long for the fires of judgment only when you have faith in a justifying judge. You can face death with the confidence of a Christian only when you are confident that ending this thorny life isn't such a bad idea at all.

No matter who you are, your life won't end just because the world does. All the edges of Holification add up to the bizarre gift, the alien freedom, of learning to embrace this. To rest on it. To let your disappointment with God vent. To find it, to feel it, to admit it, without fear of condemnation for it, because you now know that there is no condemnation for those who are in Christ Jesus.

This doesn't mean you relish your hatred. This doesn't mean you try to justify this disappointment with not being God yourself. It only means that, as unjustifiable as your disappointment is, you believe that you've nonetheless been justified by Jesus.

Deliver us from evil teaches us to pray the final, fearful truth of Christianity: I have no lasting hope so long as I remain the *Me* who lives in this thorny body and its resulting broken age. It's all my fault. My burden. It's even my daily desire to keep it this way, to stay here, to get as much out of this thorny life as I can, and avoid leaving it at all costs. But **I believe** that wrong has already been crucified in the body of Jesus. So now my capstone prayer, the final edge that all the other edges have prepared me for, prays for an end to everything I might build, everything I might be, everything I work so hard to become. Trusting God's work, Jesus' name, and the Spirit's words, I believe that even while *Me* will refuse to believe right up to the day I die, the hard-love hope is that one day soon God Himself will finally stop me from harming others by divorcing my body from this age of darkness and vale of tears.

ECHO

Seeing the darkness, feeling the evil, being the disappointment, I ask God to come sooner rather than later. While one thorny finger points at the world and blames God for the mess, the other redeemed hand grips tight on that poisoned splinter protruding from my breast and yanks at it with all the power of God's Word.

It is forgiven.

You, who were dead in your trespasses and the uncircumcision of your flesh, God made alive together with Him, having forgiven us all our trespasses, by canceling the record of debt that stood against us with its legal demands. This He set aside, nailing it to the cross. Colossians 2:13–14

THE HARD UNWORK OF WAITING

Day by day, I continue to strive against God's will, to see through it all and make-believe in a different Him. I try to replace His words with my own, to put myself in the deciding authority, to take for my body before my neighbor's good, to make of community and family a set of tools for serving my flesh, to have whatever I desire no matter whether I've earned it or not, and to be lauded and praised while I deride and chastise all others around me. All of this I do because I covet what I am not: God.

The Seventh Edge awakens me to rejoice in the condemnation of this. It lets me **echo** it. It is the euphoria of the regeneration that exults in the final damnation of *Me*. *Me* is going to burn. But it has happened already in Jesus. Now **We**, the **Assembling of Believers**, walk day-by-day in the obedient hope that this Lord who began the good work of delivering us from evil by taking it on Himself in the cross will finish it off by killing *Me*, whether in the present or on That Day. But He won't kill *Me* in such a way that I do not rise. No. I will look on God with my own eyes. For as bad as *Me* will continue to be until the day that God puts him in the ground, even so I've been given the words: "**I know that my Redeemer lives**" (Job 19:25).

It is only natural to think that Jesus' taking our cross would mean that your cross would vanish. The Seventh Holification is the honest awareness that your cross hasn't vanished. But every time you confess your sin, you take up your cross in a way set apart from the world. Every time you look for the next life, you set your stake on freedom from this one. Every time the flickering wick of hope wavers within you, you believe that you are exactly what Jesus has promised you to be.

Sin, death, and the devil are the problem, but only because I let them be so. And I cannot—I will not—put an end to it. The Holification of the Christian is the constant recentering of your disappointment from where you naturally project it back to where it really ought to be: in *Me*. In yourself. You must decrease, while Jesus increases. The sin that so easily entangles, the endless habits of your thorny heart, are not overcome by a perfect, active fulfillment of the Ten Important Things as they are written, but in their inversion as they are prayed. Jesus, ever forgiving and patient, says, **"Ask the Father to do what you cannot."**

In putting everything in subjection to Him, He left nothing outside His control. At present, we do not yet see everything in subjection to Him. But we see Him. Hebrews 2:8–9

Pray: "True God, whom we know only through Jesus, make it so that we pray only to You. Speak Your Word so that we hear and believe it. Bend our wills so that they are in line with Yours. Give us only what we truly need most. And forgive us for wanting everything else. Forgive us into forgiving one another. Let the covetousness of our hearts not overwhelm us, but teach us to hope for the end of the world, rather than ever seek to avoid it."

Pray then like this. Matthew 6:9

The more you pray the words Jesus taught, the more you are acknowledging you do not yet have what they compel you to ask for. But you are set apart to believe that you will have these things. You are awakened to know that your faith in the promise is greater than your sight in the present. Your new bondage to the Sanctified One is a freedom greater than any present answer to prayer could ever pretend to be.

When we admit in the same breath both our hatred of God and our need for Him, the First Important Thing—which we have beat our heads, hearts, and minds against from the start of time and the start of this book—is restored to its proper place. It is not the world-altering experience *Me* would create. It comes with no fire, wind, quake, angel dust, or prophetic wonder to tickle the fancy of your thorns. But the First Important Thing is eternally more powerful in its invisible, untestable moment of believing the unbelievable. Yes, **there is a God**, and yes, **I am not Him**, and yes, **because of Jesus, this is a very good thing after all**.

THE SEVENTH EDGE OF HOLIFICATION

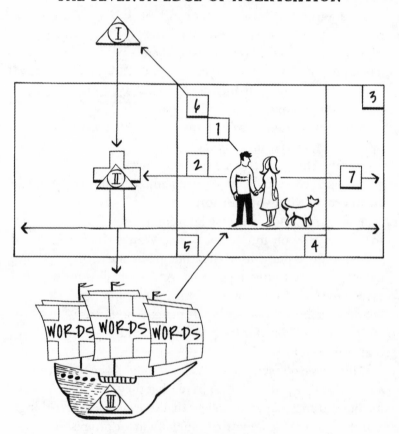

Prayer for the world to end. Soon.

THE SEVEN EDGES OF
CHRISTIAN HOLIFICATION

* **THE ONE HOLIFICATION OF THE CHRISTIAN:**
  THERE IS A GOD, AND THROUGH JESUS,
  HE IS YOUR FATHER.

* **THE FIRST EDGE OF HOLIFICATION:**
  PRAYER FOR MORE PRAYER

* **THE SECOND EDGE OF HOLIFICATION:**
  PRAYER FOR GOD TO SPEAK MORE

* **THE THIRD EDGE OF HOLIFICATION:**
  PRAYER FOR THINGS I DON'T WANT BUT NEED ANYWAY

* **THE FOURTH EDGE OF HOLIFICATION:**
  PRAYER FOR ENOUGH, BUT NO MORE

* **THE FIFTH EDGE OF HOLIFICATION:**
  PRAYER FOR PATIENCE TO OVERLOOK TODAY

* **THE SIXTH EDGE OF HOLIFICATION:**
  PRAYER FOR OTHERS TO BE PROTECTED FROM ME

* **THE SEVENTH EDGE OF HOLIFICATION:**
  PRAYER FOR THE WORLD TO END. SOON.

PART FIVE

UNBROKEN TRUTH WORTH REPEATING

THE CHRISTIAN ECHO / THE CHRISTIAN CATECHISM

> *Oh, what mad, senseless fools are we! While we must
> ever live and dwell among such mighty enemies as
> the devils, we still despise our weapons and defense,
> . . . and we are too lazy to look at or think of them!*
>
> LC Preface 15

THE CRUX OF THE MATTER

Resetting the Mold

Christianity has **Three Foundational Realities**. They are the Ten Important Things about Being Creation, the Three Elements and Five Results of the Gospel, and the Seven Edges of Christian Holification. As I gave away a few chapters ago, these aren't any spectacular insight on my part. They are the ancient Christian *catechism*: the Ten Commandments, the Apostles' Creed, and the Lord's Prayer, spun just enough to hopefully get you to engage them from a new direction.

No matter which faction or tradition of Christianity you find yourself in, this Echo has always been repeated in one form or another. Any "*Christianity*" that does not have at least the substance of them is, quite frankly, not Christianity. It is a *distorted echo*. A mimic. A facsimile. A sect. A schism. A heresy.

A lie.

A small misstep at the beginning will eventually change the entire direction of a journey. These Three Foundational Realities are the road map. The compass. The north star. The pavement of the road itself. They are the *mere* Christianity that many claim to believe, even as they just as surely are quickly fading from view in the postmodern "church" landscape.

And now, O sons, listen to me, and be attentive to the words of my mouth. Proverbs 7:24

If you lose one, you will eventually lose the others. For they are also a whole. A symbiotic, connecting, overlapping, informing, and interpenetrating total. Their attributes ebb and flow and are shared, so that at times all that they teach can be reduced to one of them. But they are distinct, not to be confused or mingled so as to destroy their clarity, ever expandable, with more layers to discover beneath their surface.

Shallow enough for the smallest child to be washed with their words, their depths are fathomless enough to drown the whole world in a flood that brings both death and life at once. We've barely begun to plumb their depths. To begin with, the Creed contains much more than just the Three Elements of the Gospel. **Who Jesus Is** begins before His incarnation and birth. Before He is the Son of David, He is first the Son of His Father in heaven. That Father is a person, the fountainhead of the eternal Trinity, the Divine Majesty beyond all we could ask or imagine. Yet we have almost ignored Him so far.

In the same way, **What Jesus Did** when He ascended into heaven was more than just sit down on a throne. As He told His apostles, "If I do not go away, the Helper will not come to you. But if I go, I will send Him to you" (John 16:7). So it was that yet another person, the Holy Spirit, proceeded from the Father and the Son down to earth to be another comforter, the eternal preacher of all the words Jesus left us.

This mysterious relationship of the three persons who share the triune majesty of God is simply beyond the scope of this book to explore. But what we can see is how the roles of the Father and the Spirit extend the central Echo of the Gospel up and out into two separate "articles." With Jesus at the center, their work presses both forward and backward into the wider Echo.

The Father, "who created heaven and earth," is the **designer** of the Ten Important Things about Being Creation. The entire world, with all its moral and natural laws, is really just an extension of that most basic **First Article of the Creed**: "I believe in God, the Father Almighty, Maker of heaven and earth." From those words, His work leaps forward through **there is a God** and **God speaks**, displaying who He is in the order of His perfect design, and ultimately driving all minds back to our need for Him with the covetous discontent that springs only from our negligence in acknowledging His place. So the Ten Commandments tell us everything we need to know about the Father, including how we have failed Him, how we have broken His world, and how surely we bear a burden of guilt in this matter.

In the same way that **God the Father** extends **Who Jesus Is** back to the original design of the Ten Commandments, **the Holy Spirit** ties **What Jesus Did** forward to the present, manifesting the Results of the Gospel in the Lord's Prayer. The Spirit, as Paul tells us, "helps us in our weakness. For we do not know what to pray for as we ought, but the Spirit Himself intercedes for us" (Romans 8:26). The Spirit inspires us to pray the Lord's Prayer, not our own wills, for all of the edges of that prayer rub against

THE FIVE RESULTS OF THE GOSPEL		THE THIRD ARTICLE OF THE APOSTLES' CREED	
		I believe in the Holy Spirit,	
The First Result of the Gospel:	The Assembling of Believers	the holy Christian church,	
The Second Result of the Gospel:	(around) The Fellow-Shape of Believers	the communion of saints,	
The Third Result of the Gospel:	(to deliver) The Divorce from Evil	the forgiveness of sins,	
The Fourth Result of the Gospel:	(which results in) The Immortalization of the Body	the resurrection of the body,	
The Fifth Result of the Gospel:	(and) The Eon of Replenishing	and the life everlasting.	

our nature. Rather than the vain kind of spirituality that only babbles and repeats magical words without understanding, the Spirit's work within us is to awaken us to pray with our minds, to believe that the words mean something, and to seek that meaning once again in Jesus.

All the requests built into the Lord's Prayer are petitions for the Five Results of the Gospel to come into your midst. Those effects that Jesus guaranteed in His cross, His Spirit teaches us to long for and to ask of Him. The Lord's Prayer is thus the **Third Article of the Creed**, which makes us hunger for the future, where our hope will be transformed into sight. Jesus will come again,

THE SEVEN EDGES OF HOLIFICATION		THE LORD'S PRAYER
The One Holification of the Christian:	There is a God, and through Jesus, He is your Father.	Our Father, who art in heaven,
The First Edge of Holification:	Prayer for more prayer	hallowed be Thy name,
The Second Edge of Holification:	Prayer for God to speak more	Thy kingdom come,
The Third Edge of Holification:	Prayer for things I don't want	Thy will be done on earth as it is in heaven.
The Fourth Edge of Holification:	Prayer for enough, but no more	Give us this day our daily bread;
The Fifth Edge of Holification:	Prayer for patience to overlook today	and forgive us our trespasses as we forgive those who trespass against us;
The Sixth Edge of Holification:	Prayer for others to be protected from me	and lead us not into temptation,
The Seventh Edge of Holification:	Prayer for the world to end. Soon.	but deliver us from evil. For Thine is the kingdom and the power and the glory forever and ever. Amen.

and the Seven Edges of our Holification all turn out to be one sanctification that hungers for That Day to hurry up.

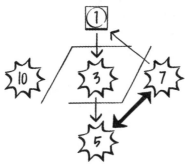

As God extends Himself among the fallen children of mankind in order to make His name holy once again, He is assembling for Himself a people restored to faith. The Bible calls these people the Church, a word that originally meant "gathering." Set apart and unified in Jesus' teaching, **the Church** is a "kingdom . . . not of this world" (John 18:36). This kingdom is not a place but a people, priests formed into the fellow-shape of trusting Jesus as sufficiently capable of dealing with that wall between us and the Father.

> For all have sinned and fall short of the glory of God, and are justified by His grace as a gift, through the redemption that is in Christ Jesus, whom God put forward as a propitiation by His blood, to be received by faith. Romans 3:23–25

Brought under Him, a new common-unity emerges, a community founded on the mutual desire to submit our wills to His will. This desire is both created and amplified by the promise that His highest will is to divorce us from our evil without also destroying us. Rather than condemn us, what God wants more than anything else is to forgive us our debts. To that end, His great holifying work to set us apart from the present evil age is done by waking us up to our jeopardy, convincing us that "sin" is **sin**, a threat to the joy and peace of both ourselves and others.

By this faith in our problem, we are driven to cry out for protection from temptation to cast ourselves off the boat. Even as we recognize that the danger will not end so long as we wait with this treasure of faith kept in jars of clay, with the rest of creation, we long with eager expectation for that moment when what is mortal in our bodies will be clothed in immortality. We pray for delivery from the evils of the corruption and the futility in this age, fully knowing that its ending means the replenished incorruptibility of an everlasting life to come. To believe all this, to hear it, to look for it, to cling to it, and to long for it is the sanctifying work of the Holy Spirit upon you.

Perfection will wait. It is the chief end of Christian sanctification now to believe in your imperfection and find the answer in Jesus. His coming. His doing. His return.

Even as we saw that the petitions of the Lord's Prayer teach us to pray for the Ten Commandments to be fulfilled, so also faith, which is the Gospel's ultimate result, fulfills the Commandments now in the one sanctification of no longer looking only to ourselves like hungry little idolaters, but now looking back and forward at once. Through Jesus. To the God who made us, no longer nameless but "Our Father" from beginning to end.

WORTH REPEATING. AGAIN.

There is a God, and you are not Him.

You wish you were, and in your vain efforts to prove it, you end up naming all other manner of created things "God" instead.

But getting God's name wrong has no power over Him. His essential desire for good cannot be dissuaded by the evil imaginations of our hearts. Our lies have not stopped God from speaking true things to us anyway.

Rather than destroy us all with a flick of the wrist, God has sustained His design of the cosmos, keeping it rutted like a well-laid track through a ravine.

No matter how hard we might try to overturn His design, we are always funneled by its natural authority back into what He made us to be.

Our bodies remain who we are, whether we despise them or worship them. The needs of the body remain the most pressing, present experience of every personal life. No matter how grossly the modern mind may have taught us to disdain the production and rearing of children, none of us escape the natural urges for touch, for trust, for nature to take its course.

No one desires to live an entire life forever alone. No one truly wants only *Me* and no other.

Authority, body, and community are the roots on which every society must be built. Everybody must be fed, and any man who randomly kills other bodies must be stopped. Just as no one can escape the natural implications of mating, neither can the mass self-sterilization of young women keep them from believing that their carnal lover ought to be committed to something more than a passing act, that sexuality should in some manner be connected to "love," and that "love" should come with some element of "trust." When children are not murdered in the womb, bearing them consistently compels both parents to face the reality of the **other**, to commit some portion of life to something other than *Me*. While some will always reject this sacrificial shift, the majority of us are still curbed by our design to see our authority over children as a duty to care, oftentimes against our personal interest and benefit.

None of these are mere opinions. When they are assumed to be options, it is because they are laws designed into us. They are more than just an idea on which to build civilization. They are its definition. Societies fall when they abandon the design that makes them, and they are inevitably replaced by new civilizations that build on that design instead. But human good increases when we believe in what we are designed to be and seek it.

Where this happens, where the quality of life for everyone improves because of it, it is only natural to look for reasons and times, places and chances to enjoy the things of this earth with one another.

Whether it is watching stars fall on a summer evening or enjoying the warm crackle of a dead tree set ablaze midwinter (chestnuts optional), joy exists for us to share in the endless stuff of the cosmos and the benefits that stuff brings to body, community, and civilization. Our present gluttonous consumption and over-industrialized hoarding of these goods is not the fault of the goods themselves, but of our rebellious greed.

It is that self-driven hunger, shared by us all, that is the reason a good name is not just hard to find.

A good name is impossible to keep. Whether it is stealing my neighbor's donkey or getting a speeding ticket from the authorities, my name is destroyed when I break obvious laws. No matter how you might feel about it, you have likely earned the majority of criticisms and complaints that have been leveled against you, even as you have likely slandered many people who did not deserve half of what you said about them. Even so, none of us abandon our names. Though tarnished, they still remain our greatest pride. This is because your name is more than a bare, primal sound. It is no bark or cry. In a broken world—full of lies, thefts, adulteries, hurt, harm, rebellion, ignorance, false gods, and unbelief—no matter who you are, words still mean something.

Your name is still who you actually are because it is a law. The world is **commanded** to be this way. The God who is not you, who is His own name, has made it so. He has spoken it into being, encapsulating all that He has called us to be as His creatures in this life of body, society, and creation.

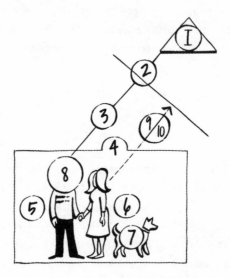

By design, this is all you need. Nothing can make us happy apart from this simplicity, which is always given freely as a gift. It is a whole, healthy, and sound. Only our twisted hunger to be more than mere **creature** has turned the experience into the thorny mess that it is. But it is that twist, that covetous belief that what should have been **very good** could be *better*, that has caused us to embark on the foolhardy quest to make gods out of everything except for the God who made the rest of it.

Even now, our broken experience is still sustained by Him. He **allows** it. He has allowed the problem of our evil to plague us, but only in order to save us from it. Creation continues to be tied to these Ten Important Things so that even all our thorns combined together cannot undo them.

All our chaos cannot unhinge the harmony. All our lawbreaking cannot overturn the laws, and this is **good news**. Your body will stop. Not only your body, but your family, your town, your civilization, your things, your name. All that you build, all that you do, all that you give, no matter what they say about it at your funeral or engrave on your tomb, will be forgotten, buried beneath the pile of dust. *But* the almighty hand that first created the heavens and the earth will go on. The God who is the **First Foundational Reality**, the Creator who first **commanded Ten Words** to be the way the world is, is bigger than all our chaos. More! He has, in sheer goodwill, also revealed the **Second Foundational Reality**: the stunning revelation that He sent Himself to become one of us.

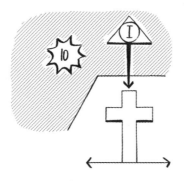

It is not the history of Jesus that defies the law and structure of the universe. It is not His resurrection from the dead that is unbelievable. It is not His incarnation's inversion of physics, time, and space that truly breaks the mold of human reason. Rather, it is the fact that God could have built a second creation from scratch, right at the beginning, right when we fell. He could have swept aside the old, broken order of the Ten Things and made a new order perfected to stand on its own.

But He didn't.

Instead, He spoke the **Second Foundational Reality** into the midst of the first one. Rather than destroy our *less-than-good-but-now-worse* (and certainly *not-very-good-anymore*) universe, He fulfilled and completed it. He looked down on the world that wanted to be its own god, the man who wanted to replace the God who made all things, and in His mind-bending mercy, He chose to become one with us to save us from the attempt. He overturned and absorbed the thorniness of Adam, the brokenness of earth, by taking humanity up into Himself, into the very inapproachable

Godhead. He did not change who He was. He changed who we are. God mingled with His creation. He became the human race.

Jesus. One man who is all men. Everything that will ever be, reduced to one person. One person who existed as God before it all began, who, in order to save both the present and the future, chose to exist within His creation as well. A new heavens and earth born of His flesh are now also an eternal inheritance He is giving away to all. Purified by the deep majesty of His name, satisfying the cosmic requirements of justice on His cross, remade in the newness of His body risen from the dead, everything else that will ever be will only be because it is His reflection.

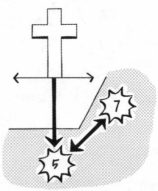

Christianity believes this. What does it mean? **Who Jesus Is** (His person), **What Jesus Did** (His work), and **What Jesus Is Coming Again to Do** are extended to us now, but not yet, as the **Five Results of the Gospel** lead to the **Third Foundational Reality** for which the Lord's Prayer teaches us to pray.

The only-begotten Son of God was born a man in order that He might suffer, die, rise, and ascend to the highest heaven, and there reign, the firstfruits of everything else that will ever be. But before He ascended, He breathed a very special breath. From Him proceeded a Holy Wind. Within that Spirit-filled moment, what He had done and what He was going to do fused the future and the present together, two epochs overlapping in a promise that did more than *say* it would drag the entrapped present into the age to come. This Spirit and these **words** actually are that age come early.

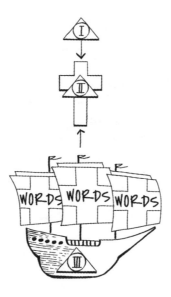

Sharing Himself, sharing His Spirit, Jesus is already doing for and through faith what He will soon enough come again to do for sight. He is joining us former, fallen creation to the endless, eternal authority He has claimed over us. This One Holification, breathed into you upon the oaths of Jesus, conjoins you into His person and works. This is the war God is waging against the devil. God the Spirit is given to **set apart**, to **Christian**, to bind you and me to Christ by calling out your death for what it is, until you see it fulfilled and taken from you in Jesus.

But for that reason, the Spirit must only ever do so exclusively through words about Jesus. The Spirit will not preach Himself. He preaches Jesus. Jesus, the one man. Jesus, the King revealed. Jesus, the author of particular faith, scrupulous words, narrow spirituality first breathed, and then breathed again, but soon written.

The holy writings, the **Scriptures**, are script **set apart** from all the other words of the world in order to set you apart from the world. They were not set down as cavalier acts of various men, all grasping after an unknown God, but as the inspired acts by directed men, commissioned by the Holy Spirit.

There will always be those who insist on disbelief, up to the day that Jesus returns. But disbelief in God has never stopped God from being God. In the end, no matter how we might try, His ship cannot be scuttled. You can jump off it. You can shipwreck yourself, climb some ladder to nowhere until it has become a plank by which you walk overboard. A ladder in the water will do you no good. No matter how many rungs you climb, it will only press further into the sea. But even there, the ship will keep sailing, the Spirit will keep breathing, the oaths of Jesus will keep getting sworn to you. The Scriptures will still be preached, and even one who has thrown himself overboard may yet hear, repent, and believe again.

It is the

that matter most, the unseen but heard **Results of the Gospel**, assembling us as the christened ones into the

of being

from our evils by Jesus' verdict alone. He has sworn to us the double certainty of a divine promise, so that with eager expectation we may await the pending

of our flesh and the

all things, all received now in the euphoria of faith, all prayed for now in the hope of things not yet seen.

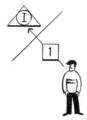

Because Jesus has already given you everything as an expression of His name, you ask for that name in which you are washed to distinguish yourself from our thorny age once and for all.

Because Jesus has already given you everything as the action of His reign as King, you ask Him to act again—both in the present miracle of making you believe Him when He says, "This is true," and also in the coming miracle when you will experience the truth in all its glory.

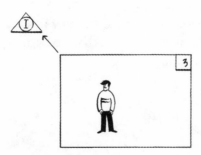

Because Jesus has already given you everything, because giving you everything is what He most wants to do, you ask Him to diminish your own will, to subject it to His own wherever it would assert itself as a distraction from the better good.

In all these things, in the faith that resulted when Jesus divorced you from your sin by declaration alone, you find yourself awakened to no longer take God's name only in vain, but also to call on it in prayer, praise, and thanksgiving. His words are no longer only forgotten or profaned by you, but you also desire to hold them sacred and gladly learn them. His design is no longer seen only as an unfair tyranny worthy of your rebellion against it, but is also seen as an ordered pattern of vocational goods, a design to give you purpose and to remind you that there is always an honor more valuable than your own.

As a result of this awakening, faith believes, accepts, knows, and decides that it is worth living for, worth dying for, worth waiting for, and worth praying for. Because Jesus has already given you everything, the Spirit also compels you to learn to believe that bread and home today, wife and child today, neighbor and town today, are of far more value than all the castles made of sand tomorrow.

Even as all things perish with their use, even as this broken life together exposes the remaining flaws of our chronic disbelieving and selfish *Mes*, even as our vocations remain crosses and the present corruption remains an overall experience of futile suffering, because Jesus has already given you everything, the Spirit teaches you to acknowledge the great benefits of living in God's creation, even as you perceive ever more clearly your need for Him to divorce your evil from you.

Still. Today. Tomorrow. When you wake. As you sleep. Always. Our constant need for mercy rather than justice, for forgiveness rather than wrath, opens our eyes to see the same need in others.

Faith sees the same thorny slavery that is always seeking an antidote through violent assertions. But faith also starves for the saving fertility of charity, for the tender touch of patience, for the graceful willingness to overlook the debts of others.

This **Us** of forgiveness, this common-unioned state of believers waiting for mercy while mercifying one another, is the closest to imitating God that we will ever come in this age. It is incomplete, but it is a wonderful reflection nonetheless. The great endurance that He has shown to us throughout our bloody, broken history, constantly staying His hand from ending us (even as we constantly raise our hands to create bloodshed on His earth), can and does have an effect on us once believed.

Because Jesus has already given you everything, because beneath that everything you are still constantly fostering destruction and living a dying life of wrath and bitterness, because you still need to live as one ever-waiting beneath the mercy of God's forgiveness, the Spirit also teaches you to abhor the many casualties your thorns create when they pierce those around you. Your sins cease to be a laundry list of arbitrary *should nots* or *I'll get in trouble if I dos.* Your sins are the real, painful, negative effects of your faithlessness on others who are already suffering just as much as you. As you see this, know this, and believe this, the Spirit awakens in you the desire to create less of it, to do less harm, to wreak less damage, to in our evil state fight to keep our evil from affecting others around us as much as we possibly can.

The Spirit's great war against us is not for our passions, but against them. Evil happens not when I have an accident, but when I choose what I most naturally want. You are led into temptation not against your own will, but **by it**. Yet now you are being **set apart** against *yourself* and for the sake of others.

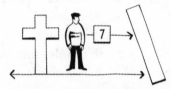

This can have only one final effect, one final Edge. That Edge is the desperate plea of the one whose belief about what he is and what this age has become has come into full alignment with God's words about it. It is the prayer of a man who hungers that he be led not into temptation in a more permanent way. It is the prayer of a woman who desires that the threat of her internal evils be removed entirely, that the thorns die at last, that faith give way to sight, that Jesus return with all His justifying recompense to deliver us from evil once and for all.

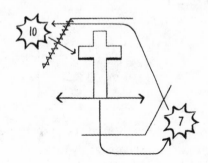

So we find ourselves thrust back into history, at the center of which sits the facts of Jesus' cross. It is fitting then, that the cross also lies at the center of our Echo. The First Foundational Reality—the creation, the Ten Commandments—sets the bedrock of what we were made to be, what we should be. But we are not. So the Second Foundational Reality—our redemption, the Creed—enters history as the story of what God is willing to do rather than condemn the world He made, no matter how bad we've become. That story's results, the Third Foundational Reality—our sanctification, the desires we learn to pray in the Lord's Prayer—press us back to the First Foundational Reality, but only through the cross. There, the Law is not abolished but fulfilled. There, the First and Third Foundations meet. There, the Commandments and Lord's Prayer are bound, two sides of a coin, the middle of which is Jesus. He is the crux of the matter, the center of all things.

This framework, these **Three Foundational Realities**—the Ten Commandments, the Creed, and the Lord's Prayer—are the entirety of Christianity boiled down to its most potent and memorable being. All the Scriptures contain no differing revelation or idea. They are to be mined and digested as testimonies to this one, constant expression. Any modern prophet who thinks to add or subtract shows himself falsely sent. Any assembly that does not believe these Three Foundational Realities, that fails to hear them preached or centers their life together on some alternative story, is no church, but yet another pagan temple dedicated to the death of all men. Any Christian who cannot repeat the **Echo** of these things among the din of the present age is a man in a war zone without either shield or weapon, a woman in a desert without water or food, a child of nothingness with nothing to save him from it.

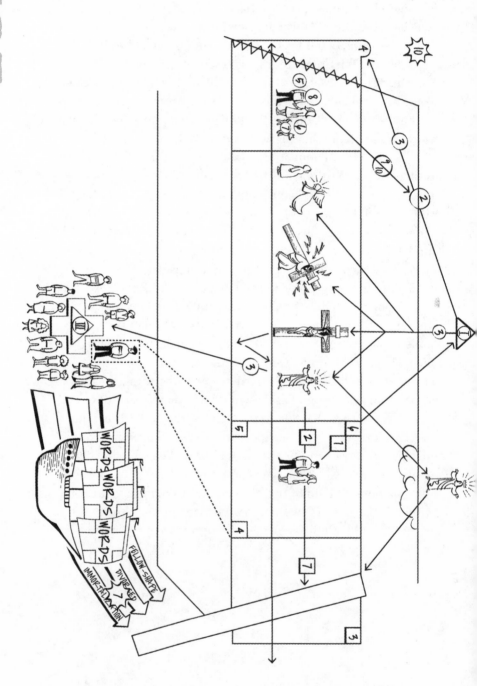

God Himself is not ashamed to teach these things daily. He knows nothing better to teach. He always keeps teaching the same thing and does not take up anything new or different. All the saints know nothing better or different to learn and cannot finish learning this. Are we not the finest of all fellows to imagine that if we have once read or heard the catechism, we know it all and have no further need to read and learn? Can we finish learning in one hour what God Himself cannot finish teaching? He is engaged in teaching this from the beginning to the end of the world. All prophets, together with all saints, have been busy learning it, have ever remained students, and must continue to be students. (LC Preface 16)

The End

This is not the end.
There is no end to the Echo of Christianity.
It is new every morning.
It is there to convert you.
Again.
It is there for you to convert others with.
Always.

I get it. *Catechism* is a very crunchy word. But I don't really care what you call it. I only want you to know it. To study it. To **believe** it. I wrote this book simply to encourage you to stop judging it based on some mediocre set of adolescently twisted memories and reconsider that its depths hold no end to wisdom and comfort. It's **gold**. Solid gold. It is the everlasting worldview. God's own opinion. Therefore absolutely **true**. Changeless. Timeless. Perfect.

This Echo cuts through all things. It subjects them to itself, like a lamp piercing the dark fog to demonstrate in unavoidable terms the difference between the path and cliff. It is the ship on which Life Himself sails among us, casting His net to pull the helpless aboard His journey to the new land that knows no dangers of the sea or depths, no chaos or death.

It is all Jesus. Who Jesus Is and What Jesus Did. All the time.
It is all Jesus. What Jesus Is Coming Again to Do. All the time.
You are not God.
But **He** is.

Far from being a reason to despair or an annoyance that ends your quest for happiness, far from being the end of you, this **Echo** is the eternal beginning, the everlasting "Again!" As He increases, you decrease. Yet the result is not less, but more. Not death, but life. Not *Me*, but **Us**, and ever **Us** as those given to one another that we might enjoy all things given in and from Him.

THE MUSCLE OF FAITH MEMORY

Christianity is not the ability to memorize and recite mindless incantations. If your goal is to repeat them *ad nauseum*, thinking God will hear you because of your many words, or if your goal is to simply recall them long enough to pass the quiz and get this confirmation thing over with, mindless rattling off of the syllables in ritualistic obligation gains you nothing. The Echo is not magic. It is **truth**.

The human heart is filled with poison. The antidote is the Echo. What these words mean. What they contain. They extract the entirety of Jesus' Scriptures into a form you can pray in less than five minutes. Even a child can learn it, yet no man masters it. This is wisdom so bottomless that it never fails to teach. There is always another edge, always an enhanced nuance, always a greater connection. The surface is elemental, like a set of wooden blocks cut to the most basic shapes. But from those shapes any host of greater forms becomes possible. But always with the same, evident order. Always with the repeated, steadfast clarity. Always the same Echo.

Like the primitive forms of martial arts that are taught to the white belt, or the simple steps of a layup drill repeated on a basketball court, the Echo appears at first to be "too easy." The early student impatiently believes himself capable of more than he ought. He demands faster progression on the mat or spends his free time lobbing up shots from well beyond his range. But if he will trust the master and coach, if he will drill the basics, if he will practice them, never dissipate from them, they will become embedded as the foundation of every move he makes.

The black belt knows that the forms of the white belt still lie beneath and undergird his most advanced attack. The superstar—piercing the lane and finishing the impossible shot despite three defenders to tie the score at the buzzer—does not hit his awkward, twisting, off-kilter layup *in spite* of all the normal layups he has drilled since childhood. He hit it **because** of them.

In the same way, in the midst of life's many trials the muscle memory of faith stands on the words of the Echo without needing to pause and call them to mind. Recall is instantaneous. Faster than awareness. No longer thinking only *about* the Echo, but thinking **with** it. It is not a list but a **mind**, not a rite of passage but a spiritual second sight.

The mixed martial arts fighter in the champion bout does not stop the fight to decide which move will best be used next. The MVP with seven seconds remaining and down a point does not take a time-out to plot his footwork intellectually. They rely on the echo of their training. The hard work is already done so that in the heat of battle there is no question. What was repeated countless times before is now repeated again, without question.

So also in these gray and evil days, in this age assaulted by all the forces of darkness, among the flurrying tantrum of constant messages, motives, and declarations on endless channels and mediums, all conspiring to drown out your trust in the true God, the Christian cannot afford to have a faith that only recites the Ten Important Things the way a child counts to ten on his fingers, or to pray for the Seven Edges the way a child has to struggle to color within the lines. That is why the purpose of this book has been to pique and challenge your convictions, to convince you to repeat the journey.

Again.

Take your religion seriously. Whatever level your training may be today, train it again tomorrow. Consider your spirituality more than a hobby for weekends, more than a relic of some dead people that you have to put up with on Wednesday afternoons to keep your mother off your back. It is **a weapon for your singular stand in the greatest war ever waged**. It is power for disarming the world, even as the world cannot see it or know it. It is a sword for your heart and your mind, to pierce them both and bind them together, killing *Me* and raising **Us**. It is the **christening**, the immortalization's root, invincibility on your lips, the conduit of divinity: God's own **words**.

REPEAT

We shout **"Amen!"** and in so doing crucify the world. Dying to it, we live. Believing, we wage the beautiful war. It is not all glory and gleaming light. No. War is not the glory the boys dream it to be. It is dirt, blood, thorns, and tears. But as you lie dying in whatever hospital they drag your already rotting carcass to, a fallen soldier in a foreign field, watching on helplessly as all that you were and all that you wanted slips through your fingers with that final, fleeting, struggling breath, **what will you say**?

Will you sit there, at the gates of *hades*, muttering empty platitudes about how it was all better than it really was? Will you tell your sons and daughters—if they are even willing to still talk to you—that you are proud you did it your way? Will the new toilet or the wallpaper at the lake house matter? Or will you have no qualms, pose no question, but like the trained man of war, the confident daughter of Zion that you are, unsheathe your sword, open your mouth, and meet every empty consolation of the pagans attending you with the Echo?

Christ has died.

Christ is risen.

Christ is ascended.

Make no mistake.

Christ will come again.

So say it!

Say it once more.

Respeak it.

Echo it!

For it is most certainly **true**.